REFORM CINEMA IN IRAN

FILM AND CULTURE SERIES

FILM AND CULTURE
A series of Columbia University Press
Edited by John Belton

See Series List, page 257

REFORM CINEMA IN IRAN

Film and Political Change in the Islamic Republic

BLAKE ATWOOD

COLUMBIA UNIVERSITY PRESS
NEW YORK

Columbia University Press
Publishers Since 1893
New York   Chichester, West Sussex

Copyright © 2016 Columbia University Press
All rights reserved

Library of Congress Cataloging-in-Publication Data
Names: Atwood, Blake Robert, 1983- author.
Title: Reform cinema in Iran: film and political change in the
Islamic Republic / Blake Atwood.
Description: New York : Columbia University Press, 2016. |
Series: Film and culture | Includes bibliographical references and index. |
Includes filmography.
Identifiers: LCCN 2016013376 (print) | LCCN 2016019805 (ebook) |
ISBN 9780231178167 (cloth) | ISBN 9780231178174 (pbk.) |
ISBN 9780231543149 (e-book)
Subjects: LCSH: Motion pictures—Iran—History—20th century. |
Motion pictures—Iran—History—21st century. |
Motion pictures—Political aspects—Iran. | Motion picture industry—
Political aspects—Iran—20th century.
Classification: LCC PN1993.5.I846 A89 2016 (print) |
LCC PN1993.5.I846 (ebook) |
DDC 791.430955—dc23

Cover image: Film director Abbas Kiarostami. © A. Abbas/Magnum
Photos. IRAN. Tehran. 1997.

CONTENTS

A Note on Transliteration vii
Acknowledgments ix

Introduction: Revolutionary Cinema and the Logic of Reform 1
1. When Love Entered Cinema: Mysticism and the Emerging Poetics of Reform 27
2. Screening Reform: Campaign Movies, Documentaries, and Urban Tehran 61
3. Video Democracies: Or, The Death of the Filmmaker 95
4. Who Killed the Tough Guy? Continuity and Rupture in the *Filmfārsi* Tradition 136
5. Film Archives and Online Videos: The Search for Reform in Post-Khatami Iran 166
Conclusion: Iran's Cinema Museum and Political Unrest 197

Notes 207
Bibliography 229
Filmography 243
Index 245

A NOTE ON TRANSLITERATION

For the transliteration of Persian words, I have followed the *Iranian Studies* transliteration scheme. Diacritical marks have been excluded on all proper nouns. I have done my best to ascertain the preferred or standardized spelling of Iranian names (e.g., Khomeini, Ahmadinejad, and Khamenei). In those cases in which I could not determine a preferred spelling, I have transliterated the name according to the *Iranian Studies* scheme but have not included any diacritical marks.

ACKNOWLEDGMENTS

So much of my intellectual work over the last decade has taken place in the Department of Middle Eastern Studies at the University of Texas at Austin, and I cannot begin to thank all of the wonderful people with whom I have interacted at UT, first, as a student and, later, as a faculty member: Kamran Aghaie, Mahmoud Al-Batal, Samer Ali, Katie Aslan, Denise Beachum, Kristen Brustad, Mia Carter, Tarek El-Ariss, Michael Hillmann, David Justh, Briana Medearis, Na'ama Pat-el, and Faegheh Shirazi. Several people at UT deserve special thanks. M. R. Ghanoonparvar has tirelessly encouraged my work since I first showed up in his office as a first-year graduate student, and I could not have asked for a better adviser. Tom Garza has shown me unbounded kindness, and our lunches once a month make my life much better. Karen Grumberg is a good friend and encouraging colleague, and I feel very lucky to have an office next to hers. Karin Wilkins's guidance has made navigating the academic waters at UT much easier, and I am very grateful for her friendship. I have also had the good fortunate of working with several exceptional graduate students at UT: Shahrzad Ahmadi, Claire Cooley, and Laura Fish, whose enthusiasm, research, and comments have pushed my ideas further and enriched my own work. I would also like to acknowledge a University of Texas at Austin Subvention Grant awarded by the Office of the President, which supported the publication of this book.

ACKNOWLEDGMENTS

I am very lucky to have a network of professional support that extends well beyond the Forty Acres, and colleagues around the world have contributed to this book in innumerable ways: Zeina Halabi, Nili Gold, Mikiya Koyagi, Neda Maghbouleh, Drew Paul, Kelsey Rice, Lior Sternfeld, and Richard Zettler. I am particularly grateful to Nasrin Rahimieh, whose work and kindness inspire me, and Peter Decherney, who has been a great collaborator, friend, and mentor to me over the last five years. Farzaneh Milani and Zjaleh Hajibashi nurtured my early passion for Persian at the University of Virginia, and I cannot begin to thank them enough. At Columbia University Press, I'd like to thank John Belton and Philip Leventhal for believing in this book and my work. Jinping Wang has been the greatest friend and intellectual interlocutor that any academic could hope for; our many conversations about history and the world have marked every page of this book in some way.

Many good friends have given me the space to work on this book but have also reminded me that there is life outside of it. Dena Afrasiabi, Beeta Baghoolizadeh, Raha Rafii, Sahba Shayani, and, Anousha Shahsavari have all been pillars of support when I needed them most, and all of them have reminded me in their own way of the importance of friendship. Anthony Ferraro is the kindest person I know, and without his friendship, this book would not have been possible. Erin Micheletti, my oldest friend, read every page of this manuscript, and I am so appreciative not only for her critical eye but also for our adventures in Austin. Sadaf's enthusiasm for this project, Khatami, Tehran, and Persian inspired me to keep writing, and her help with sources made all the difference. Vrouyr Joubanian is my favorite person in the world, and there are no words in any language to express my gratitude for everything he does for me.

I am eternally grateful to my family, who has contributed to this book and to all my pursuits in so many ways. My father always prioritized education, and I attribute my career as an educator to him. My siblings, Seth, Jessica, Ashley, and Tyler, love me unconditionally, which makes me feel like I can do anything in the world. And, finally, I owe so much to my mother, who has always encouraged me to be myself and who came all the way to Iran with me to understand what I do. Her bravery and open-mindedness never cease to surprise and inspire me. Thank you.

REFORM CINEMA IN IRAN

Introduction
REVOLUTIONARY CINEMA AND THE LOGIC OF REFORM

Film, since its inception, has danced in the shadows of wild political change. With early examples like the "conflict" implicit in Soviet montage theory of the 1920s and Benito Mussolini's Cinecittà Film Studio (est. 1937), whose motto was "Film Is the Most Powerful Weapon," the history of world cinema is also a history of violence. Third Cinema, an aesthetic movement that emerged alongside the Latin American liberation struggles of the 1960s and 1970s, redirected this history of violence to the service of anti-imperialism, in which film was no longer just an apparatus for propaganda but also an agent of resistance and opposition. The political implications of such a project were vast, and the possibility of resistance through filmmaking fueled, and still propels, the efforts of filmmakers around the world, especially in non-Western cinemas. The Syrian Abounaddara Collective, for example, reminds us of the continuing relevance of cinema to the violent struggles that seek political change. The collective's ongoing "emergency cinema" has sought to provide an alternative to the Assad regime's narrative by releasing one short video of the conflict each week since the civil war began in 2011.[1] At a time of unprecedented access to visual information, as guns and cameras seem to battle for authority around the world, it is important to remember that for more than a century cinema has been ideologically and technologically entangled with the idea of revolution.

INTRODUCTION

Nowhere has the relationship between cinema and revolution been more evident than in the Islamic Republic of Iran. In his first speech on returning to Iran after fourteen years in exile, Ayatollah Ruhollah Khomeini, the leader of the Islamic Revolution of 1978–1979, spoke unexpectedly of cinema. On February 1, 1979, after being rushed from the airport to Behesht-e Zahra Cemetery, he addressed a large, captive audience and declared, "We are not opposed to cinema. . . . It's the misuse of cinema that we are opposed to, a misuse caused by the treacherous policies of our leaders."[2] That Khomeini would mention cinema during this momentous speech signaled its centrality to the revolution that had ousted the shah, Mohammad Reza Pahlavi (1919–1980). Unlike in Latin America, however, where filmmakers such as Thomas Guiterrez Alea, Nelson Perreira Dos Santos, and Glauber Rocha were carving out a space for opposition to neocolonialism within cinema, in Iran up until that point, revolutionaries had viewed cinema not as an institution of resistance but rather as an uncomplicated imperial project, a cultural consequence of Mohammad Reza Pahlavi's ties to Europe and the United States.

Movie theaters were at the center of revolutionaries' efforts to dismantle the corruptive force of cinema. Theaters across the country were attacked and vandalized, and their patrons, hassled and harassed. In the context of this animosity toward cinema, the Cinema Rex fire stands not just as one of the most haunting events in Iran's long film history but also as a turning point in the revolution. On August 19, 1978, as protests against the shah swept the country, flames swallowed the Cinema Rex movie theater in the southern city of Abadan. Unknown agents chained the doors shut and lit the building on fire as a full-house audience sat down to watch Masud Kimiai's *Gavazn-hā* (The deer, 1974). While some patrons fled to the roof, narrowly escaping death, hundreds of others were caught in the flames and died slow, painful deaths. Immediately following this tragic incident, the shah's government and revolutionaries began pointing fingers, each claiming the other was responsible for starting the fire and locking the doors. Although scholars, filmmakers, documentarians, journalists, and even playwrights have attempted to locate the blame for this event, no report has thus far definitively identified the motivations behind the arson. Despite the uncertainty that continues to shroud the Cinema Rex fire, this episode exemplifies the extent to which cinema and the film industry were unwittingly, and perhaps unwillingly, implicated in the Islamic Revolution.

If violent ambivalence marked society's attitude toward cinema during the protests leading up to the revolution, then Khomeini's speech at Behesht-e Zahra fixed the revolution's official stance on film. "Cinema is a modern invention," Khomeini affirmed, "that ought to be used for the sake of educating the people."[3] Perhaps inspired by Dariush Mehrjui's *Gāv* (The cow, 1969), which he had praised for its ability to shed light on social plight,[4] Khomeini, with just a few words, changed his own position on cinema and reset the revolution's terms of engagement with the film industry.[5] Film was no longer a vessel of encroaching American values, the embodiment of Pahlavi corruption, or even simply a mode of entertainment. Instead, it was an educational tool, and within this scheme the film industry could be reformed and incentivized to accommodate the repurposing of film.

To refashion the cultural status of film required unprecedented state control of the industry. The creation of a new cinema was gradual, as Hamid Naficy reminds us, and its creation took nearly a decade.[6] The project included both legal and extralegal policies that enabled state intervention in every aspect of the film industry, from the training of filmmakers and access to equipment to the oversight of scripts and control over exhibition, including imported films. The state intended each of these interventions to force cinema into modeling its new vision of an idealized Islamic subjectivity. To educate society about what it meant to live in an Islamic republic was to affirm the republic's power. These policies and the film aesthetic they sought to produce depended on the same anti-imperialist rhetoric that had fueled the revolution. Cinema in the early years of the Islamic Republic maintained revolutionary fervor and helped the new state assert its legitimacy by keeping the ideals of the revolution alive. The success of this project can be measured in Naficy's assessment that "the Revolution led to the emergence of a new vital cinema, with its own special industrial and financial structure and unique ideological, thematic, and production values."[7]

Today, as film festivals and distributors try relentlessly to sell us a "post-revolutionary" Iranian cinema, it is nearly impossible imagine Iranian cinema outside of the Islamic Revolution, which sought to establish new standards for filmmaking in the country almost forty years ago. But the inescapable truth of revolutions is that they are, by definition, momentary events. Despite the Islamic Republic's attempt to leverage cinema to keep the spirit of the revolution alive in contemporary Iran, revolutions cannot last forever, and their fleeting nature challenges us to understand what happens to the relationship between revolution and cinema once the revolutionary dust has settled. In the case of Iran, how can we conceive of a history of contemporary cinema that isn't necessarily "post-revolutionary"? What has happened in the approximately thirty years since the revolution succeeded in consolidating the Islamic Republic's power through cinema? And what negotiations have determined the relationship between the state and the film industry during that time, especially since Ayatollah Khomeini's death in 1989?

Whereas scholars like Hamid Naficy and Negar Mottahedeh have determined that the revolution established new industrial and aesthetic film practices,[8] *Reform Cinema in Iran* examines what happened next in the politics of cinema in Iran. Starting in the early 1990s, an intimate relationship developed between the popular reformist movement and the film industry. The two supported each other in an unlikely partnership, and as revolutionary discourse gave way to policies of reform in the political sphere, cinema began to change as well. *Reform Cinema in Iran* makes two central arguments in this regard: First, the film industry and the reformist movement helped shape each other, and their interactions functioned on an ideological level. The reformist movement marked a change in the political landscape and at the same time signaled a new period in the country's cinematic history. Second, a reformist history of Iranian cinema exposes the inadequacy of the popular category "post-revolutionary Iranian cinema," which positions the Islamic Revolution as the most transformative event in Iran's film history. In contrast, *Reform Cinema in Iran* argues that discourses of reform have equally affected the course of Iranian cinema over the last three decades.

To write a reformist history of film in the Islamic Republic is not to overlook or devalue the revolution and its impact on the film industry. On the contrary, the discourse of reform in Iran, by seeking to work within the institutions of the Islamic Republic, depends on and regularly asserts the authority of the revolution. Cinematic reform, even as it attempts to position itself against the revolution, is also in constant dialogue with the revolutionary policies that established cinema as a propaganda machine within the Islamic Republic. A reformist history of film instead asks that we consider how the momentum of revolutionary cinema is reconfigured as power consolidates and the force of revolutionary ideology becomes tempered. Is cinema's revolutionary fervor redirected in support of the state, or does it continue to provide a space for critique? When a film industry falls under state control, is a kind of engagement with politics other than resistance possible? Might collaborations and partnerships between the state and the film industry instruct us about how cultural institutions work within state control to critique political power in newly established societies?

REIMAGINING REVOLUTIONARY CINEMA

These questions are pressing not just to the study of Iranian film but also to the historiography of world cinema. The intersection of sociopolitical reform and motion pictures has existed almost as long as film technology. In the United States, for example, the end of the twentieth century's first decade witnessed the growing popularity of politically driven reform, as the American Progressive Era took hold under William Taft's leadership (1909–1913). At the same time, the way that society understood the role of film within the country's social fabric also began to change. The widespread acceptance of motion pictures had started to grow beyond just working-class audiences, and because the consumption of films took place in public spaces, various reform factions battled to control films' content and the conditions of their exhibition.[9] The year 1909, with the establishment of institutions like the Board of Censorship of Programs of Motion Pictures Shows in New York City and the Board of Censorship (or the Board of Review after 1915), signaled early examples of collaboration between motion picture trade workers and reformist groups.[10]

Such institutions also became sites where political reform began both to transform film industry practices and to guide aesthetic concerns. This reformist moment in American political history coincided with a profound change in the status of cinema as the motion picture trade transformed into a full-fledged industry. The industrialization of American cinema occurred as trade attention shifted away from nickelodeons and toward narrative films. Whereas motion pictures before the consolidation of the American film industry often depended on spectacle, the need to keep paying audiences entertained drove the narrativization of mainstream films, which in turn demanded a complex industrial structure. That these changes to the industrial and aesthetic structures of cinema were occurring alongside collaborations between the motion picture trade workers and reformists demonstrates how political reform was wrapped up in the very ontology of cinema at this time, and Scott Simmon has shown how narrative films in the 1910s were thematically tied to the Progressive Era reformist concerns.[11]

This particular moment in American film history—as so-called early cinema transformed into industrialized mass culture, short nickelodeons became narratives, and political reform gained traction in the country—functions as an early instance of reform cinema. This precedent, however, cannot accommodate the idea of reform cinema as a reaction to revolution. Indeed, any discussion that seeks to understand the fate of cinema following tremendous political change must also include Soviet cinema following the Russian Revolution of 1917, not just for what it tells us about how film industries grapple with encroaching state control and aesthetic concerns following revolutions but also for the expansive effect that Soviet film of the 1920s had on cinema worldwide. The historical and political conditions surrounding the Russian Revolution are strikingly similar to those of the Islamic Revolution in Iran. Whereas in Iran the revolution immediately preceded the Iran-Iraq War (1980–1988), the longest traditionally fought war of the twentieth century, in the Soviet case war bookended revolution, first with World War I (1914–1918) and then the Russian Civil War (1917–1922). In both contexts, political upheaval and the material realities of wartime meant shortages of resources, including specialized film crews, film stock, and electricity, and day-to-day instability simultaneously threatened and demanded leisure activities, such as the cinema.

These periods of violence following both revolutions were, despite their material limitations, also ideologically charged, and reports of early Soviet institutions encouraging revolutionary filmmakers to make imaginary "films" without any film or film equipment have become commonplace.[12] This kind of initiative, which privileged the ideological orientation of a film over its materiality, speaks to the immediate effect that the Russian Revolution had on cinema. Initially, the Russian Revolution destabilized the film industry's material resources at the same time that it imbued it with revolutionary fervor. Vladimir Lenin, like Ayatollah Khomeini many years later, targeted cinema as an area worthy of development, stating, "Of all the arts, cinema is the most important." The Communist Party saw the most potential in cinema because it was a new medium and therefore less susceptible to past corruption. The nationalization of the cinema in 1919 and the New Economic Policy (1917–1922)—a more open policy that sought to rebuild an economy destroyed by war and revolution—enabled the Bolsheviks to use cinema for propaganda during the Civil War. However, most of the work being done in Soviet cinema at this time was theoretical as various factions of critics and director-theorists competed to establish the aesthetic practices that best spoke the ideals of the revolution. Within this context, avant-garde filmmaking, as promoted by Aleksei Gan, Dziga Vertov, and others, reigned supreme as the premier revolutionary aesthetic. Ultimately, though, as Denise J. Youngblood notes, aside from this abstract theoretical work, "very little . . . happened in Soviet cinema" in the half decade following the revolution; instead, "literally everything was" left to "the future."[13]

These five years alone, however, did not determine the nature of early Soviet cinema in its entirety. The 1920s marked an "inexorable move from organizational chaos to total centralization and from aesthetic radicalism to Socialist Realism."[14] What we witness in the post-revolutionary period is markedly different from the institutional and aesthetic structures of the film industry that we commonly associate with Soviet cinema as whole, and as Vance Kepley Jr. warns, the collapse of "revolutionary socialism" with the film industry is too "intellectually tidy" to be historically accurate.[15] Instead, the transformation to a centralized film industry that—by and large—privileged a realist aesthetic grew out of economic reform policies of the 1920s and not the immediate fervor of the revolution. The film industry and institutions charged with encouraging cinema, including Goskino (1922–1924), Sovinko

(1924–1930), and the Association of Revolutionary Cinematography (ARK), necessarily had to appeal to mainstream audiences in order to provide capital flow to fund future film projects. The need to reach mass audiences also spoke to the new state-determined ideological focus of cinema as an educational institution. The ability to appeal to a largely illiterate population was one of the draws of cinema for Lenin and other party members. Without being able to reach these audiences and without being able to fund itself, cinema might fail its new ideological purpose.

These concrete financial needs were in constant competition with the aesthetic ambitions of filmmakers who positioned an avant-garde style as in line with their political beliefs. While director-theorists like Sergei Eisenstein sought out a radical cinematic mode that, in their view, better accommodated their revolutionary politics, socialist realism ultimately won out as the aesthetic that would define silent and early-sound Soviet cinema. This success was tied to the economic reform policies of the time. Youngblood, for example, locates 1924 as the "turning point" in Soviet cinema as the post-revolutionary period (and its institutional disorder and radical aesthetic) gave way to what we might call a reform cinema, which was grounded in a "more realistic appraisal of the vast problems facing Soviet cinema."[16] This aesthetic mode would find forceful articulation with the advent of sound technology beginning in the 1930s. Silent Soviet cinema thereby ended in a place vastly different from where it had begun. Whereas the period immediately following the revolution was abstract and ideologically charged, a decade later it was grounded, both institutionally and aesthetically, in the practical economic concerns that had overtaken Soviet society by that time.

The history of early Soviet cinema urges a reimagining of the relationship between revolution and film by reminding us that revolutionary ideology is just one aspect of the overdetermined reforms that ultimately reconstitute film industries following tremendous political change. Yet this Soviet history does not necessarily account for the role of state control in post-revolutionary film industries. Although film historiography has long positioned Soviet cinema as the earliest example of state-controlled cinema, Lenin's 1919 decree nationalizing cinema actually did more to decentralize filmmaking than to consolidate control over it.[17] In fact, a common complaint among members of the early Soviet film community was the lack of financial and ideological intervention on the part of the Communist Party, despite the leadership's rhetoric about the importance of cinema. The Soviet case comprised filmmakers who, despite documented political differences,[18] were still committed to the ideals of the revolution and to communist rule, even as they succumbed to more moderate economic policies. Many filmmakers, for example, decried the semicapitalist New Economic Policy as an ideological failure,[19] but this policy, which excluded state subvention in cinematic matters, revived the economy and cleared the way for the artistic successes of Eisenstein, Pudovkin, and Vertov in the mid-1920s.[20]

To view the absence of state control as cause for criticism rather than for celebration may strike us as incongruous with our understanding of film industries today, particularly in those cinemas where the state and filmmakers seem to be at constant odds. And, indeed, the history of early Soviet cinema does not tell us much about what happened to the resistance implicit in revolutionary cinema as it made its way through the apparatuses of state control, just as the historiography of early Soviet cinema cannot accommodate the global technological and economic flows that have consumed political turmoil since the mid-twentieth century. But to study state-controlled film industries in our current era of globalization is to acknowledge a genealogy of revolutionary cinema. From censorship in contemporary Chinese cinema to the financial backing of the film industry in the early years of the Islamic Republic of Iran, many contemporary states' vested interest in cinema can be traced back to the cultural and political revolutions that preceded them.

In Iran the revolution that redefined state control of cinema was part of a global series of anti-imperial struggles. Throughout the 1960s and 1970s, from Central and South America to the heart of Africa and onward to the furthest reaches of Asia, liberation movements redrew the borders of sovereignty on the world map as nations sought to expel colonial control and influence. These upheavals also transformed the political value of cinema, and world cinema of the 1960s, 1970s, and 1980s became implicated in the political movements of the time not just with its ability to educate and propagate but also in its willingness to resist hegemony by refusing to participate in economically powerful and culturally privileged film industries, especially Hollywood. Third

INTRODUCTION

Cinema, a theory and practice of filmmaking first coined by Fernando Solanas and Octavio Getino, powerfully spoke to this new direction in world cinema. Solanas and Getino, in their treatise "Towards a Theory of Third Cinema" (1969), built on Frantz Fanon's call in *The Wretched of the Earth* for the creation of a national culture that is entrenched in revolutionary struggle.[21]

Because early theorists of Third Cinema initially conceived of it as an instrument for anti-imperial revolutions, the movement could not be sustained forever. Just as the liberation movements of the 1960s and 1970s eventually came to an end, by this logic so too must the aesthetic movements explicitly tied to them. Scholars have theorized a number of models for thinking about the continued relevance and legacy of Third Cinema. Teshome Gabriel, for example, expanded the definition of Third Cinema to focus less on "where it is made" and more on how it opposes "imperialism and class oppression in all their ramifications and manifestations."[22] In this way, African American independent cinema could be just as much a part of the ideological project of Third Cinema as Patricio Guzman's *The Battle of Chile* (1975–1979). Other scholars have begun to question how the energy of Third Cinema has transformed in light of the globalization that grew directly out of the postcolonial movements of the late twentieth century. Hamid Naficy, Ella Shohat, Robert Stam, and others have looked to transnationalism, including diasporic filmmaking and hybridity, to examine how the critiques of power from Third Cinema have been reconfigured in the late twentieth and early twenty-first centuries.[23]

At the same time that these works construct valuable frameworks for thinking more expansively about world cinema systems, we also need fresh approaches that account for the fate of national film industries and their engagement with local and global discourses following the revolutions of the mid- to late twentieth century. *Reform Cinema in Iran* uses cinema in the Islamic Republic of Iran as a case study to propose a model for analyzing post–Third Cinema aesthetics that are organized nationally rather than transnationally and invested in local political and legal debates rather than just in the economic flows of globalization. Such a framework does not, however, attempt to undercut the real effect that the global movement of media has had on the Iranian film industry, nor does it attempt to devalue the cultural

INTRODUCTION

and financial role that international film festivals have had on film production in the country. Instead, *Reform Cinema in Iran* demonstrates that even those art films destined for the festival circuit found articulation in the country's trade publications and contributed to the discourse of reform that swept through Iran at this time. The model used here, which integrates film analysis with archival sources and industry research, ultimately seeks to understand how film industries reconfigure the momentum of Third Cinema outside of revolutionary ideology. Whereas Robert Lang's recent work *New Tunisian Cinema* powerfully reminds us of the continuing importance of resistance to these postcolonial cinemas,[24] the present book, by tracing the transformation from revolutionary cinema to reform cinema in the Islamic Republic of Iran, asks that we imagine a state-controlled postcolonial cinema that is political not just in its ability to resist but also by the very nature of its collaboration with mainstream political movements.

A CINEMA OF REFORM

That theories of Third Cinema "undergird" Iranian cinema is significant insofar as it suggests the extent to which the political and aesthetic revolutions that we witness in the Islamic Republic are wrapped up in larger global trends, in the anti- and postcolonial struggles of the so-called Third World.[25] As much as cinema within the Islamic Republic is a national cinema, determined by unique policies, industrial structures, discourses, and filmic grammar,[26] it is also representative of the reform cinemas that have transformed film industries around the world. *Reform Cinema in Iran* thereby attends to the particularities of Iranian cinema in order to posit a reform cinema as the logical aftereffect of revolutionary cinema globally.

The history of Iranian cinema during the Islamic Republic's first decade, as the revolution of 1979 gave way to the Iran-Iraq War of 1980–1988, especially spoke to the ideals of Third Cinema as the recently established state developed new economic structures and systems of control in order to resist the financial and cultural logic of Hollywood. This project was paramount because the United States had been one of Mohammad Reza Pahlavi's

INTRODUCTION

strongest allies and revolutionary discourse collapsed American values with the monarchy's corruption. To resist Hollywood (and other North American and European) aesthetics and structures was, therefore, to reaffirm one's commitment to the revolution. Just as in the Soviet case, the revolution initially created instability for the film industry, so immediately following the revolution audiences depended largely on foreign imports, particularly those films that had been banned during the shah's reign. The most popular of these films, such Guzman's *The Battle of Chile* and Pontecorvo's *Battle of Algiers* (1966), fit squarely within the Third Cinema movement and thus gestured to the Islamic Republic's early commitment to revolutionary cinema.

The consolidation of the Islamic Republic's power and the escalation of the Iran-Iraq War in the early 1980s, however, demanded that the state encourage local filmmaking that would attest specifically to the Islamic citizenship that the young republic imagined for itself. From its very conception, this goal faced a number of interwoven challenges, both financially and ideologically. First, the film industry needed a supply of new filmmakers, producers, actors, and technicians who were committed to the ideals of the revolution, especially since the Pahlavi-era film industry was still associated with the monarchy's decadence. Second, a system of "supervision" (*nezārat*) needed to be established to ensure that the films produced spoke to the Islamic Republic's new value system. Finally, because audiences preferred imported films, a new financial model needed to be developed so that the film industry could start making movies that would successfully compete with foreign films. In order to address these concerns, the government institutionalized filmmaking in 1982 and 1983, when it relocated all cinematic affairs to the newly established Ministry of Culture and Islamic Guidance (Vezārat-e farhang-o-ershād-e Islāmi) and established the Farabi Cinema Foundation (Bonyād-e sinemā-ye Fārābi), a joint-stock company within the ministry that, like Sovinko of early Soviet cinema, provided funding and equipment for film projects. These two institutions implemented a series of policies that sought simultaneously to encourage and to limit filmmaking. Their initiatives included workshops to train future filmmakers, especially to make films to support war causes; financial incentive policies; and, perhaps most importantly, a rigid and systematic system of censorship that included

INTRODUCTION

eight steps and oversaw every aspect of filmmaking, from scripts to production to exhibition.[27]

These policies and the film aesthetic they sought to create depended on the same anti-imperialist rhetoric that had fueled the revolution. Cinema in the early years of the Islamic Republic thus maintained revolutionary fervor and helped the new state assert its legitimacy by keeping the ideals of the revolution alive. During the first several years of the Iran-Iraq War, the film industry more or less accepted these regulations. A number of the Islamic Republic's most successful filmmakers were trained in this model, and their early work benefited from the incentives program. Mohsen Makhmalbaf, for example, was a committed revolutionary who had been jailed for political activity before the revolution and claimed that he had never seen a film until Ayatollah Khomeini sanctioned cinema after the revolution. He received training as a filmmaker as part of the war effort, and his early films, such as *Towbeh-ye Nasuh* (Nasuh's repentance, 1983), are didactic explorations into the nature of morality and the centrality of Islam to the redemption of both the individual and the nation. Makhmalbaf's early career exemplified the Islamic Republic's early efforts within the film industry, what we might call "revolutionary cinema," which sought to create a new Islamicate cinema that supported the revolutionary ideology that continued to affirm the Islamic Republic's authority at this time.

Toward the end of the war, however, filmmakers and producers began to push back against the censorship that had come to define film production. The release of Bahram Beyzaie's *Bāshu, gharibeh-ye kuchak* (Bashu, the little stranger, 1989), for example, was delayed by three years because the director refused to implement more than eighty changes that the censors had demanded. When the film was finally released, it became the first film produced in the Islamic Republic to feature a female character gazing directly at the camera, a scene that challenged the modesty laws that had previously informed patterns of censorship.[28] And this battle between state control (e.g., censorship) and the filmmaker has come to characterize our understanding of contemporary Iranian cinema. More recently, for example, when *Jodāi-ye Nader az Simin* (*A Separation*, 2011) won an Academy Award for best foreign-language film in 2012, the director, Asghar Farhadi, used his acceptance speech to make a political statement. He claimed that Iranian culture had been buried under a "heavy dust of politics," and the international response to his speech encapsulates the way in which audiences have come to understand the relationship between cinema and politics in the Islamic Republic of Iran. Commentators lauded Farhadi's bravery and suggested that he might not be able to return to Iran because of his remarks.[29] The idea that an award-winning director would not be able to go home because he publicly mentioned politics captures the exotic appeal of Iranian cinema for international audiences. A thriving cinema has developed despite a government that seems to work against it with rigid censorship policies and an unfair legal system, and within this scheme film becomes a site of resistance, pushing back against an oppressive theocracy.

Although it might appear that the revolutionary cinema of the 1980s completely redirected itself to condemn the very state that created it, the history of the Iranian film industry between 1989 and 2011 tells a different story. During this period, film was a force in mainstream politics and not just part of its opposition. Starting in the early 1990s, an intimate relationship developed between the popular reformist movement and the film industry, and the two institutions supported each other in an unlikely partnership. This relationship is far more complex than scholars have acknowledged, and it exposes a reformist history of Iranian cinema that has been obscured by research and popular discourse that privilege the cultural effects of the Islamic Revolution over the reformist policies that emerged a decade later.

In our effort to acknowledge revolutionary cinema's transformation into a cinema of reform, the year 1989 stands paramount both because it marked the start of reconstruction efforts following the destruction of the Iran-Iraq War and because Ayatollah Khomeini died on June 3, 1989. The end of the war and the death of the revolution's charismatic leader signaled a new period in the young republic's history as society suddenly faced the challenge of imagining the Islamic Republic outside of war and revolution. The urgency of wartime politics meant that most Iranians had been forgiving of strict and often invasive laws, and during the war they had acknowledged that the Islamic Republic's need to consolidate its power in order to fight a war momentarily superseded individuals' private liberties. The tempering of nationalist discourse following the end of the war, however, opened up new possibilities to critique the state, its rigid laws, and its failure to address the economic and social problems that the revolution had promised to solve. The opportunity to critique was further made possible by the death of Khomeini, the Islamic Republic's first Supreme Leader and the authoritative voice of the revolution. His death initiated political factionalism in Iran as competing political factions attempted to reconcile the often contradictory policies that they inherited from Khomeini's leadership.[30]

Political reform (*eslāhtalabi*) was a loosely connected political faction that emerged during this transformative moment in Iran's contemporary history. What began as a philosophical and theological project by the likes of Mehdi Bazargan and Abdolkarim Soroush, who argued in favor of pluralistic interpretations of Shi'i Islam,[31] soon became a moderate political movement that broadly supported democratic reforms. The discourse of reform, a moderate move within the political system, demarcated a transformation in the epistemological value of revolution as its meaning turned away from radical politics and instead came to represent conservative policy within the Islamic Republic. In other words, the presence of political reform, which was necessarily more moderate than the utopic ideals of the revolution, relocated revolutionary ideology within Iranian discourse as a conservative stronghold rather than an articulation of the leftist, radical movement it had once been.

Reform within the Islamic Republic, since its inception in the late 1980s, has shared a special relationship with cinema and the film industry, and this unique partnership is exemplified in the career of Seyyed Mohammad Khatami, whose presidency between 1997 and 2005 marked the height of political reform in the country. Khatami, who was born on September 29, 1943, and was trained both in Western philosophy at the University of Isfahan and in a traditional seminary in Qom, was serving as the head of the Islamic Center in Hamburg, Germany, when the events of the revolution escalated. After the success of the revolution, Khomeini personally urged Khatami to return to Iran in order to serve in the new Islamic Republic's administration. He returned in 1980 and has since held a number of high-level posts within the Iranian government, including a stint as a representative in the Iranian parliament or Majles (1980–1981), the chief of Keyhan Publishing (1981–1982), the head of Islamic Propagation (1986–1989), and the director of the National Library (1992–1997).

Khatami's special relationship with the film industry, however, began during his two terms as the minister of culture and Islamic guidance (1982–1986 and 1989–1992), and it continued during his presidency (1997–2005). The partnership that developed between Khatami and the film industry during these periods was multifaceted and included support but also contempt, policies that helped create a globally successful national cinema but also apparatuses that controlled, limited, and discouraged filmmaking. Above all, this partnership was in fact a partnership, one that comprised negotiation, mutual support, and censure on both sides. Khatami's first term within the ministry was particularly fraught with the emotions and contradictions that would come to define this partnership. Khatami took his position within the ministry the same year that it took on oversight of the film industry, which foresaw the political, ideological, and philosophical entanglement that would ultimately change the course of both political reform and cinema within the Islamic Republic. When Khatami assumed control of the ministry in 1982, filmmakers hailed it as "the year that love entered cinema."[32] Khatami and his team, including Fakhreddin Anvar as the deputy of cinematic affairs and Mohammad Beheshti as head of the newly established Farabi Cinema Foundation, initiated a plan to encourage quality filmmaking by sponsoring instructional workshops, creating a rating system, and offering tax breaks and other financial incentives.[33]

At the same time, though, as Saeed Zeydabadi-nejad notes, the ministry during this period viewed its mission as providing "support" (*hemāyat*) and "guidance" (*hedāyat*), on the one hand, and "supervision" (*nezārat*), a euphemism for censorship, on the other.[34] On July 3, 1982, the Majles, with the support of the ministry, passed the resolution "Nezārat bar nemāyesh-e film va eslāyd va vidiyu va sodur-e parvaneh namāyesh-e ānhā" (Supervision over the exhibition of films, slides, and video and issuing their exhibition permits). This document, which would be updated and revised over the years, set the standards for film censorship in the country, and it included, among other stipulations, regulations that films and other visual media could not "disparage Islam," "encourage corruption," or "assist in spreading the cultural, political, or economic influence of foreigners."³⁵ Khatami's first term as minister of culture and Islamic guidance thereby contributed to the creation of a revolutionary cinema, one in which the ideological fervor of the revolution was privileged alongside the status of film as an educational tool.

If Khatami's first term as minister of culture and Islamic guidance consolidated the film industry's efforts into a revolutionary cinema, then his second term was the genesis of a reform cinema. His reentrance into the ministry, of course, coincided with Khomeini's death in 1989, and the political landscape in Iran was undergoing tremendous change. The period between 1989 and 1992 is well documented as a golden period for filmmaking in Iran because the ministry, at Khatami's urging, offered a looser interpretation of its duty to "supervise" film production.³⁶ During this period, some of the most controversial films in the Islamic Republic's history made their way successfully through the ministry's censorship process, including *Bāshu, gharibeh-ye kuchak* and Mohsen Makhmalbaf's *Nowbat-e 'āsheqi* (Time for love, 1991). Khatami would ultimately resign from the ministry in 1992, and his resignation letter cited his frustration with what he considered a "violation of all legal, religious, ethical, and secular norms . . . in the field of culture and art."³⁷ Khatami's work in the ministry between 1989 and 1992 and his resignation together signaled a major shift in his personal politics, and cinema played an important role in this development. Conservative policy makers were critical of the Ministry of Culture and Islamic Guidance during this period, and with the release of certain controversial films, such as Makhmalbaf's *Time for Love*, Khatami was forced publicly to defend the films and his ministry's decisions. In these statements, he began to articulate his emerging reformist ideas for the first time. Cinema thereby became a rallying point for early discourses of reform. Khatami's second tenure within the ministry established the dialectical dynamic of reform cinema as the film industry benefited from but also contributed to Khatami's evolving political beliefs.

Following his resignation from the ministry, Khatami took up a much less visible position as the head of the National Library. As a result, when he emerged as a presidential candidate five years later in the spring of 1997, he was virtually unknown. The film industry, however, had not forgotten his support during his last several years as the minister of culture and Islamic guidance, and it is not overstatement to suggest that the film industry's participation in his campaigning efforts helped ensure his election to the presidency on May 23, 1997. That was the first year that candidates were allowed to broadcast campaign movies, and established filmmakers such as Seyfollah Dad, Behruz Afkhami, and Ahmad Reza Darvish directed movies in support of his platform and also later found success in Khatami's administration. These efforts transformed the way that voters interacted with politicians, and they also set the precedent for a series of documentary and narrative films that explicitly represented Khatami and his reformist movement. Filmmakers not only used their technical expertise to support Khatami but also leveraged their popularity to espouse him publicly. For example, Mohsen Makhmalbaf recorded an interview with Khatami that highlighted his support. Khatami's campaign managers released the interview two days before the election in order to heighten its impact.[38] Khatami's campaign marked reform's entrance on the screen at the same time that it signaled the film industry's attempt to steer political change in the Islamic Republic.

Khatami's supporters collectively became known as Jonbesh-e dovom-e Khordād, or the Second of Khordād movement, a name that referenced Khatami's unexpected victory in 1997. The movement gave body to a reformist effort in Iran, and political reform moved from an abstraction to a critical mass of supporters who had rallied around Khatami. His campaign had sought to reset the terms of public discourse in the Islamic Republic, and Ervand Abrahamian notes that, because of Khatami, terms such as "democracy," "rule of law," "civil society," "human rights," and "citizenship" supplanted the country's revolutionary rhetoric, which had included terms such as "imperialism," "jihad," "*gharbzadegi*" (Westoxification), "revolution," and "martyrdom."[39] This important semantic shift also signaled the changing and liberalizing cultural atmosphere in the country at the time. The terms of Khatami's campaign were not, however, only his domain, nor were they stable or fixed categories.

The film industry became an institution that facilitated the movement of this language into public discourse, and certain filmmakers sought either to translate the philosophical underpinnings of these concepts for public audiences or to challenge or refute Khatami's use of them. Of the concepts in Khatami's political platform, civil society and dialogue among civilizations most captured the film industry's imagination. Civil society, or *jāme'eh-ye madani* in Persian, was the main pillar of Khatami's political platform, but it was also the most nebulous of all his proposals. He understood the factional nature of Iranian politics at the time—the extent to which a single decision or even a word could fracture the entire political system—and, as a result, he refused to explain the term in much detail. In one particularly famous example, Khatami, in an interview with the progressive journal *Zanān* (Women), suggested civil society as the answer to the problems that Iranian women faced, both politically and socially; however, he never explained exactly what he meant by "civil society."[40] In the absence of a fixed definition, the term lawlessly swept through society, open to debate. Mohsen Kadivar, a reformist theologian at the time, would argue that civil society operated in opposition to *velāyat-e faqih* (guardianship of the Islamic jurist),[41] the system of governance within the Islamic Republic that Khomeini put into place to consolidate his political power. As *velāyat-e faqih*'s antidote, civil society became a stopgap for all of the Islamic Republic's problems, and young people in the country understood it as the key to freedom, tolerance, and respect between citizens and the government. Within this indeterminateness, the film industry was particularly captivated by civil society as an opening to freedom of media and as a corrective to the social problems that plagued life in the Islamic Republic.

If civil society sought to reset the terms of political and social life within the young republic, then Khatami's 1998 proposal to the United Nations for a dialogue among civilizations, or *goftegu-ye tamaddon-hā*, was an effort to reintegrate Iran into the international community. The United Nations was so enthusiastic about Khatami's call for worldwide cultural exchange that it declared the 2001 the "Year of the Dialogue Among Civilizations." The Iranian film industry was implicated in this new policy in a number of ways. In his first speech to the UN in November 1998, Khatami used film as an example of thinking about ways of encouraging intercultural understanding,[42] and there is historical evidence to suggest that filmmakers and enthusiasts picked up on Khatami's recommendation. The Search for Common Ground (SFCG) organized the "US-Iran Cinema Exchange" in 1999 in collaboration with Iran's House of Cinema. The meetings to plan this exchange took place in Cannes in 1998 and 1999, and planners identified a number of events in both Iran and the United States at which Iranian and American representatives would be present. Whereas the impact of such an exchange on cultural dialogue is clear, the political exchange it facilitated is also noteworthy. As a part of the agreement, both parties agreed to facilitate entry visas, the United States agreed to waive fingerprinting for participants, and the possibility of equipment donations made through a third party was also suggested.[43] These successful exchanges were the culmination of Mohammad Khatami's call to international dialogue. At the same time, Khatami's emphasis on repairing Iran's international reputation became a point of critique for filmmakers, who felt like he was ignoring the country's domestic problems.

Khatami was elected president just days after Abbas Kiarostami's *Ta'm-e gilās* (Taste of cherry, 1997) won the Palme d'Or at Cannes, and many pundits speculated that the win at Cannes was, in part, international endorsement for Khatami. Such a reading of Kiarostami's win shows how international film festivals and the circulation of capital that they facilitate contributed to the development of a reform cinema in the Islamic Republic of Iran. Khatami continued his support of the film industry during the course of his eight-year tenure as president. At certain points, the film industry even encountered freedom similar to what they had enjoyed during Khatami's final years in the Ministry of Culture and Islamic Guidance. During this time, a number of films that had been previously banned—most notably Davud Mirbaqeri's *Ādam barfi* (The snowman, 1994), a film about an Iranian man stranded in Turkey so desperate to get to the United States that he decides to dress up as a woman in the hopes of attracting an American suitor to secure citizenship—were reissued exhibition permits. This period also witnessed new thematic possibilities within film, including explicitly political subject matter, critiques of the Iran-Iraq War, and love stories.

But films from this period did more than simply benefit from the liberal cultural policy that Khatami's presidency encouraged; they also actively engaged the rhetoric that formed the base of his political platform. They participated in defining terms like "civil society," "democracy," and "rule of law" within the context of the Islamic Republic. This work was particularly important because Khatami, walking a thin political line between moderates and conservatives, never explicitly outlined what he meant by some of these terms, especially "civil society."⁴⁴ The most common criticism that Iranians launched against Khatami during his eight-year presidency was the futility of his efforts. His reformist politics remained largely abstract, and his attempts to change specific laws failed because he faced a largely conservative parliament, especially after his first two years in office. Filmmakers also critiqued Khatami and his ineffectualness. The fact that their films were released despite this explicit political critique affirmed the moderate cultural atmosphere that Khatami sought to foster. Civil society, democracy, and even a dialogue among civilizations required freedom within media, and the film industry's role in determining that freedom was unparalleled.

During Khatami's presidency, films by Rakhshan Bani-Etemad, Masud Kimiai, and others sought to visualize a place for "a dialogue of civilizations" and the "rule of law" in contemporary Iranian society, and films by Abbas Kiarostami and Bahman Farmanara spoke to the ways in which changing technology, especially the rise of digital video, participated in the democratic ideals that Khatami's presidency promised. Filmmakers also produced films in order to influence specific policies, like Mohsen Makhmalbaf's *Alefbā-ye afghan* (Afghan alphabet, 2002), which brought the plight of Afghan refugees in Iran to the public's consciousness, particularly the fate of children who were denied access to Iranian schools because they entered the country illegally. Makhmalbaf has stated, "By showing the film to the government of Iran, during Khatami's presidency, we managed to change the law in favor of these innocent refugee children. And as a result the following year, the door of the Iranian schools were opened to half a million of these children."⁴⁵ All of these efforts within cinema from this period demonstrate the extent to which the film industry was ideologically wrapped up in Khatami and this discourse of political reform.

At the same time, the film industry's entanglement with reform during this period was not just limited to discursive operations. Khatami's presidency oversaw the rise of institutional support for cinema. For example, in 1998, just a year after Khatami's election, reformist politicians founded the Cinema Museum (Muzeh-ye sinemā), the only museum in Iran dedicated to the exhibition and preservation of the history of the Iranian film industry. The museum officially opened its doors to the public in its current location in

INTRODUCTION

Ferdows Garden in 2002, and Khatami was present at its inauguration. Between 1997 and 2005, there was also a surge in cinema-related publications, including film journals and book publications, and in the eight years that Khatami was president there were more cinema-related publications than the sum total of such publications during the Islamic Republic's first eighteen years. Together these developments marked the emergence of the robust film culture that we typically associate with Iranian cinema today.

Khatami's work within the Ministry of Culture and Islamic Guidance and his two-term presidency thus reveal the extent to which Iranian cinema since the early 1990s has been a cinema of reform, wrapped up in the reformist philosophies and politics that sought to reconcile Islamic governance with democratic ideals. Whereas scholars have acknowledged that the film industry benefited from Khatami's moderate politics, especially within the cultural realm, the reform cinema that I am proposing is far more complicated than modes of permissibility wherein the film industry was simply a beneficiary to the liberal cultural sphere fostered by Khatami's reform efforts. Instead, *Reform Cinema in Iran* recognizes the film industry as part and parcel of reform, and in such an assessment film is a political force that has not only tracked the development of the reformist movement in the Islamic Republic but also contributed to and helped determine the discourse of reform within the country since the early 1990s.

Reform Cinema in Iran opens an archive of political speeches, religious sermons, newspaper editorials, and films that engage Khatami's relationship with the film industry in order to establish reform cinema as the inheritor of the revolutionary cinema that determined the Iranian film industry during the first decade of the Islamic Republic. This book is organized chronologically, and it proposes a series of case studies that together tell the story of reform cinema in the Islamic Republic. Although any number of films might gesture toward Khatami and the reformist movement that he helped inspire, only those films with an explicit relationship with Khatami form the basis of the case studies that appear in this book. Such connections include representations of Khatami on screen or within the narrative, films about which Khatami made public statements, or instances of reception in which audiences made a connection between Khatami and a particular film. Each case study places archival research and, where available, industry data alongside film analysis in order to bring forward a history of reform in Iran's contemporary cinematic tradition. Limiting the book's empirical evidence in this manner helps clear the way for future efforts to classify or understand films vis-à-vis their relationship to reform cinema.

Iran's reform cinema, which began in 1989 with the death of Ayatollah Khomeini and the end of the Iran-Iraq War, depended on a dialogue between the film industry and Mohammad Khatami. *Reform Cinema in Iran*, in addition to telling the history of this transformative period of Iranian film, theorizes the visual language that developed alongside this partnership. Reform cinema in Iran was determined by aesthetic decisions that privileged the revival of mystic love, the use of Tehran as a metaphoric site of political and social reform, reconfigurations of perceptions of time, and the democratization of filmmaking with the use of video technology. To this aim, chapter 1 establishes the genesis of reform cinema in the Islamic Republic by examining the circumstances leading to Khatami's resignation from the Ministry of Culture and Islamic Guidance. This chapter investigates the case of Mohsen Makhmalbaf's controversial film *Time for Love*. The release of *Time for Love*, which openly depicts a married woman's affair, sparked a media frenzy. Conservative religious leaders, policy makers, and commentators blamed Khatami for its release because the film had gone through the ministry's inspection process. The criticism launched against Khatami became so severe that he was forced to respond publicly and defend his support of the film. In this chapter, I examine the debates about *Time for Love* as they unfolded in newspaper editorials, political speeches, and religious sermons. These debates instruct us that the film industry helped to shape certain reformist ideas in the early 1990s, and *Time for Love*'s appropriation of a mystic aesthetic appealed to these budding reformists. During the early 1990s, for those intellectuals who had devoted themselves to Khomeini, the revolution, and the Islamic Republic, mysticism represented a means of reconciling commitment to Islamic governance with the need to create a more flexible system for political reform.

Chapter 2 takes as its starting point the 1997 policy that allowed campaign movies for the first time, and it examines how filmmakers have represented Khatami during elections. This chapter considers two films by Rakhshan

INTRODUCTION

Bani-Etemad—*Zir-e pust-e shahr* (Under the skin of the city, 2000), a feature film that takes place during the 1997 elections, and *Ruzegār-e mā . . .* (Our times . . ., 2002), a documentary about the 2001 elections—and it charts Bani-Etemad's critique of the reformist movement by analyzing her portrayal of urbanism and her appropriation of the documentary form. Before Khatami's election a complicated process of censorship ensured that politics remained offscreen, but these films both openly represent and criticize the political system. In this way reform cinema participated in the very democratic ideals that undergirded Khatami's reform efforts.

Whereas chapter 2 demonstrates new political opportunities that were possible within reform cinema, chapter 3 speaks to the ways in which reform cinema was wrapped up in the technological changes during Khatami's presidency. In particular, video technology, which was banned in Iran between 1982 and 1993, gained widespread acceptance during Khatami's presidency. Meanwhile, the proliferation of digital video at the beginning of the twenty-first century was changing what it meant to make and watch movies around the world. Abbas Kiarostami's *Taste of Cherry* and *Dah* (10, 2002) and Bahman Farmanara's *Bu-ye kāfur, 'atr-e yās* (The smell of camphor, the scent of jasmine, 2000) speak to this changing technology, and they play with video in order to show how this technology was democratizing filmmaking in Iran. This chapter contextualizes Kiarostami's and Farmanara's films by suggesting a history of video technology in Iran, one that demonstrates that the changing cultural value of video developed in tandem with Khatami's discourse of reform.

Chapter 4 moves beyond the art-house films that typically determine the scholarship on Iranian cinema and asks how Khatami's presidency affected popular cinema as well. A comparison between Masud Kimiai's *E'terāz* (Protest, 1999) and *Qeysar* (Qeysar, 1969) foregrounds a discussion about the fate of the tough-guy film, a genre popular both before and after the revolution. Scholars and film critics have suggested that *Qeysar* captured and perhaps even incited the violence of the revolution by celebrating vigilante justice and creating a space in which one's moral code supersedes the rule of law. With *Protest* Kimiai directly addresses his earlier film, and he rewrites the narrative of violence that made *Qeysar* famous. *Protest*, which is set during Khatami's presidency, kills its vigilante character and replaces him with a new

INTRODUCTION

hero, a thoughtful, sensitive man who discusses politics and thinks critically about the reformist movement. In this way, *Protest* announces the death of the tough-guy genre in Iranian cinema, a death initiated not by revolution but rather by the rise of the reformist movement. Because *Protest* both appealed to and represented average Iranians, and not just a particular class of intellectuals, it speaks to the unfolding of reform into popular discourse, and it suggests the important role that cinema played in facilitating that move.

In 2005 Khatami's second term came to an end, and the limit of two consecutive terms precluded him from seeking reelection. His successor, Mahmoud Ahmadinejad, espoused a hardline conservative platform that radically differed from Khatami's moderate policies, and he immediately began tightening control over the film industry. Chapter 5 attends to the legacy of reform cinema by examining Massoud Bakhshi's *Tehrān anār nadārad* (Tehran has no more pomegranates, 2007), an experimental documentary, and the music video "Eshq-e sorʻat" (Love of speed, 2007), performed by the underground band Kiosk, directed by Ahmad Kiarostami, and released on YouTube. Bakhshi's film and Kiosk's video establish that reform cinema as an aesthetic movement functions outside of the temporal limits of its political antecedent. Although both works were released two years after Khatami's presidency ended and did not benefit directly from his cultural liberalism, they still participate in central reformist debates. Their experimentation with form further suggests that the reformist aesthetic possesses a momentum that permits it to develop and transform without explicit contact with the political movement that inspired it.

Finally, the conclusion of *Reform Cinema in Iran* analyzes the experience of walking through the Cinema Museum (Muzeh-ye sinemā) in Tehran, the only such museum in Iran. Visitors to the museum are immediately welcomed by a placard that explicitly positions the museum as a reformist effort, and this framing demonstrates that the changes to cinema that we witness during the reformist period were not limited to aesthetics but also included new institutions to support the film industry. Meanwhile, toward the rear of the museum is a large room filled with Iranian film posters, and occupying a central place is Jafar Panahi's *In film nist* (This is not a film, 2011). This provocative piece reacts to the twenty-year ban on filmmaking that Panahi received for his participation in the protests following the 2009 Iranian elections. *This Is Not a Film*, which was filmed partially on an iPhone by his former cameraman Mojtaba Mirtahmasb, inverts many of the normative features of filmmaking, and it demonstrates how the cry for reform in the Islamic Republic has deeply affected filmmaking and refashioned many of its conventions.

1

WHEN LOVE ENTERED CINEMA

Mysticism and the Emerging Poetics of Reform

In the late spring of 1992, Mohammad Khatami arrived at an impasse. April elections had ushered in the Islamic Republic's fourth Majles, or parliament, and the overwhelmingly conservative body would almost certainly terminate him as the minister of culture and Islamic guidance. Over the last several years, he had faced criticism again and again from the country's conservative policy makers for his moderate views on the regulation of art and culture, and the election of a new conservative Majles sealed his fate. With the first session of the new Majles looming on the horizon, set for May 28, 1992, he could either face the impeachment process or step down from public service. So on May 24, 1992, after nearly a decade within the Islamic Republic's highest administrative posts, including two stints as head of the ministry, Khatami accepted his defeat and submitted his resignation letter to the Majles. Later published in several newspapers, this letter reaffirmed the importance of cultural and artistic work both to the goals of the revolution and to the health of the Islamic Republic. He called the act of facilitating cultural innovation a "heavy" and "increasingly complicated" task, made complicated by a "violation of all legal, religious, ethical, and secular norms . . . in the field of culture and art." Responding to interference in the oversight of the country's cultural industries, especially by conservative forces, Khatami claimed that the ministry's work was now "completely outside any manner of logic or legality," and he warned of an "unhealthy and tumultuous environment" ahead and of the "discouragement and insecurity" that would threaten the country's thinkers and artists.[1]

Much had changed in the thirteen years since Khomeini had urged Khatami to return to Iran from Germany in order to participate in the Islamic Republic's new government. Khatami had been a member of Khomeini's inner circle, a part of the conservative ruling elite against which he was now positioning himself. In 1982, the same year that the Ministry of Culture and Islamic Guidance took control of cinematic affairs in the country, Prime Minister Mir-Hossein Mousavi appointed Khatami as the head of the ministry, and filmmakers dubbed his arrival "the year that love entered cinema." Despite this early optimism, Khatami oversaw the ministry as it established a series of strict regulations over the film industry, including censorship policies that still haunt film production. Although his letter of resignation indicated that his disagreement (*mokhālefat*) with Khomeini's conservative policies began with the leader's views on music, Khatami's professional work throughout the 1980s nevertheless provided a legal framework for tight control over film production in the country and attested to his commitment to the Islamic Republic's conservative values at the time.

To understand how Khatami's quiet acquiescence in the Islamic Republic's first decade became the impassioned defiance of his resignation letter requires an examination of the years immediately preceding his departure from the Ministry of Culture and Islamic Guidance. The late 1980s and early 1990s represented a particularly fraught period in Iran's contemporary history. The end of the eight-year Iran-Iraq War in August 1988 also marked the end of austere wartime politics. Less than a year later, Ayatollah Khomeini's death in June 1989 signaled the start of factionalism in Iranian politics as the country's policy makers struggled to agree on their country's direction in the absence of a revolutionary and spiritual leader to provide absolute guidance on political and social issues. Within the context of this turbulent period, the Ministry of Culture and Islamic Guidance gradually began to relax the strict censorship policies that had determined artistic production for nearly a decade. Between 1989 and 1992, the ministry allowed the publication of some of Iran's most controversial works of art, including Shahrnush Parsipur's novel *Zanān bedun-e mardān* (Women without men, 1989), an open depiction of female sexuality, and Bahram Beyzaie's film *Bāshu: gharibeh-ye kuchak* (Bashu, the little stranger, 1989), an explicit critique of the Iran-Iraq War.

Cinema played an important role in the liberalization of the Ministry of Culture and Islamic Guidance during the final stretch of Khatami's tenure. Films like Dariush Mehrjui's *Hamun* (Hamun, 1990) and Mohsen Makhmalbaf's *Nowbat-e 'āsheqi* (Time for love, 1991) not only passed through ministry and challenged the limits of what was acceptable but also contributed to the emerging discourse of reform at this time. Controversial films, especially those by Makhmalbaf, invited budding reformists, including Khatami and the philosopher Abdolkarim Soroush, to justify their politics, and these defenses became some of the earliest articulations of a clear ideology of reform. The mystic aesthetic that pervades many of these films became a point of engagement for Khatami and others, and certain films and the controversies surrounding them in the early 1990s positioned mysticism as an intellectual strategy for those liberal-leaning thinkers who had devoted themselves to Khomeini, the revolution, and the Islamic Republic. Mysticism offered a means of reconciling commitment to Islamic governance with the need to create a more flexible system in order to establish a space for reform, and in this way it became central to reform cinema.

AUTHORSHIP, AUTHORITY, AND ACCOUNTABILITY: THE POLITICS OF OWNERSHIP

The year 1982 was an important one for cinema in Iran. Khatami assumed control of the Ministry of Islamic Culture and Guidance, and the Farabi Cinema Foundation, the administrative arm charged with cinematic affairs within the ministry, began its work supporting and regulating film production in the country. This new collaboration between the ministry and Farabi culminated that year in the founding of the Fajr Film Festival, envisioned as Iran's premier film festival. Fajr, especially in its early years, aimed to continue encouraging revolutionary fervor within cinema by showcasing Iranian films that promoted a "commitment to human beings, defense of the poor, support for the liberation of the weak, conformity with the Islamic Republic's values." But, as Hamid Naficy has observed, the Fajr Film Festival eventually shed its "revolutionary ardor" to become the country's flagship international film festival.²

Perhaps unexpectedly, it was the representation of love that began to shake the revolutionary foundation on which the festival had been built, and the 1991 Fajr Film Festival program, which featured a number of films about love, revealed changing priorities within the film industry. The public's reaction to this program, however, showed that the country's policy and taste makers were not ready to leave behind the social issues and conservative values that had helped shape film production in the Islamic Republic up until that time in order to bring love stories to the big screen. As one editorialist in *Jomhuri-ye Eslāmi* wrote, "It is a shame that cheap love is taking the place of higher love at the Fajr Film Festival."³ The controversy surrounding the Fajr Film Festival in 1991 exposed the cracks forming in the unified vision of what cinema should achieve in the Islamic Republic.

No film was more controversial at the 1991 festival than Mohsen Makhmalbaf's *Time for Love*, which depicted a woman's adulterous affair and—most shockingly—absolved her. The criticism launched against the film opened up an unprecedented debate about the role of cinema in society. This debate, which played out in the country's periodicals, including newspapers and trade publications, and in religious sermons, indicted Makhmalbaf, the Ministry of Culture and Islamic Guidance, and Khatami, and it helps us understand the reconfiguration of commitment to the revolution during the 1980s into a set of reformist policies that diverge considerably from the original ideals of the Islamic Republic at the turn of the twenty-first century. At what point did revolutionary fervor begin to subside and disillusionment set in? Mohsen Makhmalbaf and Mohammad Khatami played important roles both in the propagation of the Islamic Republic's early ideals and in the period of reform that emerged two decades later, and their role in the *Time for Love* debates hinted at the discontent with the revolution that would emerge more fully several years later. Ultimately, the controversy surrounding *Time for Love* represented a pivotal moment in the transition from revolution to reform, both politically and cinematically.

At the core of the *Time for Love* debates is the question of who controlled the film industry in Iran in the early 1990s. This question was further complicated by the fact that the Islamic Republic played a significant role in the production and release of films. Beyond the practice of censorship, the government exerted control over the industry by providing huge yearly subsidies. It supplied financial backing for one-third of the country's film production and offered incentives to the industry by providing tax breaks and reduced-interest loans.[4] This dependency developed because the country's rigid censorship practices curtailed viewership and, subsequently, foreign imports drew greater audiences. Unable to generate enough revenue to cover production costs, the Iranian film industry faced extinction immediately after the revolution. The state recognized the transformative value of film and opted to support the indigenous film industry.[5] But with this support came expectations about accountability and the social value of the films that the government supported, which in turn gave rise to questions about categorization. Should a film be classified as the director's work, or does it in part belong to the government? Who is accountable for its controversial release? A study of the *Time for Love* debates, by focusing on public perceptions of the film and the film industry, illuminates emerging fissures and rising discontent among those individuals charged with the creation and regulation of art in the early 1990s.

Time for Love functions as a complicated and shifting matrix of morality and consists of three distinct episodes, each of which tells the same basic story but with a different ending. In the first section, a married woman, Güzel, has an affair, which her husband ultimately discovers. Outraged and angry, he kills her lover, and the episode ends with a judge sentencing him to death. In the second version, Güzel once again has an affair. But this time her lover kills her husband, and the same judge sentences him to death. In this version, the actor who plays the husband in the first episode plays the lover in the second. In both episodes, Güzel, distraught by the death of her lover, commits suicide. In the third and final part, the husband (the actor who plays the husband in the first part) once again tries to kill the lover, but during the course of their battle the lover grabs the husband's knife and refuses to kill him. The husband, touched by the event, decides to recognize the love between his wife and her lover and plans their wedding. The film ends with the wedding ceremony, at which the judge from the first two parts is present as a guest.

Whereas the unyielding order of these three sections marks an important feature of the film, the fluidity of the characters, the actors who play them, and the three endings suggests that each situation has a series of specific conditions that ultimately determine its outcome, a notion wrapped up in a theory of moral antiabsolutism. The film asserts that a universal set of morals does not exist and that morality instead depends on circumstance. Makhmalbaf shot and set his film in Turkey, thereby loosening the film's ties to Iran. Despite this distance, people in Iran began reacting to the film almost immediately, and the debates spread across multiple publications and even entered popular Friday sermons. The debate, like the film, unfolded in three distinct parts. Although some overlap exists, each of these three phases represents a specific set of concerns as the debate slowly evolved from a reaction to a particular film and director to a full-force critique of the Ministry of Culture and Islamic Guidance and its head, Mohammad Khatami.

At first critics targeted the director Makhmalbaf and the film *Time for Love* specifically. The lengthy debate began with an article published in *Resālat* (Mission) on February 21, 1991, in which the author, M. Shushtari, lamented, "Oh, God, what do I see? Can this be the same Makhmalbaf that criticized *Golhā-ye dāvudi* [Chrysanthemums, 1984]?"[6] Conservative groups in particular were outraged that Makhmalbaf, who had played an important part in solidifying the ideology of the new republic with early films such as *Towbeh-ye Nasuh* (Nasuh's repentance, 1983), *Bāykot* (Boycott, 1985), and *Dastforush* (The peddler, 1986), had dared to create a film that was at such odds with the Islamic Republic's interpretation of Shi'i Islam. Hamid Dabashi credits Makhmalbaf with the rise of an "Islamic set of aesthetics" that was "initially squarely at the service of the Islamic Revolution . . . and the Islamic Republic."[7] And *Time for Love* marked the initial decline of that relationship. Shushtari's disbelief suggested the degree to which Makhmalbaf's cinematic goals had changed. *Time for Love* explores the possibilities of multiple moralities rather than promoting the Islamic Republic's single interpretation of morality.

A. Nasrabadi noted this change in Makhmalbaf's approach to cinema in the article "The Film Festival of 1991: Armed with Love and the Negation of Desire," published in *Keyhān* on March 3, 1991. He argued, "It is no surprise that the Makhmalbaf of *Nasuh's Repentance* and *Boycott* has become the Makhmalbaf of . . . *Time for Love*." He further remarked on the shifting perception of Makhmalbaf among intellectuals by indicating that secular thinkers, who until recently "were shooting at his shadow," had reevaluated their position and "today have abandoned their boycott on his films and now include him in the same category as the likes of Shahrnush Parsipur."[8] Nasrabadi's alignment of Makhmalbaf with the novelist Shahrnush Parsipur is at once dangerous and in some ways appropriate. Always a controversial and anticonformist figure, Parsipur was arrested three times by the Islamic Republic. News of her 1990 incarceration for the publication of *Women Without Men* likely remained fresh in readers' minds at this time.[9] Makhmalbaf's representation of women's sexuality in *Time for Love* was similarly problematic. Critics accused him of "defending liberal women who are *gharbzade* [Westoxicated]" and "unconstrained."[10]

Yet not all parties reacted negatively to this particular depiction of love and sexuality. When asked to comment on the film, Dr. Abdolkarim Soroush, an important reformist philosopher who will be discussed in more detail later in this chapter, told *Omid* that he did not "understand why earthly love is bad." He questioned whether it "is possible to achieve a higher love without the lower love." *Time for Love*, he said, "is about this earthly love" and he "liked it."[11]

Makhmalbaf, however did more than simply represent women's sexuality. He also threatened the Islamic Republic's ethical system by proposing an alternative and relativist model for morality.[12] Critics attacked the film as a "condemnation of morality" and an attempt "to make relative morals prevail."[13] Ali Motahhari even suggested that Makhmalbaf put his filmmaking career on hold until he had resolved his "intellectual qualms regarding women and the idea that truths are relative."[14] This statement reaffirmed the extent to which the country's administrative elite believed in the influential power of film, and this view on the role of film in society served as a basis for the government's support of the film industry, an arrangement that expected cinema to function not as a site of contestation or ambiguity but rather as a medium for the propagation of a certain kind of ideology.

Political and religious leaders expected cinema to promote the Islamic Republic's conservative interpretation of Shi'i Islam, one that located the value of art in its ability to represent idealized types. This interpretation was codified within the film industry in 1982, when the Ministry of Culture and Islamic Guidance, newly equipped with authority over the film industry, began holding films to a new "rule of modesty" that sought to represent a "purified" culture.[15] The representation of women was especially contentious within this new policy, and women were to be limited to characters who embodied the "idealized" Muslim woman, especially in her role as mother and wife. *Time for Love* was problematic because it represented a woman whose extramarital affair disintegrated the family structure. *Time for Love* does more than fail to condemn her actions. It justifies them by creating a system wherein moral relativity is an idealized possibility.

By jeopardizing the "purified" culture that it was supposed to be promoting, *Time for Love* threatened public accountability, and the second wave in the debates consisted primarily of attempts to place responsibility for the film's controversial release. As the dispute began to extend beyond the film, blame initially rested on the Fajr Film Festival. Critics of the film expressed dismay that "the festival organizers inadvertently allowed the new and improved Makhmalbaf a place in the festival."[16] One editorial criticized the festival programmers for carving out a space for the representation of love at all.[17] A statement released by the festival's public relations office at this time, however, neglected even to mention *Time for Love* and therefore refused to participate in this debate.[18] As a result, people began looking higher for accountability and aimed their attention at the government, and specifically at the Ministry of Culture and Islamic Guidance.

N. Mahdiar first articulated this kind of attack in an article called "Defective Criticism Is Wrong: We Should Go After the Roots," published in *Keyhān* on March 14, 1991. The author wondered "which policy charted this downward course for Makhmalbaf." This line of questioning suggested a provocative causal relationship between official governmental policy and Makhmalbaf's cinematic work and indicated a significant reversal. Whereas previously his works influenced policy by reinforcing revolutionary values, with *Time for Love*, Mahdiar claimed, policy asserted its influential power over Makhmalbaf. He further argued, "Makhmalbaf is a shining example of the supervised governmental policy over cinema." Yet Mahdiar's harshest criticism came with his assertion that *Time for Love*, which had been trashed in the papers by this point, is "the product of your guidance and support."[19] This statement refocused his point of address directly to the Ministry of Culture and Islamic Guidance, and his choice of words—"guidance and support," which clearly referenced the ministry's name—left no room for doubt that Mahdiar was criticizing the ministry.

Gradually criticism against the ministry became more narrowly focused, and its head, Mohammad Khatami, emerged as the primary target. Said Motamedi, for example, addressed the minister directly and asked, "Mr. Khatami, if you are actually opposed to the cheapness of the West, then why is the film *Hamlet* (in which the lips of a boy and a girl come within a few millimeters of one another) being shown in cinemas right now? Your censors . . . edit the film in such a way that the viewer can easily guess what has been cut out."[20] Motamedi's question demonstrated the way that this debate, which began squarely focused on Makhmalbaf, had developed into larger commentary on ministry practices. This author expressed no interest in the lasting legacy of *Time for Love* but used its controversy to call into question Khatami's own system of beliefs and to censure loosening censorship policies. A second critic, A. Darai, also addressed Khatami directly and wrote: "Dear Mr. Khatami . . . you should have responded to central complaints that have entered the press in the Friday sermons of Qom . . . and asked for forgiveness from the people of the Shi'i community [*hezbollah*]."[21] This kind of request targeted Khatami as the agent responsible for the content of *Time for Love* and positioned him against a larger religious community.

Darai's comment also alluded to an important feature of the debate: much of the commentary entered the newspapers through the Friday sermons of Qom, Tehran, and other major cities. Ahmad Jannati, the interim prayer leader of Qom, launched the severest criticism of Khatami and the Ministry of Culture and Islamic Guidance during a Friday sermon on March 7, 1991, that was later published in the newspaper *Ettelā'āt*. During his speech, Jannati warned that there is a "movement crawling in the name of art" that threatens the "Islamic Republic, the committed artists, and the Revolution." He urged his listeners to "put up a serious fight against these kinds of movements."[22]

Jannati perhaps foresaw the reformist movement and its special relationship with art, but he also made an important distinction between those artists still committed to the revolutionary ideals and those artists who were aligning themselves with this growing movement.

Jannati's speech mirrored in some ways the larger debate at play as he shifted its focus from art and the artist to Khatami and the ministry. He claimed, "They brag that our film has been the subject of acclaim and appreciation outside of the country and foreigners conclude that art is alive and well in Iran. What a strange kind of art you've created."[23] Jannati significantly changed the subject of these two sentences, juxtaposing an ambiguous "they" with an equally indistinct "you." And yet the space he created between these two subjects remains certain as he relocates his point of address in the second person. This act placed specific blame not on an individual artist but rather on a larger system of government oversight.

Khatami took this point of address personally and responded to Jannati's remarks directly, commenting on the *Time for Love* controversy for this first time. In a speech published in several newspapers on March 12, 1991, he cautioned that these words "raise doubt and create ambiguity." He attempted to trivialize Jannati's comments and suggested that "it is unlikely that Mr. Jannati has the base of knowledge necessary to assess the cultural and artistic events of this country, including film festivals." Nevertheless, he noted that the "decisiveness" with which he "issues the angriest orders disturbs the peace of mind of the experts who are doing this sensitive work and upsets the cinema." Khatami reiterated this point and requested "forgiveness from all the people knowledgeable of culture and art" for Jannati's comments. He asked "the dear artists and men of culture to tolerate these unkind things with generosity of spirit."[24] Khatami made a powerful statement with this seemingly innocent request for forgiveness. He distinguished between the artistic community and conservative religious groups and, importantly, suggested that an individual must possess a certain kind of knowledge in order to evaluate art effectively. This claim precluded the participation of religious officials in the formation of governmental policy that oversees artistic production. Khatami's comment anticipated the 1992 publication of the Culture Principles of the

Islamic Republic, a government document that recommends "the task of handling sociocultural issues . . . be left to the 'experts' and not the clergy."[25]

The exchange between Khatami and Jannati touches on a defining feature of this period. A great deal of uncertainty ensued after Khomeini's death in 1989, and the country's leaders faced the challenge of reconciling a set of paradoxical policies that he had enacted during his ten-year rule. His various documents codified, in a sense, the aim of the republic, and in his absence administrators were left to their own instincts and powers of interpretation. Fakhreddin Anvar, the deputy of cinematic affairs, noted the difficulties that came with this uncertainty and classified "the experience of this year" as "a very sensitive and complicated episode." However, he defended the ministry's actions during this time and contended that "we have been very successful."[26] Ultimately, though, the variety of responses to the ministry's "success" that emerged during the course of these debates signified the factionalism that marked the post-Khomeini period.

Khatami's direct intervention into this controversy signaled the third shift in the *Time for Love* debates. During this final period in the debate, people initially responded to Khatami's statement and reiterated many of the same points, but the discussion eventually narrowed its focus to the reaction of the film industry. At this point, a series of directors began commenting on the controversy. Many of these filmmakers attempted to distance themselves from the two figures at the center of the storm, Mohsen Makhmalbaf and the Ministry of Culture and Islamic Guidance. Seyfollah Dad, who would later become the deputy for cinema affairs during Khatami's presidency, for example, suggested that one of the mistakes in current debates was "confusing the identity of current cinema in Iran with Mohsen Makhmalbaf." He also reminded readers that film did not serve as a "reflection of . . . the state or the Ministry of Guidance." He ended his article with a poetic warning by Rumi: "In Balkh an ironsmith sinned / in Shustar they cut the neck of an ironsmith."[27] This couplet served as a caution against the kind of generalization that rests at the center of these debates. In many ways, this wave of response represented the beginning of the breakdown of the connection between politics and cinema that was constructed in the second phase of the debate. With this breakdown came the dissolution of the perception of a heavy-handed relationship between cinema and the ministry.

As writers like Dad downplayed the significance of the interplay between politics and cinema, the notion of aesthetics reemerged as a central concern of the debate. These responses remained critical of Makhmalbaf. The director Rahim Rahimipur, critical of a cinematic trajectory that would permit a film like *Nasuh's Repentance* to give way to *Time for Love*, indicated that "if [Iranian cinema] continues down this path, only God knows where it will end up." He suggested that Iranian society should be "worried and concerned that *The Little Jungle Boy*, who has gotten married and settled down, gave up his battle to present the history of Islam and the Islamic Revolution through cinema."[28] Rahimipur offered his biting critique by playing with Makhmalbaf's film titles and insinuated that the director had gone soft with his depiction of love in *Time for Love*. Rahimipur criticized Makhmalbaf's neglect of more serious issues affecting the country at that time and lamented the fact that Iran does not "even have one example of one film in line with the goals of the regime and reconstruction after the war."[29] With this article, the debate came full circle, as it once again examined the purpose of film. However, whereas previously criticism was very much tied up in what film should not do (e.g., promote moral relativism), this artistic response was concerned more with what film should attempt to do (e.g., reinforce reconstruction efforts after the Iran-Iraq War).

At this point, the debate as a cohesive body began to break down. A unified set of concerns no longer drove the responses, and the discussion slowly tapered off. By the end of April, just two months after the film's first and only showing, *Time for Love* and the related disputes no longer appear regularly in the main newspapers. In June the monthly journal *Film* published a follow-up report that summarized some of the major exchanges of the debate and officially brought the controversy to a close. My examination charts some of the major concerns of the *Time for Love* debates and at the same time highlights the public's overwhelmingly negative response to the film. This collective response indicated that the Ministry of Culture and Islamic Guidance had, whether intentionally or unintentionally, loosened its grip on the art world and had challenged the limits of cultural expression in Iranian society at that time. The disconnect between the public criticism of the film and Khatami and Makhmalbaf's open defense suggested that whereas society in the spring of 1991 by and large situated art in the hands of the government, Khatami and Makhmalbaf provided agency to the artist.

The release of *Time for Love* and the controversy surrounding it suggested a shift in policy, both personal and political. This episode represented a critical moment for Mohsen Makhmalbaf and Mohammad Khatami. Both men had played important roles in the republic's first decade, but their support of this film revealed that their beliefs were no longer in line with the ideals of the conservative revolutionaries. With this film, Makhmalbaf declared his independence as an artist and no longer accepted his role as the propagator of the Islamic Republic's ideology. Dabashi notes that "Makhmalbaf's early career was . . . seriously implicated in . . . the Islamic Republic" and his works played an "integral" part in its reign.[30] The release of *Time for Love*, however, marked Makhmalbaf's move away from this "early career." The shift in the way that Makhmalbaf perceived himself and his relationship to the government was evident in the two public responses he issued. In the first press release, published relatively early in the debates, on March 10, 1991, he indicated that "the writer of these lines knows very well that these disputes don't even have anything to do with him and the dispute is . . . between the power-hungry forces."[31] Whereas previously Makhmalbaf's role was tied up in this struggle for power, at this point he was distancing himself from that process.

In his second statement, issued several weeks later during the wave of artistic responses, Makhmalbaf addressed an "open letter" to "Dear Mr. Mehdi Nasri, Brother who is committed and revolutionary." He quickly corrected himself, however, and wrote, "Pardon me, A. Nasrabadi, the managing director and actually the one who does everything at *Keyhān*!" With this introduction, Makhmalbaf alluded to the fact that Mehdi Nasri, the managing director of the newspaper *Keyhān*, had written a series of articles against the film, Makhmalbaf, and the ministry under the name "A. Nasrabadi." He attacked Nasri's failure to sign his articles with his own name and accused him of "benefiting from behind the curtain." Makhmalbaf asked, "If you claim to have faith, why don't you stand behind your words?" His most telling statement, however, came when he inquired, "Don't we, the artists of your country, stand like men under your beating sticks with our real names?"³² Makhmalbaf's emphasis on names and signing one's work functioned as a way of reaffirming his agency. He accepted responsibility for the controversy but also asserted the film as his own.

In his letter to Nasri, Makhmalbaf argued that the managing editor was only interested in "ridiculing the Ministry."³³ Nasri's eagerness to criticize the ministry may very well have rested in the agency's move away from the conservative policies of the republic under Khomeini. Khatami was responsible for steering the ministry in this new direction, and his reaction to the *Time for Love* debates highlighted his growing discontent in the post-Khomeini period. Like Makhmalbaf, who promoted the Islamic Republic's ideology through his films, Khatami contributed significantly to the formation of the Islamic Republic, serving in many of the country's highest administrative posts, including the Majles, the Keyhān Publishing House (under the direct control of the Supreme Leader), and the Ministry of Culture and Islamic Guidance. By the time that *Time for Love* premiered at the 1991 Fajr Film Festival, Khatami had been in the service of the republic for more than a decade.

His response to the *Time for Love* episode recalls the language that would mark his letter of resignation from the ministry a year later, and it brings into focus emerging cracks in his commitment to a revolutionary framework as the kind of governance that would best serve the Islamic Republic. In his public response to Jannati's critique of the film and the ministry, after addressing Jannati directly, Khatami attended to the film *Time for Love* and the complaints launched against the ministry. He suggested that he was proud of the ministry for "holding steadfast" as weak and narrow-minded people tried "to load their own political and cultural agenda onto society as a whole."³⁴ Khatami's charged language in this speech spoke to his defense of the ministry's new, more moderate direction.

During this course of this speech, however, Khatami did more than just defend his ministry. He also began to express a new ideology, one that diverged considerably from the revolutionary values that had marked his earlier career. He asserted that "today our society is facing great tragedies," and he located the root of these problems in the "judicious and courageous confrontation by his eminence Imam Khomeini . . . , the terror that he caused on various occasions, and the fatwas and provocative opinions he had concerning every area, especially cultural and artistic."[35] While Khatami remained respectful of Khomeini and the necessity of his drastic measures, he also felt limited by the policies of the revolution, especially with regard to artistic expression.

Just as Makhmalbaf's film *Time for Love* promoted antiabsolutism, so too did Khatami's speech advocate for the possibility of relativity in policy making. His statement on the film suggested that the policies and aims of the republic must adjust to fit the changing conditions and evolving political environment, a belief at the heart of the reformist efforts that would define the political landscape less than a decade later. The very core of the reformist philosophy can therefore be traced back to Khatami's work in the Ministry of Culture and Islamic Guidance, and the film *Time for Love* was a point of rupture that contributed to this new discourse of reform. The film and the controversy surrounding it marked a departure in the way in which certain artists and politicians, like Makhmalbaf and Khatami, understood the film industry's place within the Islamic Republic. By providing the film industry with more agency and relocating ownership in the artists themselves, these budding reformists began to reimagine what the Islamic Republic could achieve outside of the revolutionary and wartime politics that had dictated life in Iran for more than a decade.

MYSTIC LOVE, REFORMIST PHILOSOPHY

The debates surrounding *Time for Love* attest to increasing factionalism and the gradual formation of a reformist ideology. But what specifically about the film appealed to these dissenting voices? And how did the film speak to a larger set of intellectual strategies that this faction sought to deploy at this historical juncture? Just as the controversy surrounding the film suggested a move toward the individualization of filmmaking, the film stages the individual experiences of religion, morality, and ethics. *Time for Love* engages a long mystic tradition within Persian poetics in order to advocate an alternative to the Islam promoted by the Islamic Republic. Abdolkarim Soroush wrote several favorable reviews of *Time for Love*, and his open and enthusiastic support invites a comparison between his philosophies and the film,³⁶ a reading that ultimately underscores mysticism as an aesthetic feature of reform cinema.

Before expounding the political potential of mysticism as a feature of a reformist aesthetic, it is important to establish *Time for Love* as a film invested in and indebted to the Persian mystic tradition.³⁷ Two important Sufi concepts, *ma'refat* (knowing God) and *haqiqat* (reality, truth), inform a mystic exploration of *Time for Love*, and the poetry of Jalal al-Din Rumi proves instructive to any effort to classify *Time for Love* as a representative example of cine-mysticism in Iran in the early 1990s. The application of Rumi here is particularly relevant because both Makhmalbaf and Soroush have professional connections to him. Whereas Makhmalbaf has on several occasions quoted Rumi in reference to his films, Soroush is a scholar of Rumi and has edited an authoritative edition of his *Masnavi-ye ma'navi*.³⁸ By reading *Time for Love*'s engagement with *ma'refat* and *haqiqat* as Rumi understood them alongside Makhmalbaf's published philosophy on the film, the mystic qualities that underpin the film fully emerge.

The Sufi concept of *ma'refat*, as Franklin Lewis reminds us in his extensive study of Rumi, is "an intuitive and experiential knowing of God . . . achieved not by studying the law, but by loving God."³⁹ This definition collapses knowing God with the act of loving him, and it positions love as central to the mystic experience in Persian literature. Annemarie Schimmel also emphasizes this point when she argues that although Persian mystic poets draw on three categories of symbols, "the center of their thoughts is always Love."⁴⁰ The nature of this love according to Schimmel is metaphoric, and she cites the proverb *al-majāz qantaratu'l-haqīqa* (The metaphor is the bridge that leads to Truth) to illuminate the way in which Persian mystic poets imagine the relationship between love and truth. Persian mystical poetry ultimately depends on the tension between human love and divine love, wherein the former may, but does not necessarily, function as a metaphor for the latter, and Schimmel, like Lewis, also notes the opposition between love and intellect in the mystic tradition. For the mystic poets, she claims, "reason, or intellect, leads to talk while Love silently reveals the inside of the mysteries."⁴¹

The title *Time for Love* underscores the centrality of love in Makhmalbaf's film, and the public debates surrounding it similarly suggested that love was a point of concern for audiences. These published debates indicate that, by and large, the public considered the film's representation of love in earthly terms; other films at the 1991 Fajr Film Festival, Hamid Naficy has noted, were celebrated for their representations of "spiritual and mystic love."[42] Despite the way in which audiences received *Time for Love* at the time of its release, its representation of love is also metaphoric, a testament to the mystic love that marked a millennium of Persian poetry before it. Abdolkarim Soroush was the first to consider the romantic qualities of *Time for Love* in divine terms when he asked in a review of the film whether it "is possible to achieve a higher love without the lower love."[43] In a second essay, he expanded on the metaphoric power of love in the film and wrote that "being in love is not emphasized or treated topically" in *Time for Love*, but, rather, love functions as "proof" in a more complicated case study on the human experience.[44]

Mohsen Makhmalbaf's own philosophy of the film, which was published in a three-volume collection of essays and reviews called *Gong-e khābideh* (Muted dreams, 1993), picks up on Soroush's classification of the film as mysticism and, like the mystic poets of the classical Persian tradition, considers the concept of love both in metaphoric relation to the divine and as at odds with intellectualism. *Gong-e khābideh* is an idiom in Persian that describes the disorientation of waking up from a dream and recognizing the physical shapes of reality once again, and the state of *gong-e khābideh* describes Makhmalbaf's career and especially his disillusionment with the dream of the revolution. Within this framework, *Time for Love* is *the* moment of *gong-e khābideh* and attests to Makhmalbaf's recognition of the restrictive realities of the Islamic Republic, in contrast to the revolution's promises.

In *Muted Dreams*, Makhmalbaf's notes on *Time for Love* challenge and ultimately collapse two binary oppositions: *manteq-e sar–manteq-e del* (the logic of the mind–the logic of the heart) and *'eshq-e zamini–'eshq-e āsemāni* (earthly love–heavenly love). The tension generated in *Time for Love* between and through these opposing forces ultimately imbues the film with its mystic character. In his discussion of logic, Makhmalbaf begins with a statement that appeals to the rational mind: the whole is bigger than the part.[45] But according to the director, *Time for Love* allows us to image how the heart's logic functions differently from the mind's, in such a way that this generally accepted truth about the relationship between the whole and the part no longer seems rational and the whole is no longer bigger than the part.

Two moments in the film demonstrate the ways in which the heart's logic triumphs over the mind's rationale. In the film's first section, Güzel's husband accepts his death sentence and insists, "I am content because I have defended my honor." As Makhmalbaf notes, logically, one's honor represents only one part of one's life as a whole.[46] The husband's willingness to sacrifice his life to defend his honor confounds the proportional relationship between the whole and the part. Yet this act does not strike us as unreasonable, because it appeals to an emotional logic, according to which the desire to defend one's honor is greater and more urgent than life itself.

The logic of love also drives the first two sections of the film, when Güzel commits suicide because her lover dies, first at the hands of her husband and later at the hands of the justice system. Here again one might reasonably argue that love represents but one piece of life as a whole. However, Güzel's desire to forsake the whole for the benefit of the part conforms to the same emotional logic, a logic that resonates more soundly with human desire than the rationalized logic toward which humans often strive. *Time for Love* asserts the differences implicit in the mind's logic and the heart's logic, but the film also shows that human experience privileges the latter. The characters make decisions based on emotional rather than rational impulses, and it is only by deferring to the undeniable pull of an emotional logic that the viewer is able to make sense of the characters' actions and reactions. Makhmalbaf argues, "If it weren't so, we would have to consider all of the people in this story raving mad."[47]

The appeal to emotion in *Time for Love* is also an appeal to the logic of love, and within the mystic tradition romantic concerns often signal divine love. In his notes, Makhmalbaf questions the relationship between *'eshq-e zamini* (earthly love) and *'eshq-e āsemāni* (heavenly love). He observes some of the shades of gray that naturally exist between these two intermingled concepts and notes, for example, that love between a man and his wife is earthly because it is physical, but also divine because it has been sanctioned religiously. For Makhmalbaf, sex undoubtedly falls into the category of carnal desire, regardless of its relationship to love. He indicates that it is significant that Güzel's love is never consummated even after it has been sanctioned.

According to Makhmalbaf, the lack of sexuality leaves Güzel's love within the realm of mysticism because it does not close out the possibility of divine or heavenly love.[48] That Güzel's desires are not sexualized within the narrative is significant insofar as it gestures toward the mystic possibility of the love represented by *Time for Love*.

At the same time, if the representation of love in *Time for Love* is completely platonic and squarely within the realm of the divine, then why did it provoke such a furious debate about morality? Were critics and audiences shortsighted in their evaluation of the film, or does the film visually gesture toward the possibility of sex? One scene in particular fueled criticism, and viewers saw it both as explicitly sexual and as an unabashed absolution of carnal desire. In the film's first episode, Güzel and her blond lover ride in the back of a horse-drawn carriage. The camera pans down to the horses' hooves, and their rhythmic galloping on a stone road establishes a pulsating soundtrack for the scene. The camera moves back up the horses' bodies, and they neigh in seeming delight as their bodies and heads push together. A cut relocates to the view behind the horses, where only the top of the carriage and the sky above are visible; Güzel and her lover have slouched down in their seat. Suddenly the man raises his scarf in his hand and holds it still in the moving air. Güzel follows: raising her headscarf with an outstretched arm. The two scarves dance in the wind, and the long take emphasizes the intimate entanglement of the fabrics as they move through the breeze. A sudden, abrupt cut shows a medium shot of Güzel and the man lying on the grass next to the road. It appears they have just collapsed, and, out of breath, they lie almost head-to-head and pant quietly.

It is easy to appreciate how audiences at the time understood this scene in sexual terms. The rhythmic sounds of the horses' hooves seem to mimic the mechanics of sexual intercourse; the two scarves appear to be proxies for their owners, approximating the physical intimacy that cannot be shown onscreen; and the scene's final shot of Güzel and the blond man lying in the grass reasonably completes a sexual arch that ends with a climax. Although the representation of sex in Iranian cinema remains understudied, Shahla Haeri has demonstrated that filmmakers working under the strict production guidelines of the Islamic Republic have developed strategies to convey the experience of "carnal desire" onscreen.[49] At the same time, the "sex scene" in *Time for Love*, which predates the examples in Haeri's study by several years, alongside Makhmalbaf's insistence that the film never consummates Güzel's affair, invites a framework that understands the coded representation of sex on Iranian screens not just in terms of production but also with regards to consumption. Makhmalbaf's suggestion that the film never fulfills the extramarital affair's carnal desire might signal a politically minded sleight of hand, another attempt to distract censors and government officials from the film's explicit sexuality. But such a reading would also unravel the very mystical philosophy that Makhmalbaf claims for his *Time for Love* project. Instead, it is possible to understand audiences' reaction to this scene (which differed from Makhmalbaf's stated intentions) as the result of viewing practices that were developing in the Islamic Republic at the time and that encouraged viewers to find meaning in codes and allegories. In such a scheme, the "sex scene" in *Time for Love* becomes a fulfillment of some viewers' desires rather than simply a strategy on the part of the director.

The possibility of multiple interpretations of the "sex scene" and the movie as a whole is crucial to its mystic texture. The existence of multiple realities—the pluralism of Soroush's philosophy or the moral relativism of Ayatollah Motahhari[50]—is central to the film's mystic orientation. In his director's notes, Makhmalbaf insists that *Time for Love* is philosophical at its core, and for him it is the possibility of multiple avenues constructed from a set of unique circumstances and the film's interest in exploring those circumstances that ultimately lend the film its philosophical character.[51] The very possibility of different circumstances generates multiple realities and truths, and this notion in *Time for Love* self-consciously recalls a similar idea in mystic poetry. On at least two occasions, and once in direct reference to this film, Makhmalbaf has alluded to a well-known anecdote from Rumi that illustrates this idea: "The truth is a mirror that shattered as it fell from the hand of God. Everyone picked up a piece of it, and each decided that the truth was what he saw reflected in his fragment rather than realizing that the truth had become fragmented among them all."[52] In his director's notes, Makhmalbaf describes his project as an exploration into the "role of 'circumstance' on the fate of every single human being."[53] It is therefore the individualization of the reception of truth that occupies a paramount position in *Time for Love*. Soroush sees the film in similar terms and argues that the film promotes the idea that whether an event is "good or bad, right or wrong, when two people change places, they are like one another."[54] For Soroush *Time for Love* brings to focus the fact that circumstance can for two individuals create "two spheres, wherein one finds fault in the other and one is even willing to kill another."[55]

This analysis by Soroush underscores an important and often overlooked feature of *Time for Love*. Although many of the discussions and debates about the film revolve around Güzel and her honor, it is actually the two men who act as variables in the film and participate as subjects in Makhmalbaf's study. The film's actors and its mise-en-scène inscribe this feature visually. It is significant that the actress who plays Güzel remains the same in all three sections, and the character's circumstances leading up to the film's events remain similarly consistent: she has fallen in love with a man who is not her husband. The film reinforces visually the character's stability throughout the three episodes, and each episode begins with the same shot of Güzel standing in front of a house right before a train passes in front of the camera. The film also ends with the same shot, which suggests the continuation of this pattern and the possibility of other truths and realities beyond those posited by the film's three episodes.

It is ultimately the consistency of the representation of Güzel that signals to us the repetition of the film's main narrative in each of the three sections. Makhmalbaf exactly replicates certain shots of Güzel from the first episode in the second. At other times, he stages a frame in the second episode in exactly the same manner as the first, but although Güzel's placement remains the same, the male characters have switched places. Each instance further positions Güzel as a constant while the men switch and change, and their shifting circumstances are ultimately the variables that interest the director.

Because the men in *Time for Love* are only identified in the film's screenplay by their physical characteristics, *mu-meshki* (dark-haired) and *mu-bur* (blond), and not by names, when the actors switch roles in the second episode, one must assume that the characters have similarly changed places. Through the switching male actors and characters, the film imagines multiple possibilities and realities, each conditioned by a particular set of circumstances. Quite simply, *Time for Love* creates the opportunity for two rivals to act according to the other's circumstances. The film's second section, for example, creates the possibility that if fate had granted the blonde lover of the first section a taxi and a certificate of military completion (like the dark-haired man of the first episode), then he would have been Güzel's husband. By being her husband, however, he is denied her love. Similarly, if the husband in the first section possessed neither a taxi nor a certification of military completion, then he might have become Güzel's lover, privy to a love he was denied in the role of her husband. And this possibility becomes his fate in the film's second section. A complex web of circumstances and conditions thus defines both men and their relationships to Güzel, and by engendering an empathetic perspective, wherein the viewer is made to consider the circumstances of both men before reaching conclusions about their actions, *Time for Love* advocates a new relative order, one that fully rejects absolutism.

Despite their investment in the role of shifting and varying circumstances, both the first and second episodes of the film conclude similarly. The dark-haired character slays the light-haired character and receives a death sentence, and the death of her lover inspires Güzel to commit suicide in both episodes. The dark-haired man's role changes from husband to lover, but his act of violence and the violence he inspires in Güzel remain the same. With these sources of continuity between the first and second episodes, *Time for Love* considers the possibility that these moments of violence are predestined and unalterable, despite the different routes and conditions that ushered their arrival. The kind of predestination that the film posits, in which multiple paths—each conditioned by unique circumstances—coalesce at a single reality, evokes the Sufi concept of *haqiqat* (truth or reality). The mystic poets of the Persian tradition use the word *haqiqat* in a number of ways, including in its literal meaning of truth, which is the meaning suggested in the Rumi anecdote quoted by Makhmalbaf. As a concept, however, the word usually refers to the final stage of *ma'refat*, or knowing God. Sufi thought suggests that there are an endless number of individual and individualized paths, or *tāriq*s, that bring the traveler to this stage. *Time for Love*, as a contemporary interpretation of the mystic tradition, engages similar questions about the meaning of truth and the multiple and twisting roads that lead to it.

In his description of the film, Makhmalbaf argues that perfectionism in man's behavior depends on perfect conditions, and he quotes a famous couplet from Hafez (Ghazal no. 143): "If the Holy Spirit casts His blessings once again / Others too will do as Christ did."[56] This relationship between fate and circumstance, on the one hand, and legal and ethical conditions, on the other, is mediated through the character of the judge. Makhmalbaf suggests that the presence of the judge confirms the film as a philosophical endeavor.[57] The judge's role in the film imbues its mysticism with a political element as well, because within the context of the Iranian legal system, which is based on religious law and is carried out in an Islamic republic, issues of and judgments in morality always assume a political dimension.

The judge plays the only character in the film who is aware of—or at least acknowledges—the film's episodic structure. In the third section, he laments the repetition of similar but contradictory events in the first two parts and resigns from his post. As Makhmalbaf notes, in the first two episodes the judge too willingly conforms to social norms and acts in a manner too "expedient." The director describes his role as "judicial."[58] In the film's third episode, however, the judge reflects on these expedient and judicial rulings and asks, "How could I have condemned individuals whose preordained conditions are far more effective on their actions than their personal share?" He continues by emphasizing his desire to empathize, an act that cannot be carried out in the present legal system: "I carefully thought of each convict and without a doubt if I had been in their exact situation, I would have behaved exactly as they did." Issues of morality and the human ability to arbitrate them accurately become both for the judge and for us increasingly muddied once the film introduces multiple variables and dimensions into its complicated matrix.

The judge more clearly delineates the role of condition in one's ability to empathize as he defends his resignation. He says, "Whenever I contemplate the grave consequences of a criminal's actions, I condemn him at once, but when I consider the specific reasons underlying the crime, I see him as acquitted." The judge's recognition of the film's structure, which increasingly makes space for the recognition of incident and stipulation, ultimately leads to his advocacy of it. The judge's position calls into question man's ability to render proper judgment and make true decisions. The film reveals man's access to truth as conditional, multiple, and variable, and at the same time it demonstrates that by appreciating the conditions that breed a particular situation and thereby approximating a truer truth, man falls prey to the pulls of empathy and sympathy, which alter his ability to judge the situation at hand.

Makhmalbaf suggests that the film's first two episodes are intended to demonstrate the predestination of one's actions, and the final episode advocates for the "relative role of man's freedom."[59] And it is with this freedom to sympathize and act accordingly that the film ends and an unfinished fourth episode begins as the viewer is once again confronted with the image of Güzel standing in front of a house and a train passing by. The unfinished and cyclical nature of *Time for Love* adds to its mystic texture by creating a place for the interrogation of multiple truths, the literal and metaphoric powers of love, the relationship between fate and circumstance, and man's ability to know God.

MAKING MYSTIC MEANING: THE REVIVAL OF MYSTICISM

A number of other films in the late 1980s and early 1990s—including Abbas Kiarostami's internationally successful Koker Trilogy: *Khāneh-ye dust kojāst?* (Where is the friend's house?, 1987), *Zendegi va digar hich* (Life and nothing more, 1992), and *Zir-e darakhtān-e zeytun* (Through the olive trees, 1994)—similarly drew on the mystic tradition. Dariush Mehrjui's *Hamun* (Hamun, 1990), though, begins to trace a theoretical framework for the rise of mysticism among Iranian intellectuals in the early 1990s. *Hamun* premiered at the Fajr Film Festival the year before *Time for Love* and was identified in 1997 by *Film* as the best Iranian film, dethroning Mehrjui's 1969 classic *Gāv* (The cow). The film is a psychological drama that comprises a series of scenes that alternate between dream and reality, fantasy and life. The film's title character, Hamid Hamun, is an aspiring intellectual who has been struggling for years to finish his doctoral thesis on love and faith. In the meantime, he has taken on a job in the corporate world in sales in order to support his family, especially his wife Mahshid, who is accustomed to a more comfortable lifestyle.

His life begins to crumble when Mahshid demands a divorce and takes custody of their only child, and the film examines Hamun's mental state in these trying times by navigating the psychological terrain of memory on the one hand and anxiety on the other. In addition to the narrative that takes place in the present, *Hamun* features a number of flashbacks that go as far back as the protagonist's childhood but primarily chart the course and collapse of his marriage to Mahshid. The main narrative is also fragmented by a number of Fellini-style dream and fantasy sequences that express Hamun's anxiety about losing his wife, family, and ultimately control over his life. These scenes, which approach the absurd and include dancing midgets dressed as court jesters and faceless women, capture the breakdown of the character's psychological wellbeing and function as wild alternatives to the stagnation of his own existence.

The film revolves around the decay of Hamun's power as both a man and an intellectual, two identifiers that are, for the protagonist, tightly woven together. Before the complete eruption of his marriage, Hamun brings Mahshid to a psychiatrist in a desperate attempt to cure her of her inability to love him. Hamun, however, seems just as interested in availing himself of the doctor's services, cornering the psychiatrist on his way to the bathroom. Hamun reveals his state to the doctor, mixing metaphors—"sinking" on the one hand and "suspended" on the other—to create the impression of being completely stuck, but the psychiatrist matter-of-factly declares Hamun's state "unexceptional." This diagnosis allows Hamun's situation to represent a larger set of concerns in Iranian society, to mirror the stories of others who are "forty and suspended." Hamun responds to this evaluation by versifying the circumstances of his generation in one of the film's most famous lines: "Mā āvikht-hā beh kojā-ye in shab-e tire biyāvizim / qabā-ye zhendeh-o-kapak zadeh-ye khodemun ro?" (Where in this dark night should we, who are hanging [i.e., suspended], hang our tattered and rotten frock?).

That this stagnation is Hamun's starting point is significant insofar as it serves as a base from which the film's narrative visually constructs his further disempowerment. *Hamun* is significant in part because it is one of the first films after the revolution to depict a man, and especially an intellectual man, in a weakened state in a nonredemptive way. The previous wave of films attempted to commit audiences first to the revolution and the Islamic Republic and later to the Iran-Iraq War, tasks that required a strong male figure. Hamun is in many ways the quintessential Iranian intellectual hero: wrought with brooding "anguish and tortured self-examination" at the same time that he is "a man of great physical vitality and charm."[60] And yet, *Hamun* renders its protagonist socially, emotionally, and physically weak at various points in its narrative.

At one point in the film, Hamun is enraged by his wife's plans to divorce him, and he confronts her violently as she is hanging laundry on the roof of their apartment building. Their neighbors have to come and separate them. These violent moments in the film were the first time that a man and a woman touched onscreen in post-revolution cinema.[61] Far from being sexualized, this moment reveals Hamun as uncontrolled and unraveling. The film visually reinforces this conclusion with a flood of neighbors who take over the frame with scorn and condemnation.

At other points in the film, Hamun is reduced to childlike tears, ashamed of his own actions and heartbroken by his wife's. The breakdown of his physical prowess occurs as he unsuccessfully tries to complete the sale of medical equipment. The doctor in charge rejects the initial offer, so Hamun decides to stage a demonstration. He attempts to supply the necessary sample of blood himself and inadvertently passes out because he has drained too much (figure 1.1). This scene in the film is the ultimate metaphor for the collapse of the intellectual man in post-revolution Iran; he is literally dried up and unconscious.

Throughout the film, Hamun attempts to ground his life through a series of mystical journeys. Specifically, he goes in search of Ali, his *ostād*, or spiritual guide, who has achieved Sufi unity despite the tragic loss of his family. Hamun likens him to Hallaj, a great mystic figure, and explains, "You leapt into the silver pond and reached yourself and God."[62] Hamun yearns for this spiritual unity, and he believes that he can only achieve it by uniting with Ali. In this way the spiritual guide becomes a kind of beloved figure. However, as is typical of a mystical journey, Hamun never reaches his destination and never finds that for which he is searching. He travels from Tehran to Ali's village only to discover that Ali is in Tehran. Later Hamun passes Ali in a car, which leads to a frantic car chase that ends in Hamun colliding with

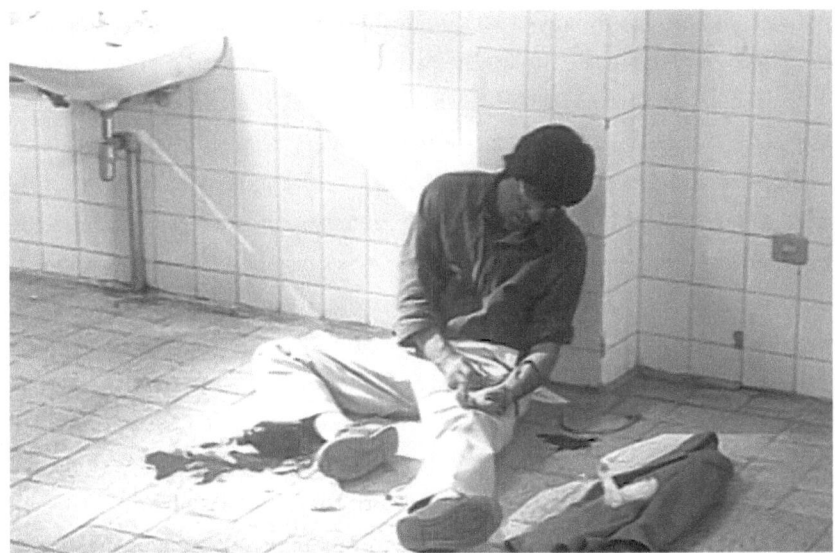

FIGURE 1.1. The Iranian intellectual bleeds out. Frame enlargement from Dariush Mehrjui's *Hamun*.

another car. This scene demonstrates how the closer one gets to the beloved the farther he actually is. Even though Hamun sees Ali in the next car, his crash ultimately causes his life to spin out of control even more, undermining his search for stability. The film's ending revisits this theme. Hamun tries to drown himself, but he is rescued by Ali. It is only in this momentary death that he can be reunited with his beloved figure.

One of the film's flashbacks returns Hamun to his childhood during *ʿāshurā*, the Shiʿi mourning ceremony for the martyrdom of Hussein. Six-year-old Hamun navigates the rituals of self-flagellation in search of Ali Abedini.[63] He eventually finds Ali, who appears to be the same age as he is during the film's present, thirty-five years later. Ali's agelessness captures the timelessness of this mystic journey. At the same time, Hamun's search represents an alternative to the communal religion represented by the mourning ceremonies.

It is the possibility of this alternative that allows us to return to mysticism as a historically grounded event in Iran in the early 1990s. The film *Hamun* theorizes how those intellectuals who felt disempowered and stagnant found purpose and meaning in mysticism, as an alternative to the religion being promoted by the Islamic Republic. The early 1990s represented a unique period in Iran's history, shaped by the death of Khomeini, the end of the Iran-Iraq War, and the gradual abatement of revolutionary fervor. After a decade of excitement and movement, the late 1980s and early 1990s represented a political and intellectual lull. Although the extreme circumstances of the revolution and the war were no longer in place, the corresponding policies, which limited economic, social, and political mobility, left many intellectuals feeling trapped, and mysticism represented the possibility of redemption.

The turn to mysticism represented in *Time for Love* and *Hamun* allows us to rethink the implications of cine-mysticism in Iran, particularly in the late 1980s and early 1990s. The appropriation of a mystic aesthetic at this juncture in Iran's history represents a point of concern for critics like Hamid Dabashi, who sees cine-mysticism as a "sad and rather pathetic outcome of the dispirited Iranian bourgeoisie's loss of confidence" in the revolutionary project.[64] He classifies this effort in Iranian cinema as "strange flirtation with . . . a belated attraction to a bourgeois version of Persian mysticism."[65] Dabashi describes cine-mysticism as a "disease" and as potentially "fatal"[66] and explains that the moment of redemption for Makhmalbaf occurred when he recovered from this illness. Dabashi finds value in Makhmalbaf's mysticism—which he describes as "ghastly"—only through the idea that this brush with cinematic death ultimately strengthened his later films. Dabashi's analysis, however, neglects the possibility that mysticism functioned as a strategic effort for Makhmalbaf as he sought to claim his own creativity, and by reducing this mystic aesthetic to bourgeois dabbling and brushing it aside, Dabashi misses the productivity that comes with considering cine-mysticism within its historical context. Indeed, his studies of Makhmalbaf represent an effort to bring about "a creative restoration of historical agency in the post/colonial subject,"[67] which he locates in the director's later films. As a result, he analyzes the director's earlier works through the lens of his later films: death avoided, illness overcome. This narrow observation, however, fails to acknowledge meaningful possibilities of mysticism within both the context of Makhmalbaf's career and Iranian cinema more generally.

The value of mysticism in films like *Time for Love* and *Hamun* extends well beyond an "exorcism."[68] The cinematic appeal to mysticism at this time also initiated profound transformations as to what could be shown onscreen and contributed to the development of an aesthetic that accepted and even encouraged multiple interpretations. These shifts in film industry practices are most visible in the representation of women; for example, cine-mysticism in *Hamun* gave way to the first contact between a man and a woman onscreen, and a mystic appeal in *Time for Love* generated the possibility of onscreen sex for viewers. As film became less dogmatic and more open to multiple possibilities and interpretations, it began to lay the discursive foundation for political reform. In this way, the cine-mysticism of the early 1990s resonated with other intellectual efforts, which also drew on the mystic tradition, and together these efforts foresaw the coming of Khatami's reformist movement less than a decade later.

The philosophical contributions of Abdolkarim Soroush are a particularly salient point of departure for this kind of argument because the film *Time for Love* clearly appealed to his philosophical, aesthetic, and political sensibilities. By identifying the mysticism implicit in his philosophies and by reading these works against *Time for Love*, it is possible to position mysticism (in both its cinematic and philosophical manifestations) as a politically potent strategy that resonated with imminent revolutionary discontent and an emerging set of reformist concerns. Soroush credits Rumi with introducing him to a "love-based mysticism" that is at odds with and ultimately saved him from the fear-based mysticism of Al-Ghazali. Historian Afshin Matin-asgari notes that Soroush's philosophies feature a "strong mystical tendency" that draws from and is structured around references to Rumi and his poetry. Matin-asgari further argues that a "deep and unresolved tension" exists between this mystic tendency and his attraction to philosophical reason.[69] The incongruities between these two modes of thought inevitably result in contradictions in Soroush's writings. Nevertheless, in the 1990s Soroush maintained that his understanding of morality appealed to "a mystical esthetics of divine beauty," and in a 1992 lecture he argued that mysticism is the "only path" out of the postmodern condition because it "doubted rationality from the onset."[70]

By the mid-1990s, Soroush's espousal of mysticism was replaced by a call for the rationality of science. Matin-asgari cites an important lecture that Soroush gave in 1996 on "Iranian identity," in which he claimed that mysticism fosters "fatalistic thinking (*jabr-andishi*) and perplexity (*hayrat*)" within Iranian society. As a solution, he advocated the rational and critical philosophy of Kant. It is within this move toward rationalism and away from nihilism that Matin-asgari locates Soroush's contribution to the secularization of Islamic thought.[71] Matin-asgari's useful delineation of the development of Soroush's philosophy brings to focus an important aspect of the study of this important figure. Soroush's philosophy comprises an expansive and expanding body of works, and each of his beliefs is grounded in a particular historical moment. To ignore that historicity is to violate the very nature of his philosophy. *Qabz va bast-e te'urik-e shari'at: nazarieh-ye takāmol-e ma'refat-e dini* (The theoretical contraction and expansion of religious law: The concept of the evolution of religious knowledge, 1999), a book published from a four-part series of articles that the author wrote between May 1988 and March 1990, speaks to the same historical circumstances that gave rise to Makhmalbaf's *Time for Love*. By reading these two cultural products side by side, mysticism emerges as a far-reaching trend among the country's intellectuals in the late 1980s and early 1990s. This mystic project corresponded both temporally and ideologically with the nascent but budding reformist discourse.

Soroush's choice of title, *The Theoretical Contraction and Expansion of Religious Law*, immediately signals the book's mystic tones. In the original Persian, the first and third words, *qabz* (contraction) and *bast* (expansion), signify two Sufi concepts that describe the movement of a mystic's heart: the literal tightening and loosening of the muscle and the corresponding symbolic desolation and elation therein. In *The Theoretical Contraction and Expansion of Religious Law*, Soroush appropriates these terms to describe "altering moments of epistemic openness and closure of Islamic societies"[72] to generate a mystic-based model that he hopes will fill an epistemological and theoretical gap in the efforts by Islamic reformists and revivalists.[73] In its most basic form, the theory of contraction and expansion aims to distinguish "religion and people's understanding of it," wherein "that which remains constant is religion (*din*)" and "that which undergoes change is religious knowledge and insight [*ma'refat-e dini*]."⁷⁴ Whereas religion itself represents perfection, human understanding of religion (or religious knowledge), as a product of the human experience, is wrought with imperfection. We can only gain access to religion through interpretation, a human science, and as Soroush notes, "defects abound in exegeses."⁷⁵ The role of reason in this theory is to acknowledge the distinction between religion and religious understanding. Reason, Soroush maintains, does not "complement" religion; "it struggles to improve its own understanding of religion."⁷⁶

Soroush describes religion as "unblemished by the artifacts of the human mind,"⁷⁷ and this description captures the temporality of religious knowledge, which is weighed down by the historical *artifacts* of the human mind. He goes so far as to state that the degree of the temporality of religious knowledge approaches "the synchronization and adaptation of this branch of human knowledge with the sciences and needs of each age."⁷⁸ The nature of religious knowledge may, therefore, more closely approximate, historically, the contours of human knowledge than the true meaning of religion. Soroush is able as a result of this supposition to reconcile a tension he detects between eternity and temporality, and by extension he renders moot debates about tradition and modernity in the Islamic world.⁷⁹ Ultimately the separation he maintains between religion and religious knowledge brings to mind the distance in Sufi poetry between lover and beloved and the divine implications of this mystic love. As Ashkan Dahlén notes, this theory "is connected to mysticism in that it renders meaning to the traditional distinction between *shari'at*, *tariqat* (the esoteric way), and *haqiqat*," and this distinction is "grounded in the eternal differences of hermeneutical methodology."⁸⁰

The critique of absolutism that surfaces in Soroush's approach in *The Theoretical Contraction and Expansion of Religious Law* echoes the mysticism put forth by Makhmalbaf in *Time for Love*. Although Soroush and Makhmalbaf interrogate slightly different terminologies (Makhmalbaf favoring "relativism" over "pluralism"), both are interested in human access to a definite, and presumably religious, truth. These models suggest the relativity of that access. Makhmalbaf's film suggests that the perfect judgment—that is, a judgment that corresponds precisely with religious truth—depends on the perfect conditions. Soroush's argument helps refine this idea as it is presented in *Time for*

Love. The observation that religious knowledge of truth is necessarily grounded in and conditioned by the historical trends of flawed human thought, which in turn shapes the mechanisms that govern societies, is significant here insofar as it suggests the impossibility of perfectionism within the human condition. In both Soroush's philosophy and Makhmalbaf's *Time for Love* this rejection of absolutism opens the door to a pluralism that accepts the possibility of multiple paths to a universal truth. In *Time for Love* this pluralism takes the form of moral relativism and is represented by the film's structure, which features a number of moral paths without imposing a privileging system on any of them. For Soroush, the resolute denial of absolutism clears the way for plurality of the religious community, which is a "shallow indicator of the plurality of souls,"[81] and he uses this indicator to call for tolerance.

Soroush's philosophies also enable us to envision the political possibilities latent in mysticism in contemporary Iran, including the kind represented in *Time for Love*. Although Soroush examines the religious and mystical nature of an Islamic hermeneutic process, the political implications of his argument are undeniable. The very call for pluralism implicit in Soroush's discussion threatened the existence of the Islamic Republic, which depends on *velāyat-e faqih*, a ruling system that privileges and enforces a single religious understanding under the guise of religion itself.[82] Soroush's use of mysticism to discredit the system of *velāyat-e faqih* is significant because Khomeini's construction of the concept drew on mystic thought.[83] Therefore, Soroush used Khomeini's own scholarly tools to refute his most important political and intellectual contribution to Iranian society. Moreover, the application of Soroush's ideas to political reform is paramount. He provided, according to Oliver Roy, "the 'political philosophy' of the Khatamists" by considering "how to secularize politics in a society which cannot afford to reject its heritage and origin: an Islamic Revolution."[84]

Whereas Roy's assessment, written in 1999, grounds Soroush and mysticism in the present (i.e., Khatami's presidency), historians have traced a long trend in Iranian intellectualism that drew heavily from the mystic tradition. In particular, the genealogy of dissent in Iranian social and religious thought reveals that the Sufis of the seventeenth century produced an intellectual model for dissent that would inform the social and political restlessness of the nineteenth century and later the Constitutional Revolution (1905–1911) and the Islamic Revolution (1978–1979).[85] This historical resonance positions mysticism within a political framework at the time that Makhmalbaf released *Time for Love*. It is clear, then, that mysticism has been epistemologically wrought with political meaning in Iran for centuries. Makhmalbaf's appropriation of mysticism in *Time for Love* is necessarily political. The film, through its critique of absolutism and its promotion of moral relativity, gently challenges the status quo in the Iranian political system by creating a complicated space for the many complications and possibilities that arise from modes of human moral judgment. As such, *Time for Love* signaled a revival of the political appropriation of mysticism. The film traces a new contour in this mystic-political trajectory as it moves away from resistance and toward the ideals of humanism.

The politicization of Soroush's philosophies and their resonance with Makhmalbaf's *Time for Love* demonstrate that mysticism in the early 1990s, far from just representing a desire to escape the Islamic Republic's interpretation of Islam, also functioned as a deliberate strategy for the enactment of political and social reform. Both Soroush and Makhmalbaf used mysticism to stress the importance of considering temporality in matters of governance and jurisprudence. Their emphasis on context represented an important step on the part of reformists to locate the Islamic Revolution as a historically grounded event, rigid but necessitated by a certain set of extreme circumstances, rather than as an ongoing and ahistorical process. As such, reform, and later the reformist movement, became a means of reconciling a glorified history with the need to move beyond the closed policies that Khomeini and his revolution enacted.

The mysticism that intellectuals began engaging with in the early 1990s became a fully formed part of reformist discourse several years later, when, on November 4, 1998, in one of his first international acts as president, Mohammad Khatami addressed the General Assembly of the United Nations in New York and introduced the concept of *goftegu-ye tamaddon-hā* (dialogue among civilizations) as an alternative to Samuel Huntington's "clash of civilizations."[86] The UN welcomed his invitation to think beyond the limiting dichotomies popular at the time—including Iranian/non-Iranian and

Muslim/non-Muslim—and declared the year 2001 the Year of Dialogue Among Civilizations. In 2000, during a preliminary UN roundtable discussion about the concept, Khatami offered mysticism as a means of clearing the way for new intercultural paths. He said, "In addition to poetic and artistic experiences, mysticism also provides us with a graceful, profound and universal language for dialogue. Mystical experience, the constitution of the revelation and countenance of the sacred in the heart and soul of the mystic, opens new existential pathways to the human spirit."[87] Khatami indicated that international cooperation and intercultural dialogue depends on an openness that approximates the expansion of the mystic's heart.

Yet quite unexpectedly Khatami punctuated this esoteric call for mysticism with an emphasis on the central role of government. He argued, "The unique and irreplaceable role of governments should never be overlooked in the process."[88] Khatami collapsed the metaphysical on the one hand and the political on the other, and the origins of the use of mysticism as an intellectual strategy for the enactment of political and social reform in the late twentieth century can be traced back a decade earlier, when examples of cine-mysticism, like Makhmalbaf's *Time for Love*, forced Khatami to articulate his changing political views at a time when mysticism formed the philosophical underpinnings of a reformist ideology. This brand of political reform would shake the political and social landscape in Iran on a spring day in 1997, when Mohammad Khatami was elected as the Islamic Republic's fifth president.

2

SCREENING REFORM

Campaign Movies, Documentaries, and Urban Tehran

The 1997 presidential campaign period marked a momentous development in the Iranian political process. For the first time, presidential candidates were allowed to release campaign movies to publicize their platforms and promote their candidacy. This new policy afforded filmmakers the opportunity to rally their support for Khatami in an unprecedented way. Not only could they use their celebrity to endorse Khatami, but they could also leverage their technical skills to campaign on his behalf.[1] This new campaigning rite also redrew the boundaries of voter spectatorship in Iran by representing candidates onscreen through a system of cuts, edits, and soundtracks typical of the film industry. Just as the 1960 televised debate between John F. Kennedy and Richard Nixon forever changed the landscape of American politics by putting the candidates on the small screen, so too did the campaign movies (*film-hā-ye tablighāt-e entekhābāti*) in Iran alter what it meant to visualize a candidate. No politician was better suited for the screen than Mohammad Khatami, the smiling *seyyed* (*seyyed-e khandān*) who, *Time* magazine suggested, "would look at home in an Armani ad."[2] From his rosy cheeks and well-trimmed beard to his tailored, chocolate-colored robes and designer shoes, Khatami challenged Khomeini's stone-cold stare, which was ever-present, plastered on buildings and billboards. The new campaign movies of 1997 allowed Khatami to redefine the face of politics in Iran, and his charismatic presence onscreen no doubt contributed to his landslide victory on May 23, 1997.

Filmmakers such as Seyfollah Dad, Behruz Afkhami, and Ahmad Reza Darvish directed campaign movies for Khatami, and many of them later found success in his administration.³ But these officially sanctioned movies represented only one avenue through which filmmakers engaged Khatami and his election. His eight-year presidency bore witness to an unexpected and unprecedented trend in Iranian cinema. For the first time in the Islamic Republic's history, a high-ranking politician became a regular feature onscreen—and not just in state propaganda but also in documentaries and narrative films, both popular and so-called art-house productions. In particular, between 1997 and 2005 a number of films were released that dealt explicitly with Khatami's campaign periods, both his initial election in 1997 and his reelection in 2001. Certainly these open representations of the political system spoke to the larger ideals of civil society that Khatami promoted during both of his campaigns. But political reform, more than just allowing cinema to push the limits of representation, became a major force or character within films themselves.

The complicated relationship between Khatami and the film industry during these electoral periods emerges forcefully in the works of Rakhshan Bani-Etemad. She once attested to her special relationship to Khatami in an interview with *Sight and Sound* when she said, "I am sure that if Mohammad Khatami hadn't been elected, this film [*May Lady*, 1998] would never have made it onto the screen."⁴ Her next two films—*Zir-e pust-e shahr* (Under the skin of the city, 2000), a narrative film set during the 1997 election period, and *Ruzegār-e mā . . .* (Our times . . ., 2002), a documentary about Khatami's reelection in 2001—foster both a theorization of what it meant for Khatami to function as a character within films and an appreciation of how certain filmmakers made sense of his election and later reelection. These two films in particular depend on the representation of urbanism, interrogate the documentary form, and reveal Bani-Etemad's ambivalence toward Khatami and his reformist movement. The films together indicate that the harsh realities of life in the city create the need for political hope but at the same time block attempts to satisfy it. Bani-Etemad's cinematic relationship with the city of Tehran ultimately betrays her critique of the reformist movement, which focused on repairing Iran's global reputation rather than addressing its local problems.

Despite Bani-Etemad's insistence that she be classified as neither a female nor a feminist filmmaker,[5] the existing scholarship on her films focuses heavily on her role as a female director and her representation of women.[6] Her body of work, however, indicates a distinctly urban style. The city of Tehran functions as both the setting and a complicated character in all of her films. By examining two of these metropolitan narratives, it is possible to move away from a strictly feminist reading of her films and to analyze her urban aesthetic. *Under the Skin of the City* and *Our Times* . . . together suggest that Bani-Etemad's cinematic city depends on three features. The director employs a fusion of documentary and narrative styles that complicate the viewer's understanding of representation and reality. She plots economic and class difference geographically on Tehran's north-south axis to suggest a multiplicity of urban experiences. And finally both films depict housing crises in the south of Tehran and locate architectural experiences as nodal points through which other economic and class struggles are mediated. Bani-Etemad's urban aesthetic powerfully attends to the complicated task of representing, promoting, and criticizing the reformist movement at election time.

DOCUMENTARY AND COMMITMENT, REALITY AND REPRESENTATION

Under the Skin of the City opened in 2001 to wide critical and popular acclaim and won the award for best director at both the fourth annual Cinema House Festival and the second annual Social Films Festival. It was also the first film by Bani-Etemad to be distributed in the United States.[7] *Under the Skin of the City*, which takes place during the 1997 presidential elections, tells the story of a house and family, whose members each try to carve out a meaningful existence in an unfair and unforgiving urban landscape. Tuba provides her family with its main source of income as a factory worker and finds comfort in the stability of homeownership. Her husband, Mahmud, once a political activist, is injured and unable to work but attempts to assert control by plotting to sell the family home to a builder who is buying all of the neighboring houses. Mahmud is encouraged by their eldest son, Abbas, who works as a delivery boy, a job that requires him to navigate all of the city's districts. He needs the money from the house to process travel documents so he can fulfill his dream of going to Japan to earn money. Ali, the younger brother and a promising student, who is teaching his mother to read, has abandoned his own studies to participate in campaigning efforts, much to the dismay of his family members, who hope that he can save them from financial hardship by going to college. The youngest child, Mahbubeh, pursues a close friendship with her neighbor Masumeh, whose drug-addict brother beats her regularly. Tuba's oldest daughter, Hamideh, is also a victim of domestic abuse. Married to an abusive husband, she has one child and is pregnant with another; she regularly returns to her family's home to escape the abuse.

The narrative comes to a head when Mahmud and Abbas sell the house, but the travel agency processing Abbas's paperwork disappears with his money. In a desperate effort to recover the money, he agrees to an underground job delivering drugs. However, Ali foils his efforts by secretly dumping the merchandise during the long drive outside the city. Meanwhile, Masumeh has fled her abusive brother, abandoning Mahbubeh and joining a gang of homeless youth. Abbas, unable to account for the missing goods, must also flee, and the film ends on Election Day with Tuba's announcement that she has lost everything. At the same time, she describes her reasons for voting and therein articulates a hope for change that remains with us long after the film's images have left the screen. This moment in the film, in which Tuba mediates her personal desires through the electoral system, signals Bani-Etemad's commitment to social commentary. Tuba makes a connection between her situation and her country's circumstances. The parallel that she draws between herself and the collective brings into focus the fact that *Under Skin of the City*'s social concern is greater than just one woman or one family.

The film's mode of representation also speaks to the social concerns that are central to Bani-Etemad's work. *Under the Skin of the City* is framed as a documentary, bookended with two documentary moments. The opening shot, which shows an image of Tuba in a viewfinder as a documentary crew prepares to interview her about the upcoming elections, signals the fact that this is a film about documentary filmmaking, and the film also ends with the film crew interviewing Tuba about her decision to vote. Her slip in this final interview—when she mentions that "people are always filming"—hints at the possibility that all of the footage between these two moments in which the film crew appears onscreen might actually represent a documentarian's visual evidence. *Under the Skin of the City* stages a documentary within the film, one whose reliability as a representation of the "real" is, at every turn, undercut by the film's professional actors and its publicity as a fictional film. The film's framing documentary moments suggest the extent to which Bani-Etemad's social and political activism, including her critique of the reformist movement, is tied to her engagement with the documentary form.

Rakhshan Bani-Etemad once described the relationship between film and reality by suggesting that the Iranian film industry is "duty-bound to attend to reality."[8] She attributed this level of commitment to the shared experiences of her generation of filmmakers, who began working and flourishing under the dire conditions of first a revolution and later an eight-year war. Bani-Etemad's statement attests to a trend in Iranian art-house cinema in which filmmakers reveal a sense of obligation to reality and at the same time interrogate the ways in which film represents it. The commitment to reality in *Under the Skin of the City* is significantly different from the style appropriated by Abbas Kiarostami and others. Bani-Etemad's film is invested in the documentary form, but it does not gather documentarian evidence or participate in a neorealist style. Instead, Bani-Etemad creates a fictional documentary crew in her film. The viewer hears the male director's voice (which clearly does not belong to Bani-Etemad) and sees the film crew's equipment. Images of the crew's "documentary" are mediated through the equipment's various screens. These images are different from Kiarostami's *Namā-ye nazdik* (Close-up, 1990), for example, in which the film *is* the documentary. *Under the Skin of the City* adds a layer of representation: the camera captures another camera capturing the documentary subject.

Unlike Kiarostami, who "intervenes" in and "pokes" at reality in his *Close-Up*, Bani-Etemad fictionalizes documentary filmmaking.[9] This technique invites a reconceptualization of the relationship between representation and reality, and specifically the ways in which film creates reality and how we access it. The reconfiguration of representation and reality in *Under the Skin of the City* reveals the director's critique of the reformist movement. The film trains the viewer to challenge the ways in which the reformist movement both has been represented and has represented itself. Bani-Etemad creates a complex system in which the documentary form is subverted in order to call into question the reality of the reformist movement.

Documentary is a complex mode because it represents rather than replicates reality.[10] Despite documentary's claim to reality, the nature of images and image making undeniably necessitates an insurmountable gap between object and representation.[11] *Under the Skin of the City*, a narrative film that introduces documentary filmmaking into a diegetic space, blurs and intervenes in the relationship between representation and reality on the one hand and narrative and documentary on the other. Bill Nichols has extensively detailed how documentaries use certain visual and rhetorical strategies to assert their authority and to collapse the boundary between reality and representation.[12] The documentary ethos—its claim to reality—has over time conditioned viewing practices within audiences, who consume documentary films differently than narrative films, and this practice of consumption, like the consumption of other mass media, is often uncritical. *Under the Skin of the City* through its representation of documentary challenges the authority that audiences have unwittingly granted documentary filmmaking and, by extension, other "discourses of sobriety" or systems of information that people assume are the truth, including politics, religion, science, and education.[13]

Bani-Etemad's *Under the Skin of the City* is not the first film to disrupt the uncomplicated relationship between documentary and reality, and by fictionally representing the mode, she references an entire history of Iranian documentary, which features reflexive documentaries that problematize their relationship to reality as a means of critiquing the social and historical worlds they index. Early documentary work in Iran during the 1920s and 1930s, which included newsreels documenting the royal court and works by foreign documentarians who came to record the country's heritage and development, eventually gave way in the 1960s and 1970s to what Nichols calls "a shift of epistemological proportions."[14] Regarding the American tradition, Nichols explains that whereas previously documentary "suggested fullness and completion, knowledge and fact," more recently it has taken on the character of "incompleteness and uncertainty."[15] In Iran, a new reflexive documentary style coincided with the New Wave movement, which is generally regarded as a trend within narrative filmmaking. These documentaries, including Ebrahim Golestan's *Kharābābād* (Ruinville, 1962), Forugh Farrokhzad's *Khāneh siāh ast* (The house is black, 1962), Kamran Shirdel's *Tehrān pāytakht-e Irān ast* (Tehran is the capital of Iran, 1966) and *Un shab keh bārun umad* (The night it rained, 1967), Nader Afsharnaderi's *Balut* (Oak, 1968), Naser Taqvai's *Nakhl* (Palm, 1970), Manuchehr Tayab's *Ritm* (Rhythm, 1972), and Parviz Kimiavi's *Peh mesl-e pelikān* (P as in pelican, 1973), attempt to unravel documentary's claim to the real by problematizing its informing logic. This corpus of films challenges the presumed indexical relationship to a lived, historical world, and it inspired a trend within Iranian cinema that uses this "truth form" to reveal, counterintuitively, a series of untruths.

Kamran Shirdel's 1967 documentary *The Night It Rained* is a representative example of the move in Iranian documentary filmmaking to call into question the representation of reality. The film provides a particularly engaging exploration into the nature of the relationship between documentary and the real within the Iranian tradition. It takes as its starting point a story from recent headlines and constructs the viewer's initial understanding of the event by showing the printed media's coverage of it. At the start of the film, a barrage of newspaper headlines and articles flash across the screen. A young boy heroically stopped a two-hundred-person passenger train outside of the village of Gorgan before it reached a bridge that had been washed out by heavy rains. The film reveals its purpose by showing a letter from the Ministry of Art and Culture that commissions the film crew to make a documentary about the event. The film primarily comprises a number of contradictory statements by journalists, railway employees, and government officials, none of whom can agree about the specific details of the event or even if it happened at all. The most contested detail is whether or not the boy would have been able to use kerosene to light his jacket on fire in order to signal the train to stop during a heavy rainstorm. Although logic prevails for many of the subjects interviewed, the most devoted advocates of the story insist that it was possible for the boy to ignite his jacket despite rains heavy enough to wash away a bridge.

Shirdel skillfully juxtaposes contradictory statements to underscore the unreliability of evidence, and in the process he casts doubt on the whole system of knowledge: how we create, access, and maintain knowledge. Early in the film, he also highlights a disconnect between the spoken voice and the corresponding images on the screen: The phrase "conversations between the men of Lamelang" signals the image of men standing silently with cigarettes in their mouths, and "Lamelang, with its pleasant climate and hospitable inhabitants" cues several shots of dogs playing in the rain. The uncertainty comes to a head late in the film, when the documentarian voice promises an interview with the heroic boy, who, the viewer hopes, will clarify the inconsistencies that the documentary has thus far uncovered. The boy's statement conforms more or less to the affirmative statements in the film. Shirdel, however, interrupts his version of the story with images and sounds of contestation: "it's a pack of lies" and "unfortunately, that is not the case." This technique breaks up and destabilizes the boy's account.

The viewer is later ushered into a one-room schoolhouse where a young boy is reading aloud from his textbook. The story that aurally unfolds is precisely the same sensational story that the newspapers and government have claimed for the boy, complete with the detail about the lit jacket, and the film never makes clear whether the boy's heroic act was inspired by the story or whether the textbook story led the boy to make up a similar story. *The Night It Rained* ends in the same pool of uncertainty it has created. A letter from the local governor to the Ministry of the Interior confirms that the event reported in the newspapers is correct, which prompts a flood of audiovisual material that points to the story's many fallacies. *The Night It Rained* demonstrates a subversive use of documentary within the Iranian tradition intended to compound the viewer's conception of reality by providing layers of uncertainty and contradictory evidence. By calling into question the category of evidence, the film also questions the construction of truth and documentary filmmaking itself. *The Night It Rained*'s appropriation of the documentary form to question these categories no doubt shaped future cinematic efforts in Iran, including *Under the Skin of the City*.

Bani-Etemad's long and complicated relationship with the documentary form has critically informed her representation of it in *Under the Skin of the City*. Like Iranian cinema, the director's career began with documentary. She directed documentaries for television early in her career and has continued to make documentaries alongside her feature films. The director noted that "documentary filmmaking is my first love," and she claimed that "it is a way of keeping in touch with the multiple layers of society"[16] by allowing her to "mediate more directly" her social "apprehensions."[17] At the same time, Bani-Etemad laments the fact that "documentaries are seen less often and discussed less frequently." As a result, she locates the value of narrative film in its ability to "relate more often and more easily to a sympathetic audience." Bani-Etemad ultimately finds the documentary medium "more appealing, and this aspect comes out consequently in [her] narrative films."[18] The director reconciles her competing desires to create documentary and to attract and affect a wider audience by blending narrative and documentary forms, and *Under the Skin of the City* powerfully attests to this composite style at the same time that it destabilizes it. The director shows the documentary filmmaking process, creates documentary-style footage, and includes sound bites from real political speeches, but the film was released as a feature narrative film and at several points makes reference to its fictional structure.

Under the Skin of the City's narrative is framed by two documentary moments. The film opens with a closeup shot of a film crew's video display. The blurry image in the display focuses to show the head of a woman. A man's voice says, "Let's roll," before reminding the woman, "Your scarf . . . Fix your hair!" She promptly adjusts her headscarf, and the man asks, "How do you assess the role of female workers in the upcoming elections?" As the woman attempts to answer, the camera moves left and settles on the display image's source: the woman sitting at a table with a man and a camera aimed at her. The woman is unable to answer the question beyond a statement of religiosity, and several women on the sideline shout their own thoughts as the man ends the interview and requests some shots of the women working at their factory posts. These images roll along with the opening credits. This first scene plays an important role in the establishment of the film's documentary ethos. Iranian censorship codes prohibit the appearance of women in closeup shots, and women must remain properly covered whenever onscreen.[19] The film's first moments push the boundaries of acceptability and provide the viewer with the sense of witnessing something unproduced and not yet ready for public consumption. The film's first active moment—the display's pull into focus—reinforces the scene's unedited, and therefore unmediated, ethos (figures 2.1 and 2.2).

The film crew never formally exits the film's narrative, and the viewer is left to wonder whether the crew has been incorporated into the film's diegetic space or if the film crew acts as a bridge between the film's narrative and the film's self-conscious documentary world. The reappearance of the same crew in the film's very last scene further complicates this distinction. A transition between a wide shot of Abbas running through the streets and a close-up of Tuba signals the film's final scene. This transition also marks the moment at which the camera once again shares its perspective with a documentarian's. Asked to explain why she is voting, Tuba eloquently articulates her reasons for voting, but a high-pitched beep interrupts her several times. Finally a familiar voice—the interviewer from the film's first scene—asks her to start over because of technical problems. Clearly frustrated, Tuba complains, "Just forget about it! I just lost my house, my son ran away, and people are filming all the time." Her final observation allows the viewer to consider the possibility that the same film crew has been following her throughout the course of the film, in which case this documentary's informing logic would hinge on the development of Tuba's political identity as enacted by the film's events. By taking on the "documentary" classification as the framing permits, *Under the Skin of the City* makes the claim that the world it represents bears an indexical relationship to the lived, historical world.

Just as easily as Bani-Etemad suggests the possibility that this film is a documentary, however, so too does she provide evidence to the contrary. In the film's first scene, when the video display pulls into focus, the viewer encounters Golab Adineh, a well-known actress in Iran. Bani-Etemad noted that she envisioned Adineh in that role when she started revising the screenplay six years before production began.[20] The director's decision to employ professional actors, including her daughter Baran Kosari in the role of Mahbubeh, runs contrary to the tendency in Iranian neorealism to employ actors

FIGURE 2.1. The first shot of Bani-Etemad's *Under the Skin of the City* shows actress Golab Adineh out of focus in the film crew's video display. Frame enlargement.

FIGURE 2.2. Actress Golab Adineh fixes her headscarf on a video display, an act audiences do not usually see onscreen. Frame enlargement from *Under the Skin of the City*.

who have little or no acting experience. The result of this decision in *Under the Skin of the City* is the viewer's simultaneous desire to read the opening scene as documentary and to acknowledge the fact that the woman in the frame does not work in a factory but is instead a popular actress. Slavoj Žižek's concept of interface, a self-conscious screen within a screen that threatens a film's delicate fictive web, further obscures the classification of cinematic mode.[21] The film crew's video display, by referencing the act of production, shows how *Under the Skin of the City* refuses to submit to the normative features of narrative film.

In the film's final scene, the director similarly complicates the audience's ability to negotiate the historical and the imagined. After noting that she is constantly being filmed, Tuba emotionally pleas, "I wish someone would come and film what's going on right here. Right here! Who do you show these films to, anyway?" Tuba thus probes the limits of the documentary form and questions its ability to capture the depths of human suffering. She also questions the ability of documentary filmmaking to reach wide audiences. The film critic Rahul Hamid argues that this criticism by Tuba "betrays Bani-Etemad's ambivalent feelings towards . . . the movie craze in Iran—and perhaps the political efficacy of cinema itself."[22] But this criticism describes too broadly the reach of Tuba's statement. Bani-Etemad instead reveals the unmediated tension between documentary and narrative modes, in which the socially committed documentary form lacks affective prowess and therefore fails to reach diverse audiences.

Hamid's misreading of this scene results from a misunderstanding of Tuba's final question, *in film-hā ro be ki neshun midin*? (Who do you show these films to, anyway?). This question, which clearly references the narrow reach of documentary filmmaking, is also an ironic and self-referential act on the part of Bani-Etemad. *Who Do You Show These Films to, Anyway?* is the title of a documentary that Bani-Etemad directed in 1993. It focuses on a poor housing community in south Tehran and shares similar concerns with *Under the Skin of the City*. This reference to Bani-Etemad's corpus of work combined with Tuba's emotional plea interrupts the informed viewer's inclination to read this final moment as documentary, because the director stages a confrontation with the artificiality of documentary filmmaking, which runs contrary to the viewer's expectations regarding the relationship between documentary and the real.

Tuba's closing statement thus captures the complexities of Bani-Etemad's composite style in *Under the Skin of the City*. Her words, which criticize the sterile question-and-answer documentary form, enact an affective desire that is perhaps satisfied by the film's fictional scenes. At the same time, this criticism creates a sense of urgency and relevance that ends the film. By creating and resolving—mediating and destabilizing—the tension between documentary and narrative forms, Bani-Etemad interrogates a relationship between truth and myth. This relationship is central to *Under the Skin of the City*, in which the city of Tehran represents an urban reality that is capable of demystifying a popular but misinformed representation of the reformist movement.

URBAN MYTH

Whereas films by Abbas Kiarostami, Majid Majidi, and Mohsen Makhmalbaf often focus on rural environments and depend on bucolic landscapes to produce a distinct poetic, neorealist style that dates back to Dariush Mehrjui's *Gāv* (The cow, 1969),[23] Bani-Etemad's films constitute a separate track in Iranian art-house cinema, one that interrogates urban spaces and experiences. For Bani-Etemad, Tehran is a site of "perplexing contradictions" that function alongside a "concentration of politics, economics and social issues" to make the city seem bigger and more "chaotic" each day. As such, Tehran serves as a complicated and unstable character in all of her films. Even in *Gilāneh* (Gilaneh, 2004), the story of a disabled veteran and his mother living in the quiet hills of northern Iran, Bani-Etemad notes that Tehran asserts its presence through the threats of displacement and urban migration.[24] *Under the Skin of the City* represents one of Bani-Etemad's most complex portrayals of Tehran. In this film, the director explores the political possibility of the metropolis, and she envisions the capital city and its many paradoxes as signifiers of a reality covered up or overlooked by the reformist movement's mythic presence.

Like documentary, urbanism allows Bani-Etemad to investigate the representation of reality and to consider the ways in which multiple urban realities coalesce. This effort resonates with a long tradition in Iranian cinema, and in particular with a set midcentury metropolitan films that use the city of Tehran to expose the realities of harsh living conditions under Pahlavi rule. Farrokh Ghaffari's *Jonub-e shahr* (South of the city, 1958) was the first film to provide a critical representation of Tehran. The film tells the story of a woman who slowly discovers a friend's secret profession as a prostitute, and this plotline lays bare the city's dirty underworld. With this gritty representation of Tehran, Ghaffari provides an alternative narrative to the Pahlavi government's promotion of the country at the time as an oil-rich, modern nation. Through displays of unjust violence, the film also criticizes the *luti* system, a code of urban masculinity that has been valorized throughout much of Iran's modern history.[25] A luti genre of films popular in the mid-twentieth century especially mythologized this urban figure and turned him into a kind of Robin Hood character.[26] *South of the City*, however, casts the luti in the role of pimp and thug and shows him as a deeply troubled character living outside of the rules of society not for the betterment of his community but rather for his own benefit.

Ghaffari's depiction of the truths that underlined modernization and the luti myths required that the director violate the thematic and technological norms of Iranian cinema at the time. Indeed, *South of the City* was the first Iranian film to leave the set behind and shoot on location in the city's streets. This innovation led to a gritty and realistic representation of Tehran's poor districts that left many viewers unsettled. The film's main actor, Ebrahim Baqeri, was even physically assaulted for his controversial portrayal of the luti system, and this act brings into focus the power of Ghaffari's realistic style. The Pahlavi regime was also threatened by the unfavorable and realistic representation of life in south Tehran, and the film was banned and confiscated shortly after its release. The government reissued the film under the title *Reqābat dar shahr* (Rivalry in the city). This version of the film was so heavily censored that it no longer bore the critical traces of its predecessor, and it was even promoted as "preserving the traditional customs and beliefs of the honorable *luti*s."[27] The case of *South of the City* functions as a precedent within the Iranian cinematic tradition for probing the city of Tehran to uncover and complicate politicocultural myth by providing urban images of the real (the real streets of Tehran, the real effects of modernization, and the real qualities of the luti) and thereby establishing a counternarrative.

Ghaffari's film had a significant impact on other directors, who began using the city in this way. Notably, Kamran Shirdel was commissioned by the shah to create a series of documentaries that exalted the government's modernization project. Instead, the director took his camera to the streets of Tehran and created an eighteen-minute documentary called *Tehran Is the Capital of Iran* that included startling images of city's poorest citizens sleeping on sidewalks and in back alleys. The message was clear: the streets of Tehran *were* the reality of the shah's modernization process, which excluded and hid a huge portion of the country's population that did not fit into the orderly system that the shah envisioned.[28]

In *Under the Skin of the City*, Rakhshan Bani-Etemad deploys the city of Tehran in a similar way and excavates the urban structures of the capital city in order to unravel the myth of the reformist movement. She attempts to expose the hopes and promises of the reformist movement as they are reflected in a sprawling and unrelenting cityscape. Tehran's spatiality is exceedingly important to Bani-Etemad's style of representation in *Under the Skin of the City*. Through a series of spatially organized fragments, Bani-Etemad's camera redeems Tehran from the reformist movement's dreamworld. The terms of the reformist myth are established early in the film. The film enters its narrative after the documentary framing by means of a bus ride through the streets of Tehran. It is fitting that as both Tuba and the viewer journey into the fictional domain, we are made to listen to a political speech delivered by Khatami. Although the 1997 elections serve as a regular feature in the film's background, it is only in this moment early in the film that the reformist movement is given voice. Bani-Etemad cleverly manipulates the authentic sound bite to highlight the movement's mythic premise. Khatami says, "And we shall broaden democracy and progress toward a civil society. We will try to strengthen continually the dignity and stability of this nation. Our developments were the product of a great revolution and our problems..." At this point, noises from a street fight drown out Khatami. The speech returns as Khatami says, "The result was first and foremost a recovery of ourselves and particularly of our youth..." before fading out once again. In many ways, this speech is very typical and likely recognizable to Iranian viewers. It pays homage to the revolution, emphasizes the importance of engaging young people, and outlines Khatami's goals for his country, including democracy and civil society, two words that frequently punctuated his speeches.

By controlling our access to the audio clip, Bani-Etemad constructs and articulates a particular view of the reformist movement that informs the film throughout. It is significant that Bani-Etemad chooses to disrupt the speech with noises from the street. This clip, like a film's soundtrack, exists in an extradiegetic space and not within the characters' lives or world. It instead plays *over* the fictional realm. The fact that noises on the streets can interrupt the speech establishes a central thesis in *Under the Skin of the City*, as it becomes apparent that our audiovisual encounters with the urban experience alter and reconfigure our understanding of the reformist movement. This rupture occurs at a crucial part in the speech, right as Khatami is preparing to describe the country's problems. The implication of this cut is that Khatami and the reformist movement have no conception of local problems. The images onscreen—a brawl between members of the *basij* (a paramilitary volunteer militia that reports directly to the supreme leader) and young campaigners—reinforces this idea by providing a visual alternative to the words "democracy" and "civil society" that play moments before. The rupture in the speech also tears the narrative's suture. In other words, the speech and the contradicting images pull the viewer's attention away from the narrative (i.e., Tuba's journey home) and toward the historical world (i.e., Khatami's election). This method heightens the viewer's awareness of the fragility of both truth and fiction, because Bani-Etemad interrupts both real, recognizable speeches and her own narrative.

Jāme'eh-ye madani (civil society) formed the basis of Khatami's moderate political platform during the 1997 elections. Understanding the limits of the political system and the nature of factionalism in Iran at the time, Khatami was careful not to define clearly what he meant by "civil society" or how he intended to deliver the country to that ideal. Mohsen Kadivar, a well-known theologian, suggested that civil society represented during the elections an alternative to *velāyat-e faqih*, the basis for the governmental system in the Islamic Republic.[29] As such, Khatami easily garnered support from young voters, who were increasingly frustrated with the political and economic status quo in the late 1990s, without ever revealing a salient civil society agenda. Shortly after Khatami's election, however, Iranians began demanding accountability and sought to understand how the new president intended to revise the Islamic Republic's legal system to include the ideals of civil society, like tolerance, freedom, and mutual respect.[30] Over the next two years, and especially after a series of violent attacks on student protestors in 1999, people became increasingly skeptical of Khatami's ability to deliver on his promise of civil society.[31]

Although *Under the Skin of the City* takes place during the 1997 elections, it was filmed and produced in 2000, as disillusionment with Khatami and his promise of a civil society were on the rise. Bani-Etemad, therefore, reexamines the historic elections and gently uncovers in Tehran's cityscape the ways in which Khatami's rhetoric of democracy and civil society failed to address the country's problems even in 1997. Scholars and pundits within Iran generally agree that conservative forces blocked Khatami's efforts to enact reform and that, had he been successful, the country would have experienced a political, cultural, and economic revival.[32] This understanding of the situation constitutes the myth of the reformist movement, against which *Under the Skin of the City* reacts.[33] In the film the city of Tehran functions as a particularly poignant example of the ways in which broad notions of democracy and civil society—reform within the existing structures of the Islamic Republic of Iran—were never able to address local and economic problems. Khatami, as a cleric and former associate of Khomeini, was attempting to create reform from the top down, but Bani-Etemad's *Under the Skin of the City* returns this political narrative to the street level, and this vantage point reveals the reformist myth's shortcomings.

The street-level perspective adds a fragmented dimension to the representation of Tehran in *Under the Skin of the City*. The film is absent of wide-angle shots that show large segments of the city and does not feature any aerial shots that attempt to capture visually the city's entirety. In a film explicitly about Tehran, the absence of an establishing shot of the capital city is telling. Bani-Etemad defies Hollywood conventions to emphasize the street-level perspective that determines her film. Michel de Certeau distinguishes between those who read the city from above with panoramic views and those who walk the city, writing it without being able to read it.[34] In *Under the Skin of the City*, Bani-Etemad's camerawork invites the viewer to identify with the latter.

In order to capture several different urban perspectives, Bani-Etemad creates a fragmented picture of Tehran, as the camera moves disjointedly from one geographic location to another but never provides a large-scale image of the space traversed. The film's visual and narrative structures depend in large part on complementary scenes from different sectors of the city. An architectural firm on the top floor of a skyscraper in downtown Tehran is contrasted, for example, with the textile factory where Tuba works. The office scene features classical music playing in the background and shows an orderly arrangement of desks and offices occupied by men and women in colorful, Western-style clothing. The noise of the machines in the factory provides an uncomfortable point of contrast for the viewer, who has just been drawn in by the soft sounds of classical music in the office. The factory only employs women, who are all dressed in traditional black veils. The vertical scan of the office's skyscraper and the camera's horizontal movements in the factory emphasize the city as a three-dimensional space. The film highlights the value of occupying the city's highest point as Abbas enters the skyscraper and his friends warn him, "Don't forget us little people on your way up!"

Under the Skin of the City similarly compares geographically diverse social structures, and the family is a particularly rich area of exploration for the film. In one scene, Tuba arrives home and discovers her granddaughter playing in the narrow alleys of the neighborhood. Explaining her unexpected arrival, the granddaughter says, "Daddy beat up Mommy and told her to get lost . . . so we came here!" The members of the family have competing approaches to Hamideh's arrival, and her presence becomes a source of contention. Their reactions range from Mahmud's anger to Mahbubeh's meddling to Tuba's pragmatism: she points out that the family does not have the physical space or financial resources to care for a pregnant woman and her young daughter. The house's architecture and, specifically, its courtyard mediate the conversation and emphasize the family's lack of space. A traditional Iranian home features several rooms or apartments organized around a central courtyard. In this instance, Hamideh stands in the small central courtyard and the family members offer their commentary from the various rooms or during their passage between them. The lack of privacy both within and outside of the home is apparent: at one point, Tuba, afraid that the neighbors will hear, reprimands Mahmud for yelling through the door.

The scene switches to a house in an affluent neighborhood in north Tehran, and the camera captures the area's desirable hilltop view of the city. Inside, the home's texture is rich with lush fabrics, and it comprises only interior spaces, unlike the traditional courtyard structure that the film emphasizes in the preceding scene. A fight between mother and son ensues; the son has been stealing car radios despite having the financial means to buy them, and the family's reputation is at stake. Abbas interrupts the quarrel, and the son mocks him for his work ethic, even though they are approximately the same age. Mother and son fight for control of the car keys; the son is eventually victorious and speeds away, nearly hitting Abbas as he walks on the side of the street.

Bani-Etemad's technique with these juxtaposed scenes resonates with the "conflict" of Eisenstein's montage theory, wherein montage represents the development of an idea through the "collision of independent shots." The dynamism that results from the collisions of independent shots acts as a site for the production of new ideas and concepts. In other words, unexpected contradictions and conclusions explode from the collision of two shots "opposite to one another."[35] In *Under the Skin of the City*, the fragmented vignettes underscore a geographically and economically diverse set of urban realities that equally constitute Tehran. At the same time, these fragmented scenes together generate some threads of continuity related to the experiences of family and reputation.

Under the Skin of the City thus fragments the city of Tehran by providing the viewer with juxtaposing sights "that are experienced on an individual scale by the man in the street in big-city traffic."[36] The film, however, is not fragmented and features a cohesive narrative structure that allows Bani-Etemad to connect different segments of Tehran. *Under the Skin of the City* was the second-highest grossing film in 2001, and this achievement indicates the ways in which the film appealed to popular audiences, including the expectation of a coherent narrative.[37] Rahul Hamid notes that "the majority of screen time is devoted to Abbas's exploits, but Tuba is at the core of the film."[38] The reason for this disparity in screen time rests in the fact that Abbas plays a functional role in the film's geographic shifts. *Under the Skin of the City* consists, for the most part, of corresponding images from the north and the south, mediated by transitional highway scenes. Abbas, as a delivery boy, possesses the mobility necessary to permeate both spaces and functions as the viewer's guide. These regional shifts encourage the viewer to make comparisons—visually and socially, spatially and economically—between the two parts of the city and to consider the different ways that people make sense of their urban spaces and the vast differences in these approaches based on their geographic location within Tehran.

Highways, cars, and traffic as points in between these various locations together constitute a distinct kind of space in *Under the Skin of the City* that generates a constitutive set of economic, political, and social features. Abbas travels the streets and highways of the capital on his small scooter. Using a car borrowed from his boss, the entire family only makes one road trip together—to north Tehran—during the course of the film. This journey, which takes place early in the narrative, plays an important role in determining the symbolic distance between south Tehran and the financial districts of the north. Before the family enters the highway, they are stopped by a passing train, which stays onscreen for more than ten seconds. The viewer is thus made to wait, just as the characters do, and the train's presence emphasizes the ways in which mobility is blocked or limited for those citizens in the southern part of the city. The scene continues with a series of shots that accentuate the highway's unrelenting size and that capitalize on north Tehran's visible appeal (figure 2.3).

Although the family begins its journey in daylight, the point of arrival is marked by the darkness of night, and Bani-Etemad thereby adds a temporal aspect to the city's spatial configuration. Tehran's structure depends on a spatial and social stratification that emerges along its horizontal axis to divide this urban space into clear northern and southern regions. The city's middle- and upper-class residents live almost exclusively in the northern half of the city, and, as geographer Ali Madanipour notes, this polarization remains "clearly visible in Tehran."[39] *Under the Skin of the City* demonstrates how this

SCREENING REFORM

FIGURE 2.3. Scenes of northern Tehran highlight its natural beauty. Frame enlargement from *Under the Skin of the City*.

visual structure maintains social stratification through spatial means and effectively keeps Tehran's poorest citizens out of the city's financial centers through a highway system that is inaccessible to those individuals without a car. The absence of car ownership in the south is revealed in the film through an aerial shot of Tuba's neighborhood. The sound of a car alarm encourages the viewer to search through the monochrome sprawl of buildings and alleyways for the source the sound: the borrowed car, uncomfortably parked in a drain. The southern neighborhood clearly lacks both the financial and spatial resources necessary to acquire a car, and *Under the Skin of the City* brings to light at several different points the difficulty of navigating Tehran's vast geography without one. The challenges of public transit emerge as Tuba and her coworkers are slowed by the sail effect of their *chādor*s while attempting to catch their bus home. Meanwhile, the perils of pedestrianism are conveyed to the viewer as Abbas walks back to work after returning a car to his boss's home and is almost hit by the same car as a seemingly endless city sprawls before him. These moments test the bounds of access to urban space while drawing attention to social and economic diversity within the city.

For Bani-Etemad, the city's ability to represent the various human experiences that exist on its concrete surfaces extends beyond spatial and even temporal dimensions. Tehran functions as an affective surface that captures and mirrors the emotional responses and impulses of its inhabitants. In this way, Bani-Etemad's cinema gives in to Walter Benjamin's notion that film opens up the viewer's perceptions of the city and, through camerawork and editing, inscribes it with features that have previously gone unnoticed. In *Under the Skin of the City*, the streets and buildings of Tehran match the characters' excitement and elation and pain and suffering. For example, after Abbas declares his love to one of the women working in the architectural office and she receives him favorably, he speeds around on his scooter, weaving through the city's streets, which have been decorated with colorful lights for the Iranian New Year celebration called Nowruz. In the absence of music, Abbas's excitement in this moment is conveyed to the viewer through the city's visual appeal. The film's background thus takes on the characteristics of the protagonist, and this scene brings into focus the fact that the city is not always a site of impasse and fragmentation but also sometimes a place of inclusion. The city supports the characters in a way in which they cannot necessarily support each other.

Nowhere do these contradictions become more apparent than within the cycles of construction and destruction that grow, rejuvenate, and paralyze every metropolis. The narrative, including the depiction of the contractor who attempts to buy Tuba's house and of Abbas's work with an architectural firm, provides the film with ample opportunity to show construction sites throughout the city, and it is never quite clear whether the viewer is witnessing a building in the process of construction or deconstruction. The visual similarities of these two in-between moments capture the fact that that they are interrelated. That the city is replete with these cyclic processes becomes clearer when they are laced with human emotion. Abbas plows through the streets of Tehran after discovering that he was the victim of a scandal that robbed him of all his savings and the money acquired from the sale of his family's home. Despite his rapid progress through space and time, he is always framed by buildings that are being (de)constructed. These shells without windows or doors, these concrete skeletons, reflect his anguish. His financial, moral, and emotional destruction is captured perfectly by the half-completed/depleted structures, and his inability to escape them suggests the city as a dynamic space that functions outside of the bounds and laws of normal spatial experience by accommodating affective as well as temporal variables.

These moments of deconstruction are redeemed only at the point of construction. As Tuba packs and prepares to move, reduced once again to the role of tenant, her house is literally being torn down around her. The house that held her life together and distinguished her as a homeowner now parallels her financial and familial ruin. However, the film's final scene reveals Tuba's political hope as she lists the loss of her house and son as reasons for voting. This political hope, examined in greater depth later, is significant here because it functions as an act of productivity born of the destruction that the film's events have facilitated. The relationship between the collapse of Tuba's house and the birth of her political identity suggests the city of Tehran as a cyclic site, a fact reinforced by the cycles in Tuba's life and especially her return to being a tenant. In her final statement, Tuba notes the historical cycles in which post-revolution Iran has also been caught: "There was a time when we complained but you said we were fighting a war. It was the truth, so we accepted it. After the war, you asked us for patience because the country was in ruins, so once again, we put up with it all. . . . Now there is someone who wants to save us, so I'm here to vote." Her use of the word ruins (*kherābeh*) is particularly interesting. Combined with the film's many demolished and collapsed sites/sights, it indicates the ways in which the city's surface encapsulates the country's social and economic problems. More than that, Tuba's final declaration, "I am here to vote," suggests that these ruins—both despite and because of their cyclical nature—can be appropriated as spots for improvement or reform.

Under the Skin of the City's representation of Tehran through geographic fragmentation, cycles of (de)construction, and an intimate relationship between building and affect sympathetically guides our gaze to the unique experiences of the city's marginalized poor, working-class citizens. As a result, the film shows particular concern for the ways in which the political system (as represented by the elections in the background) plays out in these poorer districts of south Tehran. The director reinforces the existence of a relationship between the political system and south Tehran by locating the elections' presence only in the city's southern half. References to the reformist movement and the upcoming elections only appear in the sections of the film that focus on the southern part of the city. In his examination of Paris, Benjamin also takes an interest in the city's marginalized characters. He is particularly attracted to those individuals who position themselves outside of the normal cycles of consumerism and commodity; these figures on the cityscape become essential to his effort to uncover the myth of modernity. In a similar effort, Bani-Etemad focuses on Tehran's margins to expose the reformist myth, and these characters and the neighborhoods they inhabit represent the holes left unfilled by the reformist movement's political platform.

The development of Tuba's political identity rests at the center of *Under the Skin of the City*. The film's engagement with the documentary form signals a documentary's informing logic. The documentary framing at the beginning of the film reminds us that this film requires an interpretive skill set appropriate to an argument-based structure rather than a narrative plot. If one were, therefore, to evaluate *Under the Skin of the City* as a documentary—as the film's framing structure encourages—then it is possible to see the rise of Tuba's political identity as a speculative solution to problems that the film depicts. Tuba's inability at the beginning of the film to communicate her expectations for elected officials and her articulate final political statement suggest that the film's tragic events have informed and inspired her newfound political involvement.

Implicit in her statement, however, is tension between the factors that have led her to vote and the aims of the candidate for whom she is voting. Tuba's remark that "now there is someone who wants to save us, so I am here to vote" is punctuated by references to the loss of her house and son. The reformist movement—as represented in the film by Khatami's speech about democracy and civil society—seems unprepared to handle the economic and social concerns that have affected Tuba's life. Making sense of this tension and determining the exact relationship between the hopes and needs of south Tehran and the reformist movement's proposed political shift represents one of the film's greatest challenges, and inequalities in housing and gender are two categories that prove useful to the analysis of the political incongruity that the film reveals.

Rakhshan Bani-Etemad has focused much of her career on the housing crisis in Tehran. She has directed three documentaries on the topic: *Gozāresh-e 71* (Report of 71, 1991), *In film-hā ro be ki neshun midin?* (Who do you show these films to, anyway?, 1993), and *Bahār tā bahār* (Spring to spring, 1995). Her interest in architectural and residential experiences figures into her feature films as well, including *Under the Skin of the City*. In this film, housing informs both the director's sociopolitical commentary and her cinematic style. She decided to film a large portion of the scenes as long shots, and she has stated that this cinematography was intended to create the effect of "peeping into a neighbor's house from on top of the wall."[40]

Traditional Iranian houses are surrounded and separated by walls that configure private and public spaces. That is, homes in Iran are fully private spaces, visually inaccessible to passersby on the street. Farzaneh Milani notes the relationship between this architectural feature and the practice of veiling, arguing, "Like walls that enclose houses and separate inner and outer spaces, the veil makes a clear statement about the disjunction between the private and the public."[41] *Under the Skin of the City* highlights the wall as a unique neighborly architectural feature. It serves as a meeting point for Mahbubeh and Masumeh, who climb up ladders and meet on top of the wall that separates their homes to study and gossip. The film provides the viewer with a neighborly perspective that encourages the same kind of empathy as is found in neighborly life. In this way the film's form adds force to its critical observations on the status of housing in south Tehran. At the center of this crisis is a lack of physical space and a rapidly growing urban population; these problems necessitate the reorganization of traditional horizontal living structures into vertical structures that can accommodate more people. This desire to build up motivates the constructor who ultimately buys Tuba's house, and the film reinforces this impetus with wide horizontal shots of the neighborhoods in south Tehran juxtaposed with narrow vertical shots of north Tehran. The desirability of physical space in Tehran allows the contractor in the film to buy out entire neighborhoods in south Tehran, where the immediate need for access to financial resources outweighs the stability of homeownership.

The sale of Tuba's house affords Abbas the opportunity to purchase a visa to pursue his dreams abroad (with the additional promise of financial return), and it allows Mahmud, who is unemployed, to reassert his power as the head of the home. But it is Tuba who provides for the family and finds comfort in the stability of owning a home. After Abbas and Mahmud sell the family home, she laments, "I used to carry stuff on my back, moving from one rented house to another.... Now, at this old age, when what I needed was some space, you had to do this?" Although Tuba believes that she has earned the right to homeownership, it eludes her because she is a woman, and the contractor, who tells Tuba to "go to your man. I don't deal with womenfolk," demonstrates the dynamics of gender segregation in homeownership. Tuba's name, likely a reference to Shahrnush Parsipur's novel *Tuba va ma'nā-ye shab* (Tuba and the meaning of night, 1989), similarly highlights a relationship between gender and homeownership.[42] In Parsipur's historical novel, Tuba's status as a female homeowner at the turn of the century—the result of her young marriage to an older man and the subsequent divorce—distinguishes her, and the financial and practical comforts of homeownership set her on a path of discovery that allows her to uncover within Iranian society a fully engrained patriarchy that oppresses women at every turn.[43] In *Under the Skin of the City*, it seems unlikely that Khatami's broad discussion of civil society can undo a deeply and historically determined system of economic and gender injustice.

Housing functions as a point of access to an array of gender inequalities that rise to the surface in *Under the Skin of the City*, the most important of which is violence perpetrated against women. The film engages two acts of domestic violence that together elicit a number of practical and political responses. Hamideh, who is beaten by her husband, is forced back into the cycle of violence because Tuba must accept the fact that the family does not have space in their home to accommodate a pregnant woman and her daughter. During Hamideh's stay at the house, the film includes several shots of the interior spaces, partitioned and divided with makeshift curtains assembled from old sheets; these crowded images underscore the lack of physical space in the home. Hamideh's situation is contrasted with that of Masumeh, the family's next-door neighbor and Mahbubeh's best friend. Masumeh is abused by her brother, who, although a drug addict, beats her and cuts off her hair after he discovers that she went to a concert. Masumeh breaks this cycle of violence by running away. She and Mahbubeh later meet in Mellat Park, and her style of dress and heavy makeup convey to the viewer that she is working as a prostitute.⁴⁴ When police raid the park, both girls are arrested, and Tuba is unable to bail Mahbubeh out of jail because she no longer has the deed to the house, which she needs as collateral for the bail money. In this way, Bani-Etemad ties this social problem into the economic conditions that determine the building industry.

Tuba's son Ali, a young political activist campaigning for Khatami, responds to the violence against the women around him by arguing that "these sorts of things happen as long as women are ignorant of their rights." The irony and futility of this statement are rendered apparent by Tuba's lack of rights in homeownership. More than that, Ali's statement, which accords with the reformist movement's answer to women's problems, encourages Iranian society to reconsider the way it thinks about women and their rights within an existing political structure rather than revising that structure as a whole.⁴⁵ However, Tuba's dismissive reaction to her son's statement suggests that this approach is unable to accommodate practically her socioeconomic reality. And it is ultimately this reality—the experience of one family in south Tehran—that destabilizes the reformist myth and highlights the fact that Khatami's broad vision for his country was out of touch with most of its citizens. The city of Tehran functions a particularly rich site of exploration for Bani-Etemad because its numerous complications bring to focus the many ways in which the reformist movement was never equipped to deal with the country's immediate, local problems. *Under the Skin of the City* was produced in 2000, at a time of growing criticism of the reformist movement's inability to enact broad change for a better society. The articulation of Tuba's political aspirations in this film represents nostalgia for a lost hope, covered and obscured by the reformist movement's phantasmagoria.

MAPPING TEHRAN AND THE UNTIMELINESS OF DOCUMENTARY

The lost hope that emerges in *Under the Skin of the City* is taken up and explored further in Bani-Etemad's *Our Times* . . . . Identified by the Iranian journal *Film* as one of the most important cinematic events of 2002, *Our Times*... is a documentary that examines the campaigning period preceding Khatami's reelection in 2001.[46] This film shares common concerns with *Under the Skin of the City*; in particular, it represents Khatami's reformist movement alongside housing crises in the south of Tehran and within the context of documentary filmmaking. These points of intersection between the two films enable a productive comparison that exposes Bani-Etemad's critique of the reformist movement. These two films work together first to reveal the political hope, necessitated by the urban experience, that underpinned the reformist movement's popular rise and later to reorganize our understanding of the reformist movement's failure to accommodate that hope. *Our Times*... contributes to reform cinema by underscoring the spatial and geographic features of Tehran as a means of resisting the traditional chronological and temporal markers that guide a viewer's understanding of documentary. As a result of this reconfiguration of time, Bani-Etemad freezes time as a powerful statement on the reformist movement's inability to progress or enact reform.

Our Times... comprises two seemingly disjointed parts. In the first section, Bani-Etemad follows a group of young people campaigning for Khatami. Many Iranians were disillusioned with Khatami after his first term in office. He was unable to create the changes he had promised because his efforts were blocked by conservative forces. As a result, the young campaigners meet resistance at every turn. However, in spite of these challenges, they are ultimately successful, and the film's first section ends with Khatami's reelection. In the second part of the film, Bani-Etemad tracks down the forty-eight women who had registered to run for president that year. The Guardian Council discarded their names because women in Iran, although able to run for parliament, may not seek the office of president. Bani-Etemad interviews several of them but focuses the bulk of this part of the film on one of them, a woman named Arezu. The director follows Arezu as she scourers the city looking for an apartment because she is being evicted from her current residence. Arezu's effort is complicated by the fact that she is a poor, young single mother who has no husband to petition on her behalf. Only twenty-five years old, she was married twice before, both times to heroin addicts. She eventually finds a new living arrangement, but the film ends as she returns to her job the next day to discover that she has been fired for missing three days of work to look for housing.

Determining a relationship between these two disparate parts represents one of the film's greatest challenges. How does one make sense of a film that begins as a documentary about the 2001 elections and ends as a documentary about one woman's attempt to find a place to live? The filmmaker, who provides *Our Times*... with its godlike documentary voice, initially suggests a chronological structure. In a scene that bridges the two sections of the film and shows the director driving through the busy streets of Tehran, Bani-Etemad says that she is worried that her daughter will have questions that she won't be able to answer. She never identifies the nature of these hypothetical questions, but the camera continues to follow Bani-Etemad during her drive, and the viewer gets the sense that she is moving forward, searching for these answers.

The film's second section begins with the sound of interviews being arranged; the image shifts to an office scene before quickly returning to Bani-Etemad in her car as several more interviews are lined up by cell phone. The repeated use of footage of the director in her car suggests that these interviews, and the entire second part, take place after the car ride and therefore well after the elections. We make sense of the disjointedness of the film by constructing a chronological reading facilitated in large part by this transition. The election in the first part of the film raises questions, and as a result the documentarian collects visible evidence in the second section to answer these questions. The construction of this kind of argument conforms to viewers' expectations of a documentary.

However, during the course of the second section, Bani-Etemad unravels the chronological structure that the viewer has come to accept. As the central character, Arezu, searches for a house, news of the *upcoming* elections slowly permeate the film's background. Well into her story, Arezu buys a paper and the camera focuses on the headline, which reads, "A vote for Khatami is a vote for reform." Later, a radio announces that there are "only a few more days left until the election, and the candidates have started their campaigning efforts." In Iran candidates have a limited campaigning period; thus this announcement suggests that perhaps the two sections of the film are not even synchronic and that Arezu's story, despite occupying the second position in the film, actually commences before the first section. The second section, like the first, ends on Election Day. The viewer is forced to recognize the overlap of time and as a result must question the argument-based structuring process that Bani-Etemad claims for her project.

In the absence of a linear structure, *Our Times . . .* offers structure through Tehran's topology. As noted previously, the city is divided into northern and southern regions; this division, geographer Ali Madanipour notes, represents "the main feature of the city's spatial structure."[47] The northern half of the city, home to the city's middle and upper classes, is settled comfortably at the base of the Alborz Mountains and enjoys "a wide range of social and physical privileges over the southern half." Geographically, these benefits include "a more diverse skyline and a degree of visual supremacy over the south," better flood control, and a more moderate climate. The desirability of this space means that the northern part of the city comes with "larger houses, lower densities, higher land prices, smaller households, higher rates of literacy and employment, higher concentrations of modern facilities and amenities, . . . more green space . . . a better water supply and a higher defensive value."[48] Throughout the twentieth century, city planning efforts—lead by three consecutive governments—reinforced this divide.[49] The affluent districts of the north and the poor districts of the south are, therefore, separated by an insurmountable social and physical gap.[50]

Rakhshan Bani-Etemad's work captures and is informed by this visually inscribed urban feature. Whereas the first part of the film (about the young campaigners) takes place in north Tehran, the second part unfolds in the southern part of the city. This sets up a series of juxtapositions that confirm the visual supremacy of the north. The film's representation of the north consists of scenes that show greenery, planned pedestrian spaces, and striking panoramic views of the cityscape. On the other hand, the film's focus on south Tehran emphasizes the lack of green space, an absence of pedestrian resources, and the dilapidation of physical structures (figure 2.4).

These visual disparities are compounded temporally: the first section on the north of Tehran lasts eighteen minutes, and the second section is three times as long. This distribution of time mimics the city's population. The

SCREENING REFORM

FIGURE 2.4. A young campaign volunteer stands under posters of Khatami in north Tehran. Frame enlargement from Rakhshan Bani-Etemad's *Our Times* . . . .

north of Tehran, as a privileged area, consists of a much smaller number of people, whereas the south is bigger in terms of both land space and density. Although the second part of the film tells one woman's story, it is representative of a much broader experience. The social and economic struggles that *Our Times* . . . portrays in the south of the city apply to a large number of people. However, the film's first section documents a narrow experience open to a specific class of young Tehranis who have the financial resources and support to engage in campaigning efforts. In light of the horizontal axis that the film visually and temporally sketches, it is worth reconsidering the transitional scene that connects the film's two parts. The shots of the director driving in her car, more than just representing a mystic search for the truth, suggest relocation and physical movement as she repositions her documentary subject in the south.

By laying her documentary structure over a map of Tehran's north-south divide, Rakhshan Bani-Etemad encourages a comparative perspective that illuminates how the political process that she is portraying plays out in these two distracts. The northern part of the city is alive with excitement about the upcoming elections. The campaigners are engaging people in political debates; the streets are covered in posters and other campaigning materials; and there are rallies in which Khatami addresses a stadium full of supporters. Meanwhile, in the south, the candidates' campaigns have been relegated to the background at best. They make appearances only in the form of a brief radio announcement, a newspaper headline, and a few scattered posters. The people in this part of the film are uninvolved and seemingly uninterested in the political system. For this reason, it is easy to overlook the lack of a linear chronological structure. In contrast to the heightened political activity of the first section, the political apathy of the second signals the absence of elections.

The most startling difference between the two parts of the city (and the film), however, involves the acquisition of private space. Arezu's story in the film is marked by an inability to locate housing for her family. This struggle and her frustrations are shown onscreen for almost an hour. However, the first part of *Our Times* . . . opens with the young campaigners cleaning and setting up their headquarters. They easily secure an office on a quiet residential street to use as the base for their campaigning efforts. This space is crucial to their political participation; without it, they would be unable to organize their campaigning strategies. By the same logic, Arezu's lack of private space prohibits her political participation. Rakhshan Bani-Etemad selects Arezu as a documentary subject because she was one of the few women to register to run for president. When asked why she wanted to become president, Arezu identifies a number of social and economic problems that plague poor communities in Tehran. Ironically, she is unable to participate in the very process for which she registered. In the end, Arezu is so consumed by her search for housing that she does not even have time to vote. Her urban experience, then, at once creates the need for political hope and blocks her attempts to satisfy it.

Rakhshan Bani-Etemad's geographic structure allows us to contemplate a notion of documentary time. Because documentaries construct arguments about the lived, historical world and establish what Bill Nichols calls "discourses of sobriety" that imagine their relationship to the real as "imminent,"[51] one might assume by extrapolation that documentary time is necessarily real time. However, *Our Times* . . . comprises two disjointed parts that overlap chronologically and refuse temporal cohesion. The film is premised on an argument and a reasoning logic that depend on a linear progression that is ultimately and paradoxically unsupported by its visual evidence. This documentary's temporality is, in fact, untimely. This concept of untimeliness has gained momentum recently in discussions of critical theory. Wendy Brown, who has played a crucial role in the articulation of this model, argues that untimeliness offers "a different sense of the times and a different sense of time."[52] *Our Times* . . . challenges the viewer's conception of time in order to challenge his or her understanding of the times. The film's title, *Ruzegār-e mā* . . . (Our times . . .), plays with this idea further by serving as an umbrella category for multiple narratives that are far from unified, and the director's opening commentary emphasizes this difference. She says, "Spring 2001: Strange, stormy days. The eighth presidential elections in Iran. I intended to make a record of that era, but where should I start? From what point of view? Society was filled with fear and hope, doubt and trust."

Brown argues, "Untimeliness deployed as an effective intellectual strategy, far from being a gesture of indifference to time, is a bid to reset time."[53] It is through her efforts to reset time that Rakhshan Bani-Etemad visualizes her critique of the reformist movement. By holding time still, she suggests the lack of progression, and especially the lack of improvement or *reform*. Khatami's election to the presidency in 1997 represented more than just a change in political power; it also marked a semantic shift. Phrases like "civil society" and "democracy" replaced the revolutionary rhetoric popular in the republic during its first twenty years. However, Khatami's first term proved unsuccessful in delivering the changes that these concepts promised. In fact, in four years, none of the country's economic and social problems had been addressed. By holding time constant and making geography a variable, Bani-Etemad made her film undeniably local, inextricable from the city it depicts. By fixing the viewer's gaze on the city of Tehran, she stages a confrontation with its problems. Khatami focused much of his energy on repairing Iran's global reputation through concepts like a "dialogue of civilizations." Both of Bani-Etemad's films bring into focus the local economic problems that were for many Iranians more urgent.

Bani-Etemad's effort to hold time still resonates with Walter Benjamin's concept of the "Angel of History," Thesis IX in "Theses on the Philosophy of History" (1940). Benjamin imagines a construction of history in which we look backward while being propelled forward by a "storm" called "progress."[54] Inspired by a Paul Klee painting called *Angelus Novus*, the Angel of History is caught between the momentum forward and backward and is held momentarily at a standstill. Khatami's reformist movement was similarly stuck: constantly staring back at the revolution, unable to look away but at the same time pushed forward by its desire to progress. Bani-Etemad's *Our Times . . .* demonstrates that for the reformist movement the tension between the past and the future resulted in a static present.

Under the Skin of the City and *Our Times . . .* together articulate a political hope that is discovered and later lost in the urban desires that once gave force to the reformist movement. The almost messianic quality of the reformist movement that emerges when Tuba announces, "Someone has come to save us, and I am here to vote," gives way to near negation when Arezu is unable first to run for president and later to cast a vote. Rakhshan Bani-Etemad's cinematic unraveling of the dreams and desires that paradoxically grounded and destabilized Khatami's movement endowed the reformist aesthetic with a new sense of space and time, wherein Tehran functions as a site of constant change and never-ending unchange. These spatial and temporal reconfigurations recover economic, political, and social urgencies that exist separately from the reformist myth.

Bani-Etemad's political assessment in *Under the Skin of the City* and *Our Times . . .* betrays a cinematic relationship with Mohammad Khatami and his reformist movement that is much deeper than just modes of critique. Both films depict and criticize the political process, and this level of representation is unprecedented in modern Iranian history. By relaxing the codes of cultural control and inaugurating artistic forums for open political debate and critique, Khatami made significant strides toward the ideals of democracy and civil society that he envisioned. Bani-Etemad's *Under the Skin of the City* and *Our Times . . .*—despite their criticism of the reformist movement—are, therefore, representatives of a group of Iranian films that participated in the formation, articulation, and propagation of a new set of political and philosophical reformist ideals.

3
VIDEO DEMOCRACIES

Or, The Death of the Filmmaker

In 1998 the eighteen-year-old director Samira Makhmalbaf, daughter of Mohsen Makhmalbaf, wowed international film audiences with her debut film *Sib* (Apple, 1998), and her presence at Cannes that year made her the youngest director ever to participate in the official section of the film festival. *Apple* tells the story of eleven-year-old twin girls, Masumeh and Zahra Naderi, who have been kept indoors their entire lives. Their parents, a blind mother and an unemployed father, attempt to overcome their disempowerment by exerting excessive control over their daughters' lives, especially their access to the outside world. Concerned neighbors alert social workers, who intervene on behalf of the girls, and the film covers their entrance into the outside world. *Apple*, which is based on real events and features the actual involved parties, examines issues of entrapment, isolation, and confinement and considers the psychological effects that these modes of control have on their victims. For example, because of their confinement, Masumeh and Zahra have a limited ability to communicate in Persian. Instead, the girls have developed a language between themselves, a linguistic system that keeps them isolated at the same time that it protects them. We also see the girls' reaction to observing their reflection in a mirror for the first time, and we watch them reach for an apple on the other side of the courtyard wall, dually symbolic of temptation and freedom. All of these moments in the film demonstrate the ways in which confinement has profoundly affected the formation of the girls' identities, both linguistic and social.

Mohsen Makhmalbaf, the film's writer and editor, has suggested that this individual narrative is an allegory for something much bigger, and he described the real-life events that inspired the film as "the story of our nation." He continued, "We have all been kept in a cave by our fathers. We can't even look at the sun." Hamid Dabashi notes that Makhmalbaf made this observation immediately following Khatami's election in 1997, and from this statement one might extrapolate that the film's hope—the fact that the girls do, in the end, see the sunlight and discover their freedom—reflects the hope of the reformist movement. Dabashi claims that *Apple* "may serve as the manifesto" for the director's generation, who enthusiastically supported Khatami's reforms as a postideological movement.[1] Makhmalbaf's *Apple* begins to trace the contours of this reformist aesthetic, and Mohsen Makhmalbaf's statement and Dabashi's observation point to the possibilities and insights that emerge when reform as a political and aesthetic category orders Iranian film history during this period, Khatami's eight-year presidency.

Such an ordering might reveal a "genre of the Second of Khordād," a category of films grounded in Khatami's unexpected victory on 2 Khordād 1376 (May 23, 1997). But what would such a genre look like? Whereas Makhmalbaf's *Apple* only hints at political reform, other films released during this period, including Abbas Kiarostami's *Ta'm-e gilās* (Taste of cherry, 1997) and *Dah* (10, 2002) and Bahman Farmanara's *Bu-ye kāfur, 'atr-e yās* (The smell of camphor, the scent of jasmine, 2000), directly engage Khatami's presidency and signal new thematic possibilities nurtured by his liberal cultural policies. Iranian films at the turn of the twenty-first century summon the dialectic that determined reform cinema at this time: political reform restructured aesthetic practices at the same time that filmmakers contributed to the development of a reformist discourse. In Kiarostami's works, his engagement with reform redrew the limits of his aesthetic sensibility, whereas Farmanara's film redefines the Iranian intellectual in reformist terms.

At the same time, films from this period speak to the technological innovations—including the rapid expansion of digital video technology—that were amending the standards of filmmaking and spectatorship at the time in

Iran. The proliferation of digital video technology democratized filmmaking by providing affordable access to cameras and editing software, thereby allowing individuals to sidestep the government's role as the subsidizer of expensive 35 mm film equipment. Whereas film studies has long acknowledged the democratizing effect of video technologies, the Iranian film industry's engagement with video reveals new democratic orders vis-à-vis video technology. In the United States, for example, video technology—including VCRs, Betamax players, and camcorders—democratized media culture by enabling consumers to dictate the terms of their engagement with movies and television and by allowing filmmakers to access affordable moviemaking equipment. The rise of digital video technology in Iran, however, did more than just democratize filmmaking by providing affordable access to equipment. It also encouraged a system of production, distribution, and aesthetics that operated outside of the bounds of state control. It is no coincidence that these democratizing technologies reshaped culture in Iran at the same that Khatami identified democracy as an important part of his political agenda. The convergence of these films' interest in the reformist movement and their experimentation with digital video constitutes an important attribute of reform cinema and a constitutive feature of a genre of the Second of Khordād.

As Khatami's first term came to an end, film critic Nima Hassaninasab published an article titled "Zhānr-e dovom-e khordād" (Genre of the Second of Khordād) in *Film*, Iran's foremost film trade journal. In this article, Hassaninasab suggests that Khatami's first term as president profoundly affected Iranian cinema, and he notes that "everyone who has been following cinematic production for the last two decades agrees that some of the most important and successful films over the last four years were only made possible after the appearance of the present government."[2] Hassaninasab provocatively proposes that these films together constitute a new genre, which he calls the genre of the Second of Khordād. The Second of Khordād—specifically, 2 Khordād 1376 (May 23, 1997)—was the day that Khatami was elected for the first time, but that date came to represent something much bigger in Iranian society. Following Khatami's victory, he and his followers became known as Jonbesh-e dovom-e Khordād or the Second of Khordād movement. For many Iranians, the reforms that Khatami promised represented a new beginning in the Islamic Republic, and by memorializing the date of his election in this way, this segment of Iranian society sought to reset its historical clock with the Second of Khordād as the new starting point. Hassaninasab's genre of the Second of Khordād also presupposes a new point of periodization, one that marks a new period for Iranian cinema. Whereas the Second of Khordād movement represents political change, the genre of the Second of Khordād points to changes within the film industry. This scheme suggests that cinema can do more than represent politics. A film industry, its practices and its aesthetics, can also reshape itself vis-à-vis a particular political system.

According to Hassaninasab, the films that constitute the genre of the Second of Khordād were bound together by their "engagement with themes that had previously been forgotten or unattainable."[3] Broadly surveying many of the films that were released during Khatami's first term, he outlines a number of new themes, including immigration, marginalization, love triangles, and the unanswered needs of young people, but he focuses the bulk of his analysis on four areas that best represent the thematic developments in Iranian cinema during the first four years of Khatami's presidency: (1) the rise of political content, (2) critical engagement with the Iran-Iraq War, (3) popular acceptance of stories that "engage earthly love and premarital relationships," and (4) the development of more complex female characters.[4]

A genre of the Second of Khordād that comprises films with a new set of shared concerns accepts the idea that Khatami's liberal cultural policies made possible the rise of these thematic developments. For Hassaninasab, the genre of the Second of Khordād offers the opportunity to consider what films are about when filmmakers are less restricted in what they can and cannot represent,[5] and the films that constitute the genre of the Second of Khordād in Hassaninasab's model relate to the reformist movement because they grew out of the open cultural atmosphere that Khatami's presidency fostered. And yet a study of genre must account for more than just thematic content. A definition of the genre of the Second of Khordād, whose name recalls the genesis of the reformist movement, must suggest that these films communicate with Khatami and his policies and must register the video technology that made such communication possible and that contributed to the rhetoric of democracy that swept Iran at the end of the twentieth century.

VIDEOTAPE HISTORIES

As the previous chapter demonstrated, campaign movies (*film-hā-ye tablighāt-e entekhābāti*) of the 1997 electoral period thrust Mohammad Khatami and other politicians onscreen in unprecedented ways and redrew the boundaries of political spectacle in Iran. These movies established a form of engagement between the film industry and the reformist movement, but they were also wrapped up in the technological developments of the time. For example, the director Seyfollah Dad, who eventually became the deputy of cinema affairs within the Ministry of Culture and Islamic Guidance, claimed with great pride that he shot Khatami's 1997 campaign movie with three Sony Betacam video cameras, the latest in video technology in Iran at the time.[6] These Betacam movies helped transmit Khatami's political platform to the general public and signaled the growing nexus between video and reform.

Although this confluence redefined the terms of cultural and political engagement in Iranian society at the end of the twentieth century, it would not have even been possible a decade earlier. Following the revolution of 1978–1979 and the consolidation of cinematic affairs in the Ministry of Culture and Islamic Guidance in 1982, the newly formed Islamic Republic banned all video-related technology, including handheld video cameras and video cassettes, and later VCRs and movies on video. This policy was part of a larger effort to control image making in Iran, a bold attempt to regulate viewership within the country and to curtail the unmediated circulation of images of the new republic outside of the country.[7] Even as late as 1986, the Ministry of Culture and Islamic Guidance issued a letter to all border custom agents reiterating the ban on "video cassettes and all related activity" and ordered that all blank tapes be sent to the ministry. Although in the absence of video cameras blank cassettes may have seemed harmless, the ministry warned that some of these tapes were not blank at all but rather had been "masterfully repackaged" before entering the country so that they appeared to be unopened blank tapes. The use of video technology by "individuals," the ministry declared, was "unpermitted."[8] This report reveals the government's anxiety about individual citizens accessing unregulated images and bringing them into the private space of the home, where they could no longer be controlled.

Despite clever attempts to repackage blank tapes, the ban was effective, though not absolute, in limiting access to video technology in the country. Statistics show that in 1992 there was 1 videotape per 22.5 people in Iran, compared to 1 videotape for every 3.8 people in the United States.[9] But the end of the Iran-Iraq War and the changing of the guard within the Ministry of Culture and Islamic Guidance ushered in new rhetoric and ultimately new policies with regard to video technology. In May 1993, Ali Larijani, the minister of culture and Islamic guidance, announced that the ministry intended to lift the ban on video technology. Although politicians had previously positioned video as part of an assault on culture (*tahājom-e farhangi*), Larijani argued that "we must know the qualities of mass communication in order to combat the assault on culture."[10] Importantly, he also moved beyond the Islamic Republic's anxiety about cultural onslaught from the United States and Europe and advocated for video because it would allow Iran to share its culture globally and facilitate education and research within the country.[11] The decision to legalize video technology prompted controversy,[12] especially within the country's periodicals, and one editorialist even called video a "little devil" that people welcome into their homes.[13] Nevertheless, the ministry moved forward with the legalization of video and released regulations on the production of videos in September 1993.[14] Two months later, 1,000 video clubs, owned and operated by Iran-Iraq War veterans (*basiji*s), opened.[15]

During this period of legalization, the government sought to assuage people's concern and encourage the use of video through initiatives like the subsidization of video making and the first video festival.[16] By the time that Seyfollah Dad used a Betacam to shoot Khatami's campaign movie four years later, video technology had gained tentative acceptance in society. However, it was not until Khatami's presidency that video achieved widespread popularity and became associated with the ideals of democratization that marked the use of video around the world. In his study of video, Michael Z. Newman reminds us that the history of any medium must include attention not only to technological exceptionalism but also to the changing cultural status of that medium.[17] In the case of Iran, the height of political reform witnessed a shift in the cultural value of video, as it moved away from its status as a vehicle for *tahājom-e farhangi*, the assault on culture, and toward its place alongside concepts like democracy, civil society, and the rule of law.

If the four years between the legalization of video technology in 1993 and Khatami's election in 1997 marked the gradual acceptance of the medium within Iranian society, then the period of reform between 1997 and 2005 signaled its rise to widespread popularity. Advertisements for video equipment and services provide valuable information about both the growing popularity of video and the kinds of hopes and ambitions that video technology represented for Iranian society at this time. Between Khatami's first month in office and the middle of his second presidential term, the number of advertisements for video-related products more than tripled in the monthly publication *Film* and totaled more than a quarter of all advertisements in the periodical.[18] These advertisements marketed video equipment, such as cameras, tapes, and editing software, as well as services, such as rental clubs, videography and editing services, and filmmaking organizations that used video equipment. The marketing programs that informed these advertisements, although entrenched in capitalist agendas, contributed to a new discourse about video and its relationship to the film industry. Video offered a world of possibilities, from the chance to record "the beautiful world . . . exactly as it is" and to "create and preserve happy memories" to twenty-four-hour-a-day access and immediate playback options.[19] As one advertisement boldly declared in a two-page spread, "Bring the cinema home!"[20] Video technology meant that filmmaking belonged to everyone and that the consumption of moving images was no longer confined to public spaces.

The rhetoric in these advertisements spoke to a larger global discourse about video that positioned it as a democratizing force. In the United States in the 1980s and 1990s, for example, video technology spoke to democratic goals in a number of ways. Whereas the VCR allowed people to watch television and movies on their own terms, the ability to produce moving images easily and cheaply with camcorders meant that individuals could take control of airwaves and network programming. But more than anything it was the camcorder's claim to authenticity that imbued video with a sense of democracy, and amateur video footage played a special role in the promotion of democratic ideals, including civic movements and political protests, such as the 1992 Los Angeles riots, sparked by the circulation of amateur video footage showing LAPD officers brutally beating Rodney King.[21]

In Iran, too, video came to represent democracy. In particular it afforded filmmakers the chance to operate outside of the strict polices that had previously regulated every aspect of their work. It also gave every citizen the opportunity to contribute to the nation's visual discourse, to participate in the image making that the Islamic Republic had so desperately tried to control, and it freed spectatorship from the hands of the governmental control. Samira Makhmalbaf, for example, noted that the only way to film using expensive 35 mm equipment was to rent it from the government, which required approval and constant oversight. Digital video, on the other hand, only required preliminary approval.[22] Abbas Kiarostami also saw the video camera in democratizing terms and claimed that the digital video camera "frees cinema from the clutches of production, capital, and censorship."[23] For both Makhmalbaf and Kiarostami, government control was tied to the flow of capital, and video, a relatively cheap technology, allowed the act of filmmaking to exist outside of the restraints of capitalism and state control. In general, during this period people sought to position media, including video, as fundamental to the civil society that Khatami promised.[24]

Video technology, in addition to contributing to the rhetoric of democracy in Iran at the turn of twenty-first century, opened up an unprecedented conversation about copyright law, both internationally and locally, and such a discussion would not have been possible had it not been for Khatami's emphasis on the rule of law during his presidency. Whereas debates about the ethics of video spectatorship during the period following the legalization of video technology took shape around questions about how the mass consumption of unregulated images would affect the well-being of society, during Khatami's presidency examination of the ethics of video spectatorship became a discussion of copyright and the legal right to access the work of others. For example, in 2001 the illegal exhibition of contemporary Iranian films on NITV, a U.S.-based Persian-language satellite channel popular in Iran, prompted discussions about Iran's failure to participate in one of the international copyright conventions.[25] Similarly, in 2002 a law was passed that prohibited the screening of movies on busses without written consent from the films' owners.[26] These cases highlight the role that video technology played in facilitating debates about the role of law in society and what it meant to live in a civil society.

Whereas certain segments of the film industry, including distribution companies and producers, worried about the implications of video technology from legal and financial points of view, filmmakers took a much more positivist view of the medium. As a result, their experimentation with video technology and their attempts to represent it suggest an appeal to the ideas of democracy, civil society, and the rule of law that determined video's cultural status at this important moment in Iran's history. Filmmakers like Abbas Kiarostami and Bahman Farmanara used video technology to intervene in the discourse of reform that shaped Iranian political and social engagement during the late 1990s and early 2000s. Both directors were established and successful filmmakers at the turn of the twenty-first century and, therefore, did not necessarily benefit from or require the financial affordances that video provided to amateur video makers at the time. Nevertheless, video still played an important role in their films, as both an aesthetic and a political possibility, one driven by a desire to operate outside of the hegemonic structures of power that had controlled the film industry for the better part of two decades.

GREEN AND GRAINY: KIAROSTAMI'S VIDEO CODA

On May 18, 1997, five days before Mohammad Khatami's landslide electoral victory, as his campaign video circulated in overdrive, Abbas Kiarostami's film *Taste of Cherry* momentously won the Palme d'Or at the Cannes Film Festival. Although Iranian cinema had previously enjoyed much success at international festivals, this award marked its first major win, and it catapulted Iranian cinema and Abbas Kiarostami onto the international film scene. But film critics and scholars soon began suggesting that the win was political, tied to the upcoming elections in Iran. Roger Ebert, for example, wrote a critical review of the film,[27] which Mehrnaz Saeed-Vafa positions as the critic's commentary on the political nature of the film's win at Cannes.[28] Azadeh Farahmand similarly argues that "Kiarostami's *The Taste of Cherry* won the *Palme d'Or* at Cannes in 1997, the year that Khatami was elected Iran's president, his image as a moderate leader circulating in the western Media."[29] *Time* magazine further solidified the connection between reformist politics and Kiarostami's film when it selected *Taste of Cherry* as one of the ten best films of the year and in the same issue praised Khatami for his willingness to engage in international dialogue.[30] *Time*'s suggestion that both Khatami's "dialogue among civilizations" and Kiarostami's *Taste of Cherry* attempted to engage Iran globally in similar ways hints at a deep ideological relationship that scholars have yet to excavate fully. Kiarostami has claimed that he will "never make a political film," and yet *Taste of Cherry*, although seemingly apolitical, reflects the philosophical crises that Khatami's reformist movement sought to resolve, and the film and its video coda participated in a new popular discourse that culminated with Khatami's political platform.[31]

Taste of Cherry is a minimalist film that follows a middle-aged man, known throughout the film only as Mr. Badii, as he circles the dusty outskirts of azTehran in his Land Rover. He drives almost aimlessly, looking for someone to bury him after he commits suicide. During the course of his travels, he picks up three men: a Kurdish soldier, an Afghan seminary student, and an Azeri taxidermist. To each of his passengers Mr. Badii offers a considerable sum of money to come to the grave site he has prepared for himself and cover him with dirt. All three men are visibly uncomfortable with the frankness of Mr. Badii's offer, and each passenger reacts to Mr. Badii differently, their responses conditioned by their varying ages and social perspectives. The young Kurdish soldier is made so uncomfortable that he just jumps out of the car while it is still moving. The seminary student attempts to dissuade Mr. Badii by offering Islam's perspective on suicide. The taxidermist, older and more experienced, offers his own experiences overcoming despair in an attempt to convince Mr. Badii to put off his plans and wait for something better. Once he sees that the protagonist is unwilling to change his outlook, the taxidermist reluctantly accepts the offer so that he can pay his sick daughter's medical bills.

The film's final scenes unravel the certainty of Mr. Badii's plans. He leaves his car for the first time in the film as he tracks down the taxidermist at work to request that the taxidermist shake him before covering him with dirt, because it is possible he will just be sleeping. This request is followed by uncertain and voyeuristic images that show Mr. Badii's shadow in his apartment and do not clearly indicate whether or not he takes the pills to kill himself. The uncertain momentum comes to a head when the scene changes to reveal Mr. Badii lying in his uncovered grave, and we are confronted with the possibility that we may never fully know whether or not Mr. Badii actually killed himself. The film abruptly destabilizes our investment in Mr. Badii's decision when a long black-screen sequence marks the transition from 35 mm film to digital video. What at first seems like the next morning quickly becomes behind-the-scenes footage, as the actor playing Mr. Badii interacts with the film crew and we watch the production team at work. This coda powerfully reminds the viewer of the film's fictionality, and it accords with other efforts by Kiarostami to draw attention to the camera's delicate position between fiction and reality.

Despite this point of consistency between this film and Kiarostami's previous works, *Taste of Cherry* also marks a significant departure from the director's earlier aesthetic. These points of difference coincide with several features of the reformist aesthetic that I have described so far. In particular, *Taste of Cherry* was unique at the time of its release for its urban focus. Kiarostami's neorealist style had previously depended on and drew inspiration from rural environments and settings. With *Taste of Cherry* the director reorients his camera to an urban perspective as he maps a set of concerns specific to a Tehran-based intellectual class. Additionally, although Kiarostami has a long-standing interest in the journey as a narrative strategy, *Taste of Cherry*'s emphasis on circular journeys is unique to this film and central to its examination of an urban intellectual class. These circular journeys, which differ from the more linear-based treks that defined Kiarostami's earlier films, such as the back-and-forth movement in *Khāneh-ye dust kojāst* (Where is the friend's house, 1987) and the narrative of return in *Zendegi va digar hich* (Life and nothing more, 1992), resonate with the Sufi journeys popular in Iranian cinema in the early 1990s.

Although these aspects of the film play into a larger reformist aesthetic, the film furthers our understanding of a genre of the Second of Khordād by engaging the reformist movement's most basic philosophical question about the reconciliation of a revolutionary, Islamic political system with more moderate democratic ideals. *Taste of Cherry* locates the answer to this paradox in the circular journey of reform and in video technology, which, far from punctuating the film in its final moment, opens up a whole world of new possibilities. *Taste of Cherry* reveals Mohammad Khatami's reformist movement and the democratizing value of video technology as reactions to the social and political concerns that shaped Iranian discourse in the late 1990s, as products of a particular sociopolitical moment that are ideologically tied to each other.

Taste of Cherry's global success emerged from its engagement with universal questions about the meaning of life and death. Scholars have thoroughly examined the film as a philosophical statement that engages the fleeting nature of human life, and they have made connections to the commentaries on death in the literature of Iranian authors like Omar Khayyam and Sadeq Hedayat.[32] Although the Iranian government took this candid discussion of suicide at face value, it has been suggested that the film's coda, which exposes the profilmic space, was a move on the director's part to appease censors, who otherwise saw the film as promoting suicide.[33] Despite the emphasis on the film's representation of life, death, and suicide, *Taste of Cherry* betrays a sense that the issue of suicide is less the thrust of the film and more a means through which Kiarostami probes a cross section of society, what Laura Mulvey calls the film's "social experiment."[34]

The film's delicate structure is wrought with moments in which Kiarostami wryly casts doubt on both his own and the main character's intentions. For example, the seminary student invites Mr. Badii to eat with him and a friend who has prepared a meal. Mr. Badii declines the offer by saying, "Thank you! I know he's prepared food but eggs are bad for me. Some other time! Goodbye!" Both Mr. Badii's concern for his health and his look to the future contradict the conversation he has just had about his upcoming plans to kill himself. Later, as he drives the taxidermist to work, Mr. Badii pulls out into traffic. His passenger yells, "What's wrong with you? Are you in a hurry to die?" At this point in the film, the viewer is well aware of the fact that Mr. Badii is actually in a hurry to die. By including this line in the film, Kiarostami turns the forthcoming suicide into a joke, undercutting the severity of the film's premise.

These ironic moments in the film invite us to think outside of the narrative structure and to contemplate a set of concerns not necessarily tied directly to the conversations that take place between the film's protagonist and his various passengers. These counterexamples to Mr. Badii's suicidal plans indicate that something else is at play with regard to the discussion of suicide, without necessarily devaluing the significance of the life/death discourse that the film establishes. *Taste of Cherry* undertakes philosophical inquiry, but its stakes are not necessarily life or death. Instead, the film shoulders the same philosophical project as Mohammad Khatami's reformist movement and attempts to reconcile a body of inherited policies with a contradictory set of future desires.

Taste of Cherry's premise—a man looking for someone to bury him after he has committed suicide—offers an interesting paradox within an Iranian-Islamic context. On the one hand, suicide is considered a grave sin according to Islamic law, a fact emphasized in the film by the seminary student. A person who takes his own life is denied passage into paradise. On the other hand, burial is a rite of *passage* according to Islamic tradition and functions as one step in the process of gaining entrance into paradise. Whether or not someone who has committed suicide is eligible for a proper burial remains a topic of debate within Islamic jurisprudence, and there are a number of hadiths that indicate that during his lifetime the Prophet Mohammad refused to perform funeral prayers for individuals who had committed suicide.[35] Shari'a, or Islamic law, constitutes a spectrum wherein mandatory and lawful actions (*halāl*) constitute one end, prohibited actions (*harām*) form the other end, and in between are actions that are to varying degrees desirable or undesirable. Mr. Badii's goal, suicide and burial, creates tension between these two ends of the spectrum, and his foresight and intentionality strike the viewer as particularly strange.

Ultimately, it is the tension that arises from Mr. Badii's two-part pursuit (his suicide and subsequent burial) that cinematically recreates the reformist movement's most fundamental philosophical concern. Mohammad Khatami's moderate political platform, which encouraged concepts like global engagement, civil society, and the rule of law, was in constant tension with the revolutionary system of governance that he both inherited and helped create. Olivier Roy, for example, argues that the biggest task that Khatami and his supports faced was secularizing a political system within a society that is culturally and socially invested in "its heritage and origin: an Islamic Revolution." He also claims that in broader terms Khatami's election brought to light "contradictions" about the relationship between religion and politics in the Iranian constitution.³⁶

The contradictions in Khatami's political philosophy extend beyond the constitution and reach to his leadership style. Keyvan Tabari notes that one of the great "paradoxes" of Khatami's leadership, and especially of his promotion of a rule of law, was that he claimed an "open mind" while also working from the seat of a system that limits political participation to those individuals "who pass a strict loyalty test."³⁷ Khatami's support of the Islamic Republic (as a governing system), the Iranian constitution, the *velāyat-e faqih*, and at times the *basij* did not readily accord with his promise of open democracy and civil society. Indeed, Abdolkarim Soroush, who provided a philosophical framework for Khatami's early work, criticized Khatami for these contradictions and argued that Khatami's "practical vacillation" was the result of "theoretical vacillation."³⁸

These paradoxes, contradictions, and vacillations would ultimately open Khatami up to criticism. At the time that he was elected in 1997 (just days after *Taste of Cherry*'s win at Cannes), however, the possibility of reconciling these competing desires brought hope to Iranian society.³⁹ Khatami's promise to pay homage to the revolution of 1978–1979 while also moving the country forward appealed especially to the sense of stagnation and revolutionary discontent that had come to a head in the country by the late 1990s. *Taste of Cherry* conveys this sense of stagnation while attempting to navigate through it. Like the reformist movement in 1997, the film represents the challenges of overcoming history while maintaining hope for the future.

Taste of Cherry constructs tension through its representation of journeys. The film's visual structure depends on medium shots of Mr. Badii's Land Rover circling through the dusty outskirts of Tehran. These shots, which show the car making small circles and big circles, punctuate the main character's various conversations. In his study of the film, Marco Della Grassa carefully charts the moments of silence and dialogue in the film and provides the following breakdown:

Silence: 8:14
Dialogue: 17:35
Silence: 6:42
Dialogue: 16:09
Silence: 5:46
Dialogue: 14:08
Silence: 6:06
Dialogue: 1:00
Silence: 10:24

Alberto Elena suggests that this schema is a meditative structure that forces the viewer to contemplate the nature of the discussion that has just unfolded.[40]

These contemplative periods, however, do not occur in complete darkness, and the accompanying images serve as visual clues that guide the viewer's experience. Shots of Mr. Badii circling consume a substantial portion of the silent stretches. The languid movement of Mr. Badii's Land Rover ultimately reveals the disparity between the film's visual structure and its narrative structure. The film's dialogue, which focuses heavily on suicide, establishes a life-death continuum that forms a linear structure, intersecting and overlapping the visual structure's circularity. The journey to death as a linear process is underscored by the taxidermist, who warns, "Life is like a train that keeps moving forward, and then reaches the end of the line, the terminal. And death waits at the terminal." The character's use of a transportation metaphor forces us to compare the linearity of life/death with the car's dizzying turns, which scratch circles onto the film's dusty landscape.

The film's circular movements may reference a Sufi journey, a quest whose destination ultimately becomes the experience of movement.[41] *Taste of Cherry*'s circularity also references the sense of stagnation that began developing in the early 1990s, at the same time that Makhmalbaf's *Nowbat-e 'āsheqi* (Time for love) and Dariush Mehrjui's *Hamun* (Hamun) sought to represent the inertia of Iranian intellectual life. In *Taste of Cherry*, the tense interplay between silence and dialogue helps construct this sense of stagnation. Although the long periods of silence encourage contemplation, they make us restless and uncomfortable at the same time. The film also visually inscribes stagnation through its setting, the function of which is never made entirely clear. This dirt-filled space might be a construction site. We see heavy machinery, but piles of dirt are the only things being moved around or constructed. At one point, Mr. Badii gets out of his car and the viewer only sees his shadow. A dump truck backs up and dumps a pile of dirt onto the shadow. The shot widens, and Mr. Badii is covered in a cloud of dirt. Both he and his shadow are effectively buried. Although it is tempting to read this scene as foreshadowing Mr. Badii's suicide and his burial, a better interpretation might stress the feeling of being buried alive, which captures the sense of futility that arose from the stagnation that Iranian society experienced at this time. Mr. Badii stresses this feeling during his discussion with the seminary student. He says, "There comes a time when a man can't go on. He is exhausted." The character's sentiment resonates with the discontent of a generation, the origins of which we saw in films like *Hamun* and *Time for Love*.

The presence of the film's minor characters positions this sense of stagnation and ineffectiveness not just as an individual predicament but also as a national condition. Mr. Badii's first passenger, the Kurdish soldier, suggests that he is in a rush to return to the barracks. A series of follow-up questions, however, reveal that the soldier is hastily making his return even though he is not required to report back for duty for at least another hour. Mr. Badii points out the ridiculousness of rushing back only to wait. The film's protagonist often seems to be in the position of pointing out the characters' inefficiency. At one point, he chats with an Afghani laborer, whom he invites for a ride in his Land Rover. The worker claims that he cannot leave his post even on a holiday, because he must ensure that no one steals the machinery. Mr. Badii points out that the machine he is guarding is so big that no one could possibly steal it. But the Afghani worker insists that he must remain in his watchtower. The film's main character also chats with a Lor man who collects plastic bags around the construction site. When Mr. Badii asks him for a favor, the man replies, "I just collect bags." The man walks away, and the title sequence begins. The ethnicity of these characters is significant. In this film, Kiarostami maps Iran's ethnic and cultural diversity, and he gives particular weight to those groups that have been marginalized. By showing these marginalized groups in the context of futility, the film shows how far this sense of stagnation reaches: to the outskirts of the city and of society.

The hope of the reformist movement, or what later became the myth of the reformist movement, grew out of a desire on the part of Iranian society to overcome this stagnation. By the mid-1990s, Iran found itself stuck in the historical circles that the film *Taste of Cherry* so powerfully depicts. Khatami's reformist platform offered a way out of this circular pattern by changing the popular discourse in the country. He offered a new vocabulary for discussing the changes that might help Iran to realize fully its Islamic republic, a set of terms that stressed the "republic" and built on the Islamic foundations put in place by Khomeini. *Taste of Cherry* picks up on this willingness to contemplate past decisions. The wise taxidermist, for example, tells Mr. Badii, "You think something is good, and then you realize you're wrong. The main thing is to think hard. You believe what you do is right but then you realize it is wrong." Throughout *Taste of Cherry*, Mr. Badii's fixation on suicide as a "way out" is analogous to Khatami's promise to guide Iran to reform. The discussion of suicide in the film ultimately attests to a national longing at the time for a way out.

The challenge of *Taste of Cherry* comes when one attempts to trace this metaphor to some end. The film features two narrative layers: one aural and one visual, one linear and one circular. It suggests that the linear journey between life and death might offer some reprieve from the circular patterns that haunt Iran's modern history. Yet the film confounds its own philosophical reasoning when the taxidermist says, "Of course, death is a solution but not at first, not during your youth. Forgive me for dragging you off along this rocky road." This statement throws doubt on the linear progression as a way out and redeems the circular journey as hopeful. The phrase "rocky road" is a reference to a point earlier in their conversation when the taxidermist tells Mr. Badii to take an alternative route to the city. When Mr. Badii says he does not know the way, the taxidermist replies, "I know it. It's longer but better and more beautiful. I've been a prisoner of this desert for 35 years." In this way, the film advocates the reform that Khatami's movement promised rather than revolution. In other words, the taxidermist's monologue, which is so powerful that it causes Mr. Badii to reconsider his suicide, suggests that it is not necessary to reconceptualize the idea of the journey. Sometimes the longer and more beautiful route is the way out. Khatami's reformist movement similarly recognized how young the Islamic Republic was—at that point not even twenty years old—and sought to work within the existing structure rather than completely shifting gears and advocating for another revolution.

Although no other character is able to sway his beliefs on suicide, after his conversation with the taxidermist, Mr. Badii changes his tone significantly and suggests that he may not kill himself after all, that he might just be asleep in the grave. The film positions hope outside of the linear journey to death and, in doing so, redeems the circular journey. For the viewer, who at this point is invested in the characters' decisions, the possibility that Mr. Badii might spare his life and continue driving in circles is hopeful. As chapter 5 more fully demonstrates, reform has also been a circular concept in Iran's modern history, and *Taste of Cherry* locates hope in the cycles of reformist ideology.

Tehran has functioned as a physical manifestation of the country's reformist efforts, and its representation constitutes an important feature of reform cinema in Iran. One of *Taste of Cherry*'s final scenes shows Mr. Badii moments after his conversation with the taxidermist, which throws his suicide plans into doubt. He meaningfully stares at the Tehran skyline at dusk. This scene, colorful with the sun's final moments, clashes with the rest of the film, which is literally brown with dirt. Several cranes are at work in the center of the skyline, reminders of the patterns of construction and deconstruction that define Tehran. The bright colors and the crane revive the possibility of hope and of reform. Although *Taste of Cherry* never fully advocates either, the brief possibility acts as a momentary reprieve from the film's otherwise heavy stagnation.

Our ultimate reprieve from this stagnation emerges from the film's coda, which positions video technology as a redemptive force. A shot of Mr. Badii lying in his grave as a thunderstorm rolls in fades out while the sound of the storm continues to haunt the black screen. After a minute of darkness, rain, and thunder, the chants of soldiers doing military drills replace the thunderstorm soundtrack, and the black screen gives way to a grainy, green-tinted long shot of the rural countryside, presumably the site of Mr. Badii's

VIDEO DEMOCRACIES

FIGURE 3.1. The first shot of Kiarostami's video coda shows a grainy, green landscape. Frame enlargement from Abbas Kiarostami's *Taste of Cherry*.

grave (figure 3.1). Then a sudden cut reveals a cameraman walking with a 35 mm camera. The shot pans out, and Homayun Ershadi, the actor who plays Mr. Badii, walks up to the director, Kiarostami, and hands him a cigarette, followed by a shot of a member of the sound crew squatting in the grass. These details destabilize any possibility that this scene represents the morning following Mr. Badii's suicide. In fact, this final scene does not even qualify as the film's end, because we are no longer in the film. We are now outside of it, watching its production.

This coda may have been a clever maneuver on Kiarostami's part to outsmart censors by destabilizing the story of Mr. Badii's suicide, and it certainly conforms to the director's previous self-reflexive aesthetic. But the film's final scene also makes an important statement about video technology, a point emphasized by the dramatic way in which Kiarostami ushers his audience into video spectatorship. Following a long stretch of black and thunder, the video footage, whose quality is markedly different from the previous 35 mm footage, reframes our perspective and makes it impossible to ignore the video camera's presence.

VIDEO DEMOCRACIES

Kiarostami, now a figure onscreen, provides some clues to understanding what video achieves in this coda and what it realizes within *Taste of Cherry* that conventional 35 mm film cannot (figure 3.2). After the video camera establishes the presence of the film crew, it settles on the marching soldiers, and we hear Kiarostami direct, "That's enough. Do you hear me? Tell your men to stay right there, around the tree to rest for a few minutes. Filming is done..." Although the film's English subtitles indicate that Kiarostami states that "the shoot is over," he actually says *filmbardāri tamum shod*, or "filming is done." Yet the fact that filming is complete does not mean that the movie is over, and several more minutes of footage, gathered with a video camera and set to Louis Armstrong's somber "St. James Infirmary" unroll before us.[42] Within *Taste of Cherry* filming and videotaping function separately, and video seeks to accomplish something to which film can only allude.

Because the video technology in *Taste of Cherry* operates outside of film, it can reveal truths about the "filming" whose completion Kiarostami has already declared. By rendering the filmmaking process visible, the video coda exposes the fiction of the narrative and saves us from having to face the possibility of Mr. Badii's suicide. Video as a medium explodes *Taste of Cherry*'s ending and redeems it from film's linearity. A film, even when it is wrapped in a circular canister, is a straight line, with a tangible beginning and end. But video, whether digital or analog, rejects this linear trajectory. Videotape, for example, charges endlessly in circles as it navigates the cassette's anatomy, maneuvering between guides and capstans and around drums and reels. Video provides the possibility of taping over, looping, and immediate playback, all of which overcome film's linearity. The final image we see in the video coda shows Mr. Badii's Land Rover once more rounding a bend before the cut to credits. This moment, caught on video, renders the uncertainty of Mr. Badii's suicide immaterial because it supplants the tentative shot of Mr. Badii lying in his grave as the movie's last image. Instead, *Taste of Cherry* concludes by locating video technology in the very circularity that Mr. Badii's narrative seeks to redeem.

Shot entirely with two digital video cameras mounted on the dashboard of an SUV, Kiarostami's *10* continues the theorization of video technology that began in *Taste of Cherry*, and it demonstrates how the convergence of video

FIGURE 3.2. The video camera exposes the mechanics of filmmaking, including the director, film crew, and film camera. Frame enlargement from *Taste of Cherry*.

and cinema contributed to the discourse of reform in Iran at the beginning of the twentieth-first century. Like *Taste of Cherry*, *10* was released in the context of one of Khatami's campaigns, this time shortly after his reelection in 2001. With *10* Kiarostami returns to and expands on many of the stylistic features that made *Taste of Cherry* so successful. This film also marked Kiarostami's return to the international film festival scene. After his success with *Taste of Cherry*, Kiarostami stated that although film festivals had played an important role in supporting his work, that phase in his life was over.[43] Nevertheless, he screened *10* at Cannes in 2002, where it received little attention. This movie also represents Kiarostami's return to an urban space. After *Taste of Cherry*, Kiarostami released *Bād mā rā khāhad bord* (The wind will carry us, 1999), which takes place in a Kurdish region of Iran and conforms more closely to the director's previous rural aesthetic. *10*, on the other hand, finds articulation in the streets, concrete, and traffic of the capital city.

10 comprises ten discussions between Mania Akbari, a real-life visual artist and photographer, and various passengers as she drives around Tehran. The movie takes place entirely within the tight interior space of her SUV, and the use of the car as a narrative device constitutes a striking similarity between *10* and *Taste of Cherry*. *10* was shot with two digital video cameras, and Kiarostami claimed that the video cameras' presence links *10* and *Taste of Cherry*, two films with disparate subject matter.[44] During the shooting of *10*, the cameras were fixed on the dashboard, one in front of the passenger's seat and the other in front of the driver. We only see footage from one of these cameras at any given time, and Kiarostami carefully controls the viewer's access to images of the characters.

During the first sixteen-minute sequence, for example, we cannot see the driver. Instead, we only see her ten-year-old son, with whom she is arguing. Because we only see the son and his uncomfortable movements as he accuses his mother of being selfish and of loving no one but herself, we are made to identify with him.[45] This strategy puts us in the uncomfortable position of identifying with a boy who uses what Alberto Elena calls "verbal violence" to berate his mother.[46] We must come to terms with or challenge our passive spectatorship, and this technique proposes a new kind of video spectatorship.

Whereas nearly a century earlier Walter Benjamin celebrated the development of film technology for providing audiences with endless vantage points and perspectives, Kiarostami limits those perspectives in his configuration of video spectatorship.[47] Kiarostami intentionally does not adjust the camera's zoom, so each passenger fills the frame differently.[48] This strategy draws our attention to the camera's framing, or the process by which the camera establishes its frame and chooses to include or exclude subject material.[49] In this way, Kiarostami's video spectatorship invites us to consider the nature of authenticity in the camera's presence, rather than taking its authority for granted. Empowering the viewer to determine for him- or herself the limits of the camera's frame speaks to a twenty-first century Iranian rhetoric of democracy.

Each of the ten sequences in *10* begins and ends abruptly, and these various sequences form a countdown that begins with ten and ends with one. This structure creates the impression that the movie is building up to something, that Akbari's SUV has a final destination. However, the final sequence (number one), which is the movie's shortest, simply repeats images and scenes that the viewer has already seen. *10* diverges from Kiarostami's previous works with its decisive focus on the condition of Iranian women.[50] Indeed, the director has been criticized for rendering women absent from most of his films. He has explained his lack of attention to women's issues by pointing to the codes of censorship that limit how he can represent women onscreen, and he claims that he does not "give any false impressions" that grow out of these restrictions. He later admits this omission as a mistake, one that he redeems in *10* by "giving a realistic picture of the Iranian middle-class woman as she actually is." He says, "I can assure that it is all very true to life. . . . In other Iranian films there is always someone who goes around adjusting the women's headscarves just before they start filming, but that is frankly the death of cinema."[51] His observation about women's scarves nods to the rule that all women must be properly veiled whenever onscreen, even in scenes depicting their private lives, where they would not normally be required to cover their hair. Certain films meaningfully draw the viewer's attention to the cinematic absurdity that this rule creates. For example, Tahmineh Milani's *Afsāneh-ye āh* (Legend of a sigh, 1991) features a scene in which a young woman springs from bed already wearing her scarf, and *Under the Skin of City* shows Tuba combing her long hair, but Bani-Etemad frames the shot in such a way that we cannot see her head, only her disembodied hair.

In *10* Kiarostami chooses to navigate around this trap by confining the narrative space to a car's interior, a mobile setting that he believes more closely approximates women's reality. Just as in *Under the Skin of the City*, *10* establishes the car as a specialized space, bound by its own rules and regulations. Whereas *Under the Skin of the City* brings to focus the car as a source of social and economic mobility, *10* theorizes the car in Iranian society as a semiprivatized space, susceptible to certain public laws, like those that dictate the modesty of one's clothing, but private enough for intimate conversations and sometimes the transgression of legal gender relations. Adam Ganz and Lina Khatib argue that *10* is different from other films about women that were released in Iran at the turn of the twenty-first century because it gives the audience "direct access" to a woman's space, and this perspective radically alters the relationship between object and subject. Its lack of wide shots ultimately creates a spatialized female intimacy that other Iranian films fail to achieve.[52]

10 marks a shift in Kiarostami's body of work to include the representation of women, a trend that began with *The Wind Will Carry Us*. Kiarostami's exclusion of women began before his work in film, and even the commercials he directed throughout the 1960s did not feature many women.[53] Kiarostami had remained consistent in his exclusion of women over the course of his forty-year career up until this point, despite a revolution that drastically restructured the policies regulating media industries. At the turn of the twenty-first century, however, with films like *10* he not only included female characters but also aggressively tackled the issue of women, both in Iranian society and in the film industry. This shift spoke to the consolidation of the "women's question" in society at this time and the possibilities opened up by digital video technology, both of which contributed to discourses of reform at the turn of the twenty-first century. Just as *Taste of Cherry* and Mohammad Khatami's reformist movement reacted in kind to the stagnation that weighed heavily on Iranian society in the late 1990s, *10* responded to the growing concern over the status of women in the Islamic Republic. This evolution is in step with the reformist movement's shift from being a philosophical venture to being less philosophical and more invested in specific social issues.

Women's participation in Iranian society occupied a central position in Khatami's political platform, and this particular issue distinguished him from other contemporary politicians.[54] During his presidency, in step with concepts like civil society, democracy, and human rights, Khatami addressed the oppression of women and even criticized Islamic jurisprudence for not taking into account the realities of modern life when addressing the rights of women.[55] In 1997 he famously stated that "women and men are different, but women are not the second sex and men are not superior."[56] In 2000 Khatami published a book called *Zanān va javānān* (Women and youth). The book stresses the significance of engaging both women and young people in systems of governance. Khatami argues that one role of government is to facilitate women's recognition of "their rights and capabilities" and to allow them to "acknowledge their merits."[57] With this statement he moves beyond the previously held notion that men, and their government in particular, must guard women. As a result of this progressive thinking, the feminist magazine *Zanān* (Women) endorsed

Khatami during both of his elections. During his presidency, what appeared to be women's reform marked the streets of Tehran, and the enforcement of dress codes was relaxed considerably, a move that visibly changed the visual composition of the cityscape. Press restrictions were also relaxed, and in 1998 the secular feminist journal *Jens-e dovom* (Second sex) received a permit for publication. Khatami also established the Center for Women's Participation, which was led by Vice President Zohreh Shojai and encouraged the formation of women-based nongovernmental organizations.

At the same time, Khatami's line of thinking with regard to women featured an explicit paradox. For Khatami, women played an imperative role in the home, in the family structure, and within private spaces, and he wondered whether this special place in the home would marginalize them in society. He called on Iranian society to contemplate this potential contradictory duality, asking "how we can have women in the public sphere without disintegrating the structure of the family."[58] During his presidency, however, Khatami never succeeded in solving this paradox.[59] He was also unable to overcome conservative forces to achieve the level of women's rights that he had promised. Most notably, he failed to get the Guardian Council to ratify the UN Convention on the Elimination of All Forms of Discrimination Against Women (CEDAW); many of the bills in support of women's rights that the sixth Majles (2000–2004) passed met the same fate. Despite, or perhaps because of, these failures, Khatami's presidency brought discussions about women's rights in Iranian society to the forefront in unprecedented ways.

Kiarostami's *10* responds to this heightened discourse about women. It critiques the status of women during Khatami's presidency, and more specifically it challenges the policies that regulated the representation of women onscreen. The film's penultimate segment is especially poignant in this regard. Mania chats with her friend, who rode in the SUV earlier in the movie as well. The friend has grown dependent on a man who refuses to marry her, a fact she has finally accepted. Mania comments that the woman's veil is particularly tight, a fact that the viewer has already recognized based on earlier images of her. Mania jokes, "Are you modest? Why is your veil so tight? It doesn't suit you." This observation triggers a minute-long scene in which we are uncomfortably forced to watch the friend as she plays with her scarf, slowly pulling it off to reveal that she has shaved her head. By any measure, this scene is powerful and shocking, but it is especially so within the context of Iranian cinema at this time, because even the slightest transgression in women's clothing might have been perceived as a serious moral transgression.

In this scene, we watch as Kiarostami and the actress unexpectedly and unapologetically violate the law, and at the same time we are forced to witness the women's vulnerability: her shaking hands as she adjusts her scarf, her uncertain laugh as Mania interrogates her about cutting her hair, her tears, and ultimately her bald head. The shot, generated from a mounted, stationary camera, refuses to change its perspective or alter its focus to provide the viewer with some visual relief. Instead the viewer remains an uncomfortable voyeur for a relatively long stretch of time. This scene violates and at the same time challenges the laws of onscreen modesty. At the center of the law requiring women to veil is a belief in the tantalizing power of a woman's hair. In *10* a woman unveils, but she has no hair, and this image draws attention to and undermines the very foundations grounding the laws that regulate women's public appearance.[60]

Mohammad Khatami, in his role as minister of culture and Islamic guidance, played a crucial role in establishing the film industry under the Islamic Republic, and shortly after he began his tenure as minister of culture and Islamic guidance in 1982, the ministry was charged with generating and enforcing a set of guidelines that governed the production and exhibition of moving images. These regulations demanded that films represent "chaste" women who participate in society while raising "God-fearing and responsible children," and that directors must not use women to "arouse sexual desires."[61] Khatami's ministry was responsible for interpreting these ambiguous guidelines, and at that time the Ministry of Culture and Islamic Guidance prescribed the "commandments for looking (*ahkām-e nigāh kardan*)," which took the shape of "laws that enforced the veiling of Iranian women from their male counterparts both on and in front of the screen."[62]

Kiarostami's *10* points to the restrictive policies that Khatami helped create, especially when a woman unveils herself onscreen. *10* underscores the covalence of open discourse about women's rights on the one hand and the contradictions of the laws of modesty that determine the very shape of women onscreen on the other. In this way, the movie highlights the contradictions of Khatami's leadership in the Islamic Republic, in his role both as president and as minister of culture and Islamic guidance, by drawing attention to the incongruity between his presidential policy toward women and his profound effect on the film industry. The tension that *10* creates points to the paradox of Khatami's rhetoric about women: the challenge of reconciling a woman's specialized role in private space with her right to live and work in public spaces. Like Khatami's reformist movement, *10* never provides a solution to this paradox and cannot, therefore, be part of a film industry that demands women's modesty. *10* was the first film by Kiarostami to be banned by the Islamic Republic, and it marked the first time that the director openly criticized regulations on the film industry.[63] In an interview with Shahram Tabemohammadi in 2000, Kiarostami confirmed his belief that filmmakers ought to work within the codes of censorship.[64] *10* therefore demonstrates a notable shift in the director's attitude toward the film industry, and this shift was a corollary of the paradoxes of Mohammad Khatami's reformist movement, especially its policies regarding women.

10's relationship to the reformist movement is less direct than what we see in the films of Rakhshan Bani-Etemad, which explicitly depict Mohammad Khatami. Instead, *10* and *Taste of Cherry*, released immediately before and after Khatami's two elections, helped establish and critique the discourse of reform that buttressed Khatami's political platform. The films intervene philosophically on behalf of and in opposition to the tenants of the reformist movement. But *10*'s social critique also furthers our understanding of the genre of the Second of Khordād and demonstrates how a reformist aesthetic transformed the shape of movies in Iran. Specifically, *10*'s innovative use of digital video cameras and footage has had a profound effect on Iranian cinema, and it has reconfigured what it means to operate within the regulations of the Iranian film industry.

Kiarostami's first foray into digital video occurred in *Taste of Cherry*, and the journalistic quality of the video coda opened Kiarostami up to censure by critics who believed this technology to be unbecoming of Kiarostami's arthouse style.[65] Kiarostami's decision to shoot *10* exclusively with digital video cameras must thus be considered within both the immediate artistic context and the broader cultural-political context. The director gives us further insight into his decision in the short movie *10 on Ten* (2004), originally intended to be an extra on the French DVD of *10*. The short takes place in the dusty setting of *Taste of Cherry* and represents the director's most pointed commentary on the digital form and its effect on his transforming vision for Iranian cinema. In *10 on Ten*, Kiarostami advocates on behalf of digital video cameras because they eliminate directing and directors. He claims that the digital camera, small and sometimes concealable, encourages the "artist to work alone again," because he is no longer bound to investors, capital flow, or the limitations of his technical abilities. Everything is "self-contained" in this tiny box, which frees the director and invites "new discoveries."[66] As Adam Ganz and Lina Khatib note, the digital camera "continues looking when the film camera averts its gaze," and it "does not attempt to frame the action but only [to] cover it."[67] However, the disappearance of direction does not mean the disappearance of the *auteur*, and *10*'s ninety minutes were fashioned from more than twenty-three hours of raw footage gathered over several days. The director whittled the movie's shape and controlled precisely what we see and hear.

Because of the video camera's independence—the fact that it does not require processing or specialized technical crews like film does—Kiarostami sees it as closer to reality than the 35 mm camera. He claims that video eliminates the "artifice" between his eye and reality, and that its sweeping 360-degree shots "record the truth, the absolute truth." He likens the technology to "a god: all-encompassing and omnipresent."[68] By positioning video technology in terms of the divine and as a medium through which we might discover the truth, Kiarostami returns to the mysticism that shaped reform cinema during the early 1990s. But at the same time his advocacy of digital cameras also helps us understand why he suddenly took up the representation of women in *10*. He previously stated that he avoided female characters because restrictions on the film industry rendered any representation of women unauthentic. The digital video camera, however, allowed him to operate outside of those restrictions and to get as close to his female subjects as possible.

In *10 on Ten*, during his discussion of *10*, Kiarostami claims that digital video "will bring about fundamental structural changes to the concept of film, cinema, directing, cinematography, and acting." He foresees digital cameras ushering in the expansion of cinema, a move away from "clichés, traditions, imposed forms, and pretentious aesthetics." The language that Kiarostami uses in his impassioned endorsement of digital video recalls the very democratic rhetoric that linked video to political reform during this period. He says that digital cameras provide the filmmaker with "liberty" and that they allow the filmmaker to sidestep "traps set by capital and capitalists."[69] This impetus to experiment, the commitment to re-form, is a crucial piece of the reformist aesthetic.

VIDEO CAMERAS, FUNERALS, AND THE NEW IRANIAN INTELLECTUAL

Shortly after Khatami's election in 1997, Bahman Farmanara, a contemporary and friend of Kiarostami, submitted a script to the Ministry of Culture and Islamic Guidance for a political film called *Az Abbas-e Kiarostami motenaferam!* (I hate Abbas Kiarostami!).[70] He thought he might be able to capitalize on Khatami's victory to end his forced retirement from the film industry. Although he hoped that the script's title would throw off censors, the ministry immediately rejected the script. Farmanara was particularly upset by this rejection, concerned that he might never work as a director in Iran again, because he was denied permission even after the country's most moderate president was elected into office. In response, Farmanara wrote a synopsis for a script about a dying director who has been refused permission to direct and thus decides to make a movie about his own funeral using a video camera, because such a movie would not require permission from the ministry.[71] He claimed that he submitted the synopsis "as a joke," and much to his surprise, the ministry asked for the full script, which ultimately earned Farmanara a permit to begin work on *The Smell of Camphor, the Scent of Jasmine*.

The film marked Farmanara's long-awaited directorial return to Iranian cinema after an absence of nearly a quarter century, and it is fully entrenched in the political atmosphere that ushered in his homecoming. *The Smell of Camphor, the Scent of Jasmine*, a relatively short film (ninety-three minutes), is interrupted midway by a two-minute clip of Khatami giving a speech. The main character, played by Farmanara, watches the president on TV, and the film's viewer is made to watch with him. The mise-en-scène signals a complicated relationship between Khatami and Farmanara. As Farmanara listens to Khatami, he lazily sprawls on a couch; above him hangs a picture of a man in Qajar attire whose face has been erased. Iranian audiences immediately recognize the man in the picture as Shāzdeh ehtejāb (Prince Ehtejab), the title character in a modernist novel published by Hushang Golshiri in 1969. Farmanara made his second feature-length film and a name for himself in Iranian cinema by turning the novel into a successful film in 1974. The picture hanging over the director's head in *The Smell of Camphor, the Scent of Jasmine*, a painting by Aydin Aghdashloo, bears a striking resemblance to the original cover of the book and the movie poster, and its presence places Khatami in conversation with Farmanara's career (figures 3.3 and 3.4).

The director's cinematic career literally sprawls out on the screen in front of us as Khatami's voice resonates in the foreground. Khatami effects Farmanara's career and shapes his film as we watch it. By keeping Khatami onscreen for more than two minutes, Farmanara does more than simply reference Khatami or reform. He provides the viewer with a sample of the president's philosophies, and these lessons in political reform stay with us for the rest of the film. Certainly, *The Smell of Camphor, the Scent of Jasmine* benefited from Khatami's administration. Farmanara's requests for permits had been denied previously, and he received his first permit to direct within the Islamic Republic during Khatami's presidency, no doubt a result of Khatami's support of the film industry at this time. At the same time, *The Smell of Camphor, the Scent of Jasmine* also seeks to understand how reform redefined the Iranian intellectual at the turn of the twenty-first century. The film is an exploration into mourning: private mourning, public spectacle, and the death of an older order of intellectualism. The sense of melancholy that consumes the first two-thirds of the film clears the way for a new kind of reformist intellectual, and video serves as the medium through which this new intellectualism finds hope.

The Smell of Camphor, the Scent of Jasmine is largely autobiographical, a fact reiterated by the director's role as the main character, who is also named Bahman. Farmanara was born in 1942 in Tehran and studied film first in London and later at the University of Southern California. He returned to Iran in the

FIGURE 3.3. The viewer is forced to watch a speech Khatami makes on TV. Khatami onscreen became a regular feature of cinema in Iran at this time. Frame enlargement from Bahman Farmanara's *The Smell of Camphor, the Scent of Jasmine*.

FIGURE 3.4. Bahman Farmanara frames his own career. Frame enlargement from *The Smell of Camphor, the Scent of Jasmine*.

mid-1960s and began working for Iranian national television, first promoting art films on the network and later directing short films himself. His first feature film, *Shāzdeh ehtejāb* (Prince Ehtejab, 1974), won critical and popular acclaim and instantly solidified the director's place as a serious filmmaker in Iran's New Wave. Farmanara followed *Prince Ehtejab* with *Sāyeh-hā-ye boland-e bād* (Tall shadows of the wind, 1978), also based on a story by Golshiri. Like his first film, *Tall Shadows of the Wind* was controversial and features a scene that juxtaposes images of a mullah praying and a man masturbating. A year later the revolution halted Farmanara's directing career, and he and his family eventually settled in Canada, where he successfully ran a film distribution company. His work took him to Los Angeles, where he lived for a brief period of time before returning to Iran in the mid-1980s to deal with family issues. He decided to remain in Iran rather than return to his work in Los Angeles.

Almost immediately, he began to submit scripts to the ministry in order to obtain a permit to make films in Iran. Until *The Smell of Camphor, the Scent of Jasmine*, however, the ministry rejected all of his scripts. Farmanara has suggested that the authorities took particular offense to his representation of Islam in *Tall Shadows of the Wind*, and they were suspicious of the fact that he was successful before the revolution and left immediately after it.[72] The director worked as a producer and taught in the Cinema Department at the Arts University in Tehran while continuing to submit scripts. Shortly after Khatami's election, the complex system of censorship in Iran loosened slightly, and the process no longer required the submission of scripts for preliminary approval.[73] Nevertheless, Farmanara continued to submit his scripts as a precaution, worried that the films would later be denied a permit. After eleven rejections, he found success with the proposal for *The Smell of Camphor, the Scent of Jasmine*.[74] Since then, Farmanara has directed three other films: *Khāneh'i ru-ye āb* (A house on water, 2001), *Yek bus-e kuchulu* (A little kiss, 2005), and *Khāk-e āshenāi* (Familiar soil, 2008).

The Smell of Camphor, the Scent of Jasmine, an autobiographical investigation into the nature of mourning, disillusionment, and the fate of intellectualism within Iran, tells the story of Bahman Farjami, a director who has not made a film in more than twenty years. Farmanara plays the role of Farjami, and the similarity between the director's name and the character's is striking. The word *farjām* literally means "concluding" or "near the end," and this name adds to the overall sense of death that pervades the film. Farjami suffers from a heart condition, and his death is imminent. On top of that, he mourns his wife, who died five years earlier, and his colleagues and friends, who have all died recently. More than anything, he mourns his life, his failures, and his career as a filmmaker. The film is divided into three acts: "A Bad Day," "Funeral Arrangements," and "Throw a Stone in the Water." In between each of these acts are scenes of Farjami sitting on a train, traveling to some unknown destination. The progression of acts along with Farjami's name and travel indicates that for Farmanara, like Kiarostami, the journey to death is a linear one. This understanding of death is reaffirmed in the film when characters refer to birth and death as arrival and departure, respectively.

Like *Taste of Cherry*, *The Smell of Camphor, the Scent of Jasmine* tackles issues of life and death. Throughout the film, Farjami claims that he is making a documentary about funeral rituals in Iran for Japanese television, an enterprise that no one questions, because these kinds of intercultural exchange had become increasingly common at this time as a result of Khatami's "dialogue among civilizations" and other efforts to engage the international community. The documentary, though, serves as a front that Farjami uses to gather the resources he needs to create a meta-film about his own funeral. By arranging the funeral and the details of the film, Farjami attempts to exert control over his final act, in terms of both execution and representation. However, after a heart attack and near-death experience, Farjami reassesses the value of life, and the momentum of the film's final act is driven by doubt about whether or not Farjami can call off the funeral/video project that he has arranged for himself.

The autobiographical details of the film extend beyond the reference to *Prince Ehtejab* and the naming sleight of hand. Farmanara also alludes to the beginning of his career, and the small role he played in Ebrahim Golestan's film *Khesht va āyeneh* (Mudbrick and mirror, 1965), which is about a taxi driver who discovers an infant in the back of his car. The taxi driver spends most of the film trying to find the baby's mother, and he encounters cynicism at every turn. In *The Smell of Camphor, the Scent of Jasmine*, Bahman Farjami picks up a woman walking by herself, and when she exits the car, she leaves behind her stillborn child in a plastic bag. Whereas in *Mudbrick and Mirror* the baby ultimately becomes a symbol of hope and a positive force in the taxi driver's life, in *The Smell of Camphor, the Scent of Jasmine*, the baby is another source of mourning. It is the death of a long but unproductive career.

Farmanara's personal ties to the pervasive sense of melancholy extended into the details of the film's production and publicity. After the distributor only published one newspaper advertisement to publicize the film, Farmanara took matters into his own hands. He printed ten thousand copies of a portrait of himself in the style of an obituary photograph (figure 3.5). In Iran people print such photographs in newspapers and post them publically on neighborhood walls to announce a loved one's death. Farmanara distributed these photographs to his friends and to students and requested that they post them on the walls of the city. As a result, countless people phoned Farmanara's father to express their sympathies for his death. The tactic was wildly successful, and although initially the film was slated to screen in only one theater, its distribution was extended to three theaters to accommodate the demand for the film. In the end, it was the third most successful film of the year in terms of box office sales.[75]

More than just a publicity stunt, this move demonstrates how the film mourns Farmanara's career up until that time, and in this way he joins a group of other filmmakers, including Bahram Reypur, Hajir Dariush, Jajal Moqaddam, and Sohrab Shahid-Saless, Farmanara's friends and colleagues, whose deaths and funerals are mentioned throughout the film. The presence of these deceased directors within the film's text leads Hamid Dabashi to label the film as a public means through which Farmanara privately mourns his colleagues in a format that no longer has relevance in Iranian society.[76] But *The Smell of Camphor, the Scent of Jasmine* ultimately offers something much broader than one filmmaker's elegy for his friends. The deaths of these renowned directors come to symbolize within the film the death of a certain kind of intellectualism. The film brings into focus the futility of an entire generation of artists and intellectuals, disempowered by a new governance system that evaluates their work according to new terminology and a new set of standards. After mentioning the deceased directors, Farjami describes the present environment,

FIGURE 3.5. Farmanara printed a death announcement for himself in order to publicize *The Smell of Camphor, the Scent of Jasmine*. Printed in *Film* magazine, Iran.

saying, "When a filmmaker doesn't make films or a writer doesn't write that is death. In fact, I am not afraid of dying. I am afraid of living a futile life." And this was the death that Farmanara advertised by circulating his own obituary photo, and this kind of death spoke to the anxiety of a generation of intellectuals who were prolific and celebrated before the revolution but unable to continue their work after the revolution.

The Smell of Camphor, the Scent of Jasmine's representation of the demise of the artist recalls the bleeding out of the intellectual in Dariush Mehrjui's *Hamun* a decade earlier. What distinguishes *The Smell of Camphor, the Scent of Jasmine* is its resurrection of the intellectual during Khatami's presidency. If the film had stopped at Farjami's *farjām*, his end, then it might have fallen into Dabashi's categorization, too narrowly focused to appeal to a society no longer invested in that dying intellectual generation. But the film features Farjami's funeral, which is wild and out of control, unlike anything that he had planned. Farjami is present as both a participant (i.e., the deceased) and an invisible observer, unable to change the camera angles or stop people from crying. A phone call announcing the birth of Farjami's grandson interrupts the procession. The funeral disappears—it has never happened—and Farjami is imbued with new hope and a desire to return to his childhood and to nature. Farmanara explains the name of the last act, "Throw a Stone in the Water," as a reference to a quotation from Kafka: "When you throw a stone in the water, you can't control the waves." The film ends with Farjami throwing a stone into water, and Farmanara has suggested that this act is a statement: "I am alive. I am back and I am going to keep working."[77] This ending suggests the possibility of working within the existing structure of the Islamic Republic and participating in a new kind of intellectualism.

This conclusion to *The Smell of Camphor, the Scent of Jasmine* does not strike the viewer as unreasonable, because the film provides the information and tools necessary to reconstruct (or reform) the intellectual figure. Khatami and the reformist movement play a significant role in this process and function as representative examples of the new Iranian intellectual. At the same time the film provides counterexamples to this model and examines the real-life fate of those intellectuals unwilling or unable to repurpose themselves and conform to the new standards of intellectualism in the Islamic Republic. In *The Smell of Camphor, the Scene of Jasmine*, the old order of intellectualism no longer has a function in Iranian society, and the film identifies Khatami's reformist movement as a site of new and emerging modes of intellectualism in post-revolution Iran.

Farmanara explained that after the revolution everything in Iran became politicized. Although before the revolution intellectuals were always political, after the revolution the spread of politics into almost every aspect of life demanded the democratization of intellectualism.[78] This democratization in turn required that the intellectual be well versed in and sympathetic to a number of different modes of thinking, not just one's own ideological belief set. In his film Farmanara represents this need for intellectuals to access broader sources of information through the use of newspapers. At several points in the film, we see references to conservative newspapers. Characters read them, and they are on display on tables and desks.

The most notable example is *Keyhān*, a newspaper that is under the direct control of the Supreme Leader and is one of the most influential publications in Iran. Even though Farjami is represented as an artist and intellectual, a director with a demonstrated knowledge of both Western and Iranian thought and a flawless American accent, conservative newspapers like *Keyhān* appear on his coffee table. And this moment in the film suggests the need for the intellectual to "foster a much wider connection." Although this detail may seem small, it is unprecedented in Iranian cinema, and Farmanara notes, "It is like a bombshell" that "young people will notice."[79]

Khatami similarly promoted broader connections through the press. One of his major contributions to the country during his first few years as president was a rapid liberalization of the press. Almost immediately following his election, Khatami's administration made it easier for the Ministry of Culture and Islamic Guidance to issue press permits, and within the first year of Khatami's presidency, 779 new press permits were issued, which raised the total number to 930. In other words, there was an approximately 500 percent increase in press permits and press activity in one year. However, like many of Khatami's initiatives, this one was thwarted by conservative forces, which had grown resentful of Khatami's relationship with the press.[80] Beginning in 1999 and continuing in 2000, the Majles, led by speaker Ali Akbar Nateq-Nouri, passed a series of laws that limited freedom of press and initiated the closure of several prominent reformist newspapers. The 1999 closure of *Salām*, the most popular reformist newspaper at the time, prompted student demonstrations that were violently squalled. The paper's closure incident, which remains one of the greatest blemishes on Khatami's presidency, calls attention to the contentious nature of the press in Iran at this time. In *The Smell of Camphor, the Scent of Jasmine*, which was released in the wake of *Salām*'s closure, the subtle use of newspapers is a reminder of the debates over open press and the significance of these debates to the reformist movement.

In contrast to the more restrained use of newspapers in the film, Farmanara's inclusion of a video clip of a speech by Khatami forcefully draws the viewer's attention to the reformist movement. In *Under the Skin of the*

City, Rakhshan Bani-Etemad also uses a real Khatami speech, but she uses just the sound bite in order to contrast Khatami's words with images from the street. In contrast, Farmanara inserts an entire video clip, and the effect of this technique is that the viewer is made to watch and focus on the video of Khatami without additional visual stimulus. In this video, Khatami argues that "the fate of the social aspect of religion will always depend on our viewing of religion in such a way that it is compatible with freedom." With this statement, he establishes the necessity of multidisciplinary thinking when it comes to the study and practice of religion.

Khatami studied Western philosophy at the University of Isfahan and then undertook traditional seminary training at Qom. He thus embodies the coalescence of two different modes or styles of thinking. Certainly, Khatami's attempts to introduce democracy, civil society, and the rule of law into Islamic thinking mark a significant step in the effort to bring together disparate beliefs and ways of thinking. This endeavor was one of the great philosophical contributions to Iranian society. The view of religion as something that can be pitted against or reconciled with freedom also harkens back to Abdolkarim Soroush's ideas that were discussed in chapter 1 of this study, wherein religious knowledge is a manmade tool through which humans approximate and access religious truth to the best of their abilities.

Within the scheme that Khatami describes, freedom is the undisputed champion in human societies. He says, "If you read the pages of history, you will notice that anything that has confronted freedom has suffered in the process. . . . If religion has confronted freedom, it has been damaged. If justice has confronted freedom, it has been damaged, and if development and construction have confronted freedom, they too have been damaged." Khatami cites two examples to make his point that to challenge freedom is to dismantle one's own cause. His first example is "from the Middle Ages when religion and freedom confronted one another, and religion suffered the defeat. The other one is from the world of communism in our age, when economic justice and freedom confronted one another and justice lost, even though the people might not have gained their freedom either." These two examples both reference ideologically closed periods in which political systems did not accommodate freedom and consequently suffered. The irony of this speech in the film is that the viewer watches it as Farjami lies motionless on his couch, unable to work and direct films. Farmanara has mentioned that one reason he included Khatami's speech was because he found Khatami's assertion that not every encounter with freedom is positive to be congruent with this part of the film's sense of despair. Nevertheless, the film posits Khatami as a new brand of intellectual who works within different theoretical frameworks and brings together different types of knowledge and ideologies in order to appeal to broad, popular audiences.

Whereas *The Smell of Camphor, the Scent of Jasmine* positions Khatami as the new intellectual, it also considers the fate of those intellectuals who were unable to work within the new structure of the Islamic Republic. One of the film's most daring aspects is its direct, though subtle, reference to the *qatl-hā-ye zanjireh'i* (serial murders), the name given to a number of unexplained murders of dissident intellectuals in the late 1990s.[81] These intellectuals were, by and large, what remained of the generation of pre-revolution intellectuals, who were usually socialist or communist. In the film one of Farjami's friends, presumably a fellow intellectual, disappears for several days. When he returns, he has been badly beaten, and he eventually dies. In the several years following Khatami's election, a number of intellectuals, artists, writers, and translators and their families suffered similar fates or suffered other violent deaths.

The unexplained murders of intellectuals in the Islamic Republic began as early as 1988, in a fashion strikingly similar to murders carried out by SAVAK, the shah's intelligence and security agency, in the decades before the revolution. However, the murders gained unprecedented momentum and organization once Khatami was elected president. This connection between the escalating murders and Khatami's new leadership led some people to the conclusion the murders were directly related to Khatami's victory and were a backlash against his cultural liberalism.[82]

The Smell of Camphor, the Scent of Jasmine recognizes the serial murders as a reaction to the reformist movement but also criticizes the government for allowing such defiant and violent acts against basic human rights tenants. As Farjami flips through the channels on TV, he stops at a report on violence in Sierra Leone. The program shows images of the mutilated bodies of Sierra Leoneans and explains that rebel forces cut off the arms and/or feet of those captured individuals who supported the current president. The report condemns the acts of violence as "medieval" and inhumane. Farjami changes the channel and begins watching Khatami's speech. The implication of the sequencing of these two videos is clear: the violence perpetrated against supporters of Iran's current president is just as brutal and inhumane as the political violence in sub-Saharan Africa.

The references to the serial murders, although not crucial to the development of the film's plot, provide further evidence that the old style of intellectualism, tied to a single ideology and directed at an elite class, simply cannot function within the Islamic Republic. Although more horrific, these deaths evoke the same feeling of death that has gripped Bahman Farjami because he cannot work. The serial murders are a tragic part of the dismantling of an older form of intellectualism in Iran. The new intellectualism, which emerges from the remains of the old, is born of figures like Khatami who work with Islam and within the structure of the Islamic Republic and seek reform and not revolution. *The Smell of Camphor, the Scent of Jasmine* advocates this intellectualism when Farjami discovers new inspiration to work within his confinements. As Farmanara suggests, the film's ending recognizes that "this hand has been dealt to us. What are we going to do? Either we are going to roll with it and try to make something positive out of it, or we can bang our heads against a brick wall."[83]

The Smell of Camphor, the Scent of Jasmine's investment in a reformist aesthetic involves more than just participation in the redefinition of the Iranian intellectual. The film also suggests the ways in which new mediums were reforming the film industry and democratizing filmmaking in Iran. Like Kiarostami's *Taste of Cherry* and *10*, Farmanara's film also plays with the possibilities of video as a new way of making movies in Iran. Although *The Smell of Camphor, the Scent of Jasmine* was shot using 35 mm cameras and is technically a film, it represents video as a medium full of possibility, and just as Rakhshan Bani-Etemad's *Under the Skin of the City* is a narrative film *about* documentary filmmaking, *The Smell of Camphor, the Scent of Jasmine* is a film about video making. As Farjami arranges his funeral and enlists producers and actors, he constantly faces questions about his permit. Each time he must explain that he did not receive a permit but is making a documentary for

FIGURE 3.6. The video camera at Farjami's funeral. Frame enlargement from *The Smell of Camphor, the Scent of Jasmine.*

Japanese television. However, the Japanese documentary is just a front, and Farjami really intends to videotape his own funeral (figure 3.6). But ultimately the act of preparing for the video, of serving as its director, ultimately helps revive Farjami's hope. Within *The Smell of Camphor, the Scent of Jasmine*, video functions as a conduit for a new intellectualism, a new source of productivity and broad appeal. With films like *Taste of Cherry, 10,* and *The Smell of Camphor, the Scent of Jasmine*, the genre of the Second of Khordād finds articulation in video, a medium that offers filmmakers new ways to work within the film industry and acts as a mechanism that re-forms the way that movies are made and watched within the Islamic Republic.

4
WHO KILLED THE TOUGH GUY?

Continuity and Rupture in the *Filmfārsi* Tradition

> *I heard that someone once said that in* Protest, *Kimiai represents the supporters of the reformist movement (dovom-e khordād) as a bunch of pizza-eating students. But who cares if students eat pizza and are also sensitive to the fate and status of politics in their country?*
>
> —MITRA HAJJAR, ACTRESS, *PROTEST*

Masud Kimiai's popular film *E'terāz* (Protest, 1999) represents the reformist movement as part of everyday life, as regular as pizza. Mitra Hajjar's remarks about the film show that politics were not just the domain of the art-house films of the previous chapters. Rather, popular films were also pushing the boundaries of censorship and representing the reformist movement and other political debates onscreen. In one particularly representative scene from *Protest*, a group of young people sit in a pizza parlor and discusses politics. Although a complicated process of censorship had ensured that direct commentary about the political system remain offscreen,[1] the characters in this scene reference real politicians, organizations, and newspapers, and they include Khatami and other reformists in their discussions. The young people offer critical opinions that are representative of the kinds of debates that people were having in Iran at the time, during the second half of Khatami's first term as president. This inclusion of open political discussion marks an extraordinary moment in Iran's long cinematic history.

Kimiai's camerawork reinforces the uniqueness of this political discussion. As the scene opens, a series of shot–reverse shots establish the viewer's position at the table along with the characters. Warm colors and the close proximity of bodies add intimacy to the scene, and we as viewers participate in a private moment between friends. About halfway through the scene, however, the view abruptly swings up, and we go from sitting at the table with the students, fully engrossed in their political conversation, to perching in the rafters, where we are suddenly spying on the very conversation in which we were just participating. The initial framing of this new shot, in which the ceiling obstructs part of our view, contributes to the sense that we are watching something forbidden, and this experience highlights the rarity of open political commentary onscreen in Iranian cinema.

Protest, like other films from this period, broaches political themes in unprecedented ways. However, unlike the films of Kiarostami and Farmanara, Kimiai's work echoes the midcentury popular films that made the director famous in the first place. *Protest*'s engagement with the *filmfārsi* tradition— the mode of popular filmmaking from the industrialization of the film industry in the 1950s through the revolution of 1978–1979—offers unique insights into the ways in which the film industry's interactions with political reform refashioned popular genres, and it speaks to the ways in which *filmfārsi* functions as a point of continuity that destabilizes the idea of a revolution-driven rupture within cinema. The tough-guy genre is one of the cornerstones of the popular film tradition in Iran. This genre has been popular in mainstream Iranian cinema since the 1950s. A comparison between *Protest* and Kimiai's most famous tough-guy film, *Qeysar* (Qeysar, 1969), reveals that *Protest* announces the death of the tough-guy genre in Iranian cinema, a death initiated not by revolution but rather by the rise of Mohammad Khatami's reformist movement. This announcement is particularly ominous for Kimiai, whose body of work found articulation in the tough-guy genre for more than thirty years. But the demise of his tough guy was necessitated by transformations in the codes of masculinity in Iranian society, which came out of the popular discourse on which Khatami's political platform depended. *Protest*'s investment in both Khatami and the history of popular film signals the extent to which reform affected the entirety of the film industry, and not just a select group of art-house films. Because *Protest* both appealed to and represents average Iranians, and not just a particular class of intellectuals, it speaks to the reformist movement's integration into popular discourse, and it suggests the role of film in facilitating that move.

With *Protest* Kimiai directly addresses his earlier film, and he rewrites the narrative of violence that made *Qeysar* famous. This methodology—comparing two films separated by more than thirty years—allows operation outside of the typical pre- and post-revolution dichotomy. Instead, moments of continuity and rupture in Iran's cultural history emerge, as does an explicit relationship between *Protest* and *Qeysar*, a connection that scholarship on Kimiai's work has not yet acknowledged. By locating these films in the tradition of the tough-guy genre, it is possible to understand how each represents the ideals of masculinity and how, in turn, these representations of masculinity are informed by their political milieu. The differences in how these two films represent codes of masculinity establish an important shift, both cinematically and socially, and political reform is ultimately the impetus for this complex sociocultural transformation.

Masud Kimiai's 1969 film *Qeysar* has been the subject of much critical debate, with some film critics hailing it as the start of modern Iranian cinema and others deploring it as a thinly veiled imitation of Western action films. Despite this disagreement, both the film's success since its release and general scholarly agreement that it is one of the founding films of the Iranian New Wave have ensured its relevance and staying power among scholars and audiences alike.[2] The film captures a particular moment as Iranian society grappled with the corollaries of modernity, urbanism, and the rising rule of law. *Qeysar* revolves around the title character as he seeks revenge for his sister's rape and suicide and his older brother's murder. Qeysar chooses not to turn to the police or other law enforcement for help but rather seeks out each of the three Ab-Mangol brothers himself to enact his revenge for the crimes they committed against his family. Qeysar systematically hunts and murders each of the brothers in a location that stages Iran's encounter with modernity: a bathhouse, a butcher's shop, and finally a train station. His actions are driven by his desire to protect his family's honor, a moral code that the viewer comes to respect and even accept. Despite the film's incredible violence, Qeysar avails himself as a sympathetic character, and as the film ends with the injured main character hiding in an abandoned train car as the police close in, we hold onto the hope that he might escape before the police catch him.

The celebration of violence and the viewer's sympathy make for a very dangerous film, one in which an individual's moral code supersedes the laws of the state. Of course, violence had become part and parcel of cinematic spectacle around the world by the late 1960s, and *Qeysar*'s unrelenting violence is thus part of an international appeal to onscreen aggression, fighting, and bloodshed. The rise of onscreen violence at this time, even when represented uncritically, drew attention to the social and political conditions that breed violence in the first place, and it is no coincidence that the rise of cinematic violence occurred in tandem with the Third Cinema movement. In this context, it is easy to understand why film scholars such as Hamid Naficy and Hamid Reza Sadr have suggested that *Qeysar* captures and perhaps even promotes the fervor that would eventually lead to the revolution of 1978–1979.[3]

Released thirty years later, *Protest* begins, in some ways, where *Qeysar* ends: with a man going to prison for a murder he has committed in the name of his family's honor. The film's central character, Amir, is sent to prison for murdering his younger brother's cheating fiancée. At the time of the crime and in prison, he is celebrated as a hero. When he is released from jail several years later, he discovers that society is very different, and he is no longer the hero he once was. Shortly after his release, Amir notes his confusion. "I wasn't gone for that long," he says, "but there are new words I don't understand and the old words don't mean the same things." Amir's confusion attests to the change in public discourse that Mohammad Khatami's political platform initiated, including the rule of law (*hokumat-e qānun*). Elsewhere in the film the characters debate reformist policy. So it is clear that what is unique about this period is Khatami's presidency and the moderate cultural environment that it fostered. Amir cannot function in this new environment and ultimately slips into a life of crime before quietly being murdered in a back alley.

Hamid Dabashi has suggested that *Protest* represents the "convulsive persistence of what is worst" in Iranian cinema, and he laments Kimiai for "reviving one of . . . [his] oldest character types, a man jailed for committing a crime to protect his 'honor' (*nāmus*)."[4] However, the revival of this character type is precisely the point of *Protest*. If the character of Qeysar embodies the values of the revolution, then *Protest* importantly asks what happens to those values over time, particularly following Khatami's election as president. With *Protest*, Kimiai calls into question the tough-guy genre and asks whether this category of film can occupy a place in Iranian society as the norms of masculinity move away from the violence of revolution and toward Khatami's civil society. That Kimiai ultimately kills Amir in *Protest* suggests the inappositeness of the archetypical tough guy in Iran at this time, and that Khatami's reformist platform rendered the cinematic tough guy irrelevant counters the commonly held belief that the revolution enacted the deepest changes in the course of Iranian cinema.

THE DEATH OF A GENRE

Just as Farmanara's *The Smell of Camphor, the Scent of Jasmine* redefined the intellectual in light of Khatami, Kimiai's *Protest* rethinks the ideals of masculinity during this period of political reform by resketching the quintessential hero. The significance of *Protest* depends on both its relationship to *Qeysar* and its position within the larger trajectory of Iranian popular film in general and the tough-guy genre in particular. The tough-guy genre gained momentum in the 1950s and was part of a larger category called *filmfārsi*, which included popular films that featured high melodrama, formulaic plots, and a system of stardom. Film critic Amirhushang Kavusi first coined the term *filmfārsi* in 1953 to describe the popular B-grade films, and the term denotes the belief among film critics at the time that these films were only Iranian insofar as they were in Persian, but their plots and styles were otherwise completely imported from Hollywood and Europe.[5] The use of other terms, such as *film-e ābgushti* (stew films), and qualifiers like *mobtazal* (campy) and *monharef* (deviant) to describe these films point to the critical reception of the *filmfārsi* as a whole. Hamid Naficy remarks that criticism of the *filmfārsi* genre denoted "underlying anxiety" about the status of film in the country and reflected "a simplistic understanding of Max Horkheimer's and Theodore Adorno's 'pessimistic' thesis about the work of the culture industry."[6] Despite this criticism, *filmfārsi* films were extraordinarily popular among midcentury audiences.

These popular films have never fully shaken the derogatory language that developed around them at the time of their production, and the scholarship on *filmfārsi* and its popular predecessors following the revolution has remained surprisingly thin as a result. Iranian film studies often sharply distinguish between art and popular films, especially with regard to films that were released after the revolution. Hamid Naficy, for example, speaks of a "populist cinema" that "inscribes postrevolutionary values" and a "quality cinema" that "engages with those values" and critiques "social conditions under the Islamic government."[7] Kamran Rastegar similarly mentions the "distance between art-house auteur cinema and popular cinema in Iran" and suggests that the two branches have responded to the codes of censorship in vastly different ways. Typically, art-house films address international audiences and the flows of the international film festival circuit, whereas the popular films appeal to Iranian audiences in Iran.[8] This division is at times overstated, and films by directors such as Rakhshan Bani-Etemad, Asghar Farhadi, and Dariush Mehrjui have screened successfully at both the local and international levels. Nevertheless, the way in which the scholarship has divided Iranian cinema, coupled with the classification of popular films as "lowbrow" and the difficulty of accessing films that never made it to international film festivals has meant that much of the literature in the field has overlooked *filmfārsi* and other popular Iranian films over the past century.

Scholars working on a range of international cinemas have begun to validate popular films by undertaking serious studies of non-Hollywood popular cinemas. Works on Egyptian, Hong Kong, Indian, Japanese, and Nigerian cinemas have all made the case that commercial cinema can offer complex representations of contemporary society that are at times more accessible than representations offered by abstruse art-house films popular abroad.[9] Walter Armbrust, one of the first scholars to make a case for the study of international commercial cinemas, warns that in Egypt art-house films have been arbitrarily and uncritically identified as "good," whereas critics and scholars often dismiss commercial films as "bad." However, studying only "good" films means studying only a small segment in a particular film industry. Armbrust argues that both filmmakers and audiences draw on a "fund of images" derived from both art-house and popular films. Armbrust suggests that the main difference between commercial and art-house cinema rests in technique rather than content, and especially not ideology. He claims that both kinds of films attend to the same social and cultural concerns and derive from the same "patterned narratives."[10] The study of any national cinema must, therefore, acknowledge, engage, and even overcome the division between popular and art-house cinema that often marks the study of world cinema.

Studies on Iranian cinema have only recently accounted for popular cinema. William Brown's study of Tahmineh Milani's *Ātashbas* (Ceasefire, 2006), for example, suggests that the value of commercial films can be found in their representation of the middle class, a segment of society that has been overlooked by *auteur* filmmakers, who favor stories of the downtrodden. He advocates for the study of popular films like *Ceasefire* because they offer "Western audiences" a "glimpse" of Iran otherwise absent from the art-house films that normally make the rounds at the international film festival circuits. Although Brown misguidedly describes the "glimpse" of Iran that emerges in *Ceasefire* as a "multicultural utopia," his study nevertheless encourages scholarship that contemplates how popular films reflect the values and norms of that society and in turn provide a more robust picture of a particular national cinema. However, Brown's methodology, in which he examines one financially successful comedy about a middle-class family and extrapolates that Iranian audiences must favor films with "an ostensible emphasis on wealth, freedom of movement, and indeed a light-hearted tone," fails to engage the long history of popular film in Iran at the same time that it neglects the complex social and cultural negotiations that mark any given period.[11]

Naficy's recent four-volume industrial history, *A Social History of Iranian Cinema*, rises above the shortcomings of Brown's study by adding important nuance to the scholarly portrait of Iranian cinema, which, he argues, comprises multiple histories with a variety of genres and funding sources. Popular film plays an important role in this schema, and Naficy writes *filmfārsi* into the larger history of the Iranian film industry. Accordingly, *filmfārsi* marked a significant shift as Iranian cinema transformed from an artisanal mode to an industrialized hybrid production model.[12] Commercial cinema was part and parcel of the industrialization of film, because *filmfārsi* demanded studios and labs with specialized professionals and gave rise to processes for distribution and circulation, which in turn created movie genres. Governmental institutions charged with regulating film, examples of what Naficy calls "ideological apparatuses," also emerged at this time. The *filmfārsi* enterprise witnessed the birth of the star system, and the growing numbers of professionals associated with cinema in Iran gave way to the establishment of unions.[13] In short, the financial, governmental, and technological structures typical of a film industry developed alongside commercial film in Iran.

These developments in the film industry coincided with profound changes in society, including population growth, urbanization, and urban migration. *Filmfārsi* came into its own during the reign of Mohammad Reza Shah, who ruled Iran between 1941 and 1979 and enacted one of the most aggressive social reform plans in the country's history.[14] Commercial films from this era inevitably represent and simultaneously grapple with the corollaries of these social changes. One can see that popular film since its inception has served as a gauge for transformations within both the film industry and society as a whole. Naficy capitalizes on this feature of commercial cinema and draws on the tough-guy genre to investigate the "complex and contingent social and cinematic dynamics" that have determined popular films in Iran. He engages in a kind of "cultural study of genre" and argues that attention to a particular genre reveals a dialectical relationship in which "social and ideological forces are inscribed in a specific group of films" at the same time that "genres influence social and ideological discourses and relations." Accordingly, the evolution of the tough-guy genre has less to do with "cinematic realism" and more to do with the creation of a "sociocultural encyclopedia" that charts "Iranian cultural orientation, expectations, conventions, and social and ideological formations."[15]

The encyclopedia written by this genre invariably begins with an entry on the figure of the *luti*, the foundation for most Iranian tough-guy films. The word *luti* dates back to the tenth century in Persian, and references to the word can be found in classical poetry, including Rumi's *Masnavi-ye m'anavi* (ca. 1258–1273) and works by Naser Khosrow (d. 1088). The term traditionally described any sort of rogue figure, including dervishes. However, during the Qajar Dynasty (1785–1925) the word's various meanings consolidated and came to represent a specific kind of man, a Robin Hood figure who operated on the fringes of society, sometimes outside of the law but always under a rigid moral and chivalrous code, called *javāmardi* or *lutigari*. Because lutis often frequented *zurkhāneh*s, or traditional Iranian gyms, their particular brand of masculinity included physical prowess, and the performance of violence often marked their public disputes. Although lutis operated under a strict moral code, their particular ideological and political leanings were far more nebulous. As a result, religious and bureaucratic leaders often leveraged lutis in order to enact to their own agendas. In this way, without being especially political themselves, lutis have nevertheless historically played a political role in Iranian society, and their shifting political allegiances, together with their code of masculinity, help us determine how tough-guy films in Iran understood the country's changing social and political dynamics.

Naficy divides the history of the tough-guy genre in Iran into three phases: *dāsh mashti* films, *jāheli* films, and Islamicate tough-guy films.[16] Although these phases briefly overlap, each is tied to a particular period of time and offers a unique treatment of the luti figure. *Dāsh mashti* films, popular between 1950 and 1970, provide a nostalgic look back to the early twentieth century. These films long for the fading traditions of old Iran, and in particular they mourn the loss of the premodern, preurban luti, whose morality and chivalry marked the ideals of masculinity before Iran's encounter with European modernity corrupted society and traditional values.[17] This wistful look back in time contrasts sharply with *jāheli* films, which gained popularity between 1965 and 1979. The *jāheli* subgenre deals directly with the urbanization of the mid-twentieth century and asks what happens to traditional values in post–World War II society. Whereas *dāsh mashti* films operate as conventional stories of good and evil wherein the generous luti is good and his enemy, the *lāt* (lout), is evil, in *jāheli* films we witness the collapse of the luti into the *lāt*, and the distinction between good and evil becomes much less clear. As a result, the "hopeful and lightweight" outlook of the *dāsh mashti* films fades to "bitter and pessimistic" themes in *jāheli* films.[18]

The success of the revolution and the establishment of the Islamic Republic meant the reevaluation of all films and film genres. Parallel to the gradual formation of an Islamized cinema, the tough-guy genre underwent several iterations, including a simple revival of Pahlavi-era tough guys with only slight modifications, a vilification of Pahlavi-era lutis, and finally the creation of an Islamicate tough guy. Onscreen tough guys following the revolution find themselves at the service of the Islamic community, and the moral compass guiding the luti is now decidedly Islamic. The plots of many of these new tough-guy films revolve around the reformation of luti characters to match the new Islamic ideals promoted by the Islamic Republic.[19] The various agencies overseeing cinema within the new government were charged with the very difficult task of taming the Pahlavi-era luti character, who many scholars and critics have identified as revolutionary because of his willingness to die for his beliefs. This negotiation reflected larger discussions among intellectuals and policy makers at this time about how to redirect the fervor of the revolution toward productively establishing and maintaining a new system of governance.

Naficy sees the endurance of the tough-guy trope as evidence of the dynamic and resilient nature of genres. He contends that "genres, particularly those with heavy cultural and ideological investments, do not die; they just evolve."[20] Whereas scholars often assume that political ruptures, like revolutions, also necessitate ruptures in the cultural sphere, Naficy rightly identifies this moment of cinematic continuity before and after the revolution, and his statement on generic immortality raises important questions about the nature of genres themselves. What causes genres to evolve? At what point does one genre give way to another? And, perhaps most importantly for a study of *Protest*, what happens when a filmmaker tries kill off a genre? Eventually genres outlast their utility, and locating their final moment tells us about both the genres and the societies they claim to represent. Early tough-guy films like *Qeysar*, with their roots in the historical figure of the luti, speak to shifting ideals of masculinity and society's anxiety about changing gender roles. So when Masud Kimiai announces the death of the tough-guy luti with *Protest*, what does it tell us about the anxiety surrounding masculinity at that particular moment? I argue that *Protest*'s deep investment in Khatami instructs us that reform resolved something in the Iranian collective consciousness regarding masculinity that the revolution could not.

WHO KILLED THE TOUGH GUY?

In order to appreciate what the death of the tough-guy genre means in *Protest*, one must first consider what gave rise to and drove the genre in the first place. The history of the tough-guy genre and Naficy's rigorous study of its development unravel the practice of periodization in Iran's film history. In order to delineate the various features of the *dāsh mashti* and *jāheli* subgenres, Naficy draws on two of Kimiai's films—*Dāsh Ākol* (Dash Akol, 1972), as a representative of the *dāsh mashti* mode, and *Qeysar*, as the quintessential *jāheli* film—and his selection of evidence powerfully defies linearity. Although *dāsh mashti* films generally preceded *jāheli* films, these categories do not necessarily break down neatly according to chronology, and ultimately the nebulousness of the tough-guy genre opens up the possibility of thinking of these two subgenres not as ruptures but rather as points of continuity. If these two modes represent varying aesthetic responses to a single set of social concerns, then we can examine the underlying anxieties to which this genre as a whole responds, rather than focusing on the slight changes in society that might have prompted shifts in style.

The tough-guy genre, both the *dāsh mashti* and *jāheli* modes, grew out of society's engagement with modernity. As historians have carefully documented, Westernization, urbanization, new technologies, and other changes attributed to Iranian modernity restructured society and refashioned gender norms and sexual mores.[21] The experience of modernity for the lower-class Iranian man was particularly emasculating, as family restructuring, new economic systems, and urban migration unsettled the established role of men in society, especially in lower-class families. The working-class man in the second half of the twentieth century struggled both to find his place in the city and to locate the power he once possessed within the family and the community. The tough-guy genre created a space for people affected by these changes to participate in a valorized masculinity, and the *dāsh mashti* and *jāheli* subgenres each facilitated this participation in a unique way. Whereas *dāsh mashti* films like *Dash Akol* allow viewers to ponder premodern ideals of masculinity, *jāheli* films reflect on changes to contemporary society and reimagine what a strong and powerful man might look like in light of these changes. *Qeysar*, as a *jāheli* film, thereby captures the shifting notions of gender and sexuality and reacts to them with unchecked violence.

POSTCARD SHOTS AND THE INEVITABLE VIOLENCE OF *QEYSAR*

One of the most relentless criticisms launched against *Qeysar* is the film's "touristic" view of Iran, with claims that the representation of traditional places borders on ethnographic. The wide angles and long shots of people performing rituals in spaces like bathhouses and pilgrimage sites have struck critics as foreign and instructive. Film critic Hajir Dariush accused Kimiai of planting "a foreign camera inside an Iranian décor,"[22] and filmmaker and author Ebrahim Golestan refers to *Qeysar* as constituting an imperialistic text.[23] This line of criticism echoes the concerns that filmmakers and critics have launched against Hollywood representations of certain major cities. For example, director Sidney Lumet, discussing films set in New York City, claims that a director "from California" picks "all of the postcard shots," like the Empire State Building, and in the process misses the actual experience of the city. In a similar vein, Thierry Joussee lambasts Hollywood for turning Paris into a "village for tourists." At the heart of these critiques rests the question of authority.[24] Who has the right to represent a city, and what does it look like when someone without that authority renders a particular city visible?

Yet in the case of *Qeysar*, much of the film's legitimacy hinged on the fact that its director grew up in the same south Tehran neighborhoods that he depicts. Indeed, critics often compare *Qeysar* to Golestan's film *Khesht va āyeneh* (*Mudbrick and Mirror*, 1965) and claim that the characters in *Qeysar* are more realistic because Kimiai—unlike Golestan, who is an intellectual looking in on the lower class—provides an insider's account of the social dynamics of that class.[25] Ultimately, the claims that *Qeysar* provides a "touristic" glimpse into Iran present a challenge, because Kimiai did not necessarily gear the film toward international audiences. It found success at film festivals, but only at Iranian festivals. Although the film community in Iran expected the film to fare well at the Berlin International Film Festival, it was never even screened there.[26] *Qeysar*, then, is a commercial film with no visible international audience, but it represents Iran as a strange and foreign land.

This act of defamiliarization captures the immense social changes of this period and the estrangement from Iran felt by many working-class Iranians. Issues of gender and sexuality act as a barometer with which we might evaluate social change, and in *Qeysar* shifting gender roles and new sexual mores underscore the lower-class man's new, evolving position in urban Iran. These issues highlight his powerlessness and his anxiety, and together with ethnographic images of Iran's most traditional spaces, they capture a society in transition, one whose most important cultural sites and rituals now require documentation. In this way, *Qeysar* transforms its local Iranian audience into group of tourists. However, the film does more than just capture the isolation of modernity; it also prescribes a way out of this personal turmoil through its absolution of unchecked violence, which ultimately becomes the fervor of the revolution.

In order to appreciate the film's masculinity, one must take into consideration its depiction of female characters. The female café dancer is a hallmark and nonnegotiable feature of the *filmfārsi* franchise, including *Qeysar*, and her depiction mirrors the evolution of gender roles on film. The first Persian-language talkie film, *Dokhtar-e Lor* (The Lor girl, 1933), although not technically a *filmfārsi* film, set many of the standards of the *filmfārsi* mode, including the café dance scene. In this film, a group of bandits capture the titular character, Golnar, and as the film opens, she is forced to perform. This scene features closeup shots of her dancing body, which betray the viewer's intended male subjectivity. Meanwhile, the male audience in the scene forms a tight circle around Golnar as she dances, and these shots, which are almost claustrophobic, serve as a reminder of her captivity. The actress who played Golnar, Ruhangiz Saminezhad, did not even realize that she was acting in a film; the directors tricked her into thinking that she was just playing with a toy, and she later encountered severe criticism for her role and ultimately had to change her name to avoid the negative attention she received.[27] The character and the actress both unwillingly fell into this objectified role, and this early example of a café dancer demonstrates the lack of agency of women in Iranian cinema in the early twentieth century.

At first glance, the café dance scene in *Qeysar* appears similar to Golnar's performance in *The Lor Girl*. Although Soheila, the resident dancer and singer in *Qeysar*, wears a much more revealing outfit, the same closeup shots of her moving body guide the viewer's experience of the show. However, the way that Soheila interacts with the audience signals the changes in gender roles that have transpired since *The Lor Girl* was released almost four decades earlier. Soheila performs on a stage, removed from the male audience, whose members she effectively renders immobile. Several medium shots, spliced in as reverse shots to her dancing body, reveal groups of men silent and unmoving (figure 4.1). In short, she commands the room, and she even gleefully teases the male band members and the waiter who passes by during her performance. In a similar vein, the actress who played Soheila, known by her stage name Shahrzad, was a star who, at the time, was in a public relationship with Behruz Vosuqi, the actor who played Qeysar. So although the camera stills sexualized the female body, the control that women had over the filmic audience and their forceful presence as stars in the film industry demonstrate the extent to which gender dynamics had changed over a relatively short period of time.

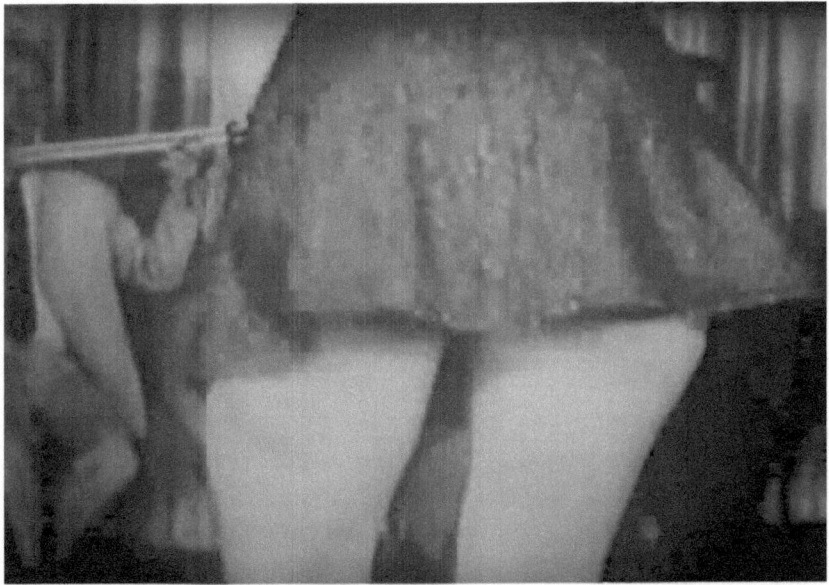

FIGURE 4.1. A shot intended to entice the heterosexual, male viewer. Frame enlargement from Masud Kimiai's *Qeysar*.

WHO KILLED THE TOUGH GUY?

The effect that these changes had on masculinity becomes apparent in the interactions between Qeysar and Soheila. He seeks out Soheila to get information about the whereabouts of the last Ab-Mangol brother, Mansur. When she approaches him after her performance, a carefully staged scene exposes his meekness in front of a strong female character. As Soheila stands by the table at which he sits, we see her from Qeysar's perspective, and she towers over him, consuming most of the frame. As he stammers to speak to her, she very forcefully says, "Speak faster, I have things to do." As their encounter continues, Soheila initiates each step. She suggests they leave the café and then tells him to stay the night with her. Once they are in her apartment, she removes her clothes in front of him and then forces him to unhook her underwear. During all of this, Qeysar sits uncomfortably in her small bed, unsure of what to do or where to look. As she stands naked in front of him, she asks what is he thinking about, and he replies, "I am thinking about tomorrow." The bedroom scene ends abruptly: a train loudly flies across the screen, and we realize that it is now the following day and Qeysar has arrived at the train station to kill Mansur. In the face of this modern woman, who is in control sexually and financially (as demonstrated by the fact that she has her own apartment), Qeysar has become an emasculated character, unable to even imagine a sexual relationship with her.

Qeysar's interactions with Soheila diverge considerably from his relationship with the only other main female character, Azam, his former love interest. Everything about Azam stands in contrast to Soheila, from the spaces she occupies (a traditional home with her family) to the clothes she wears (a chador), and in turn Qeysar's dealings with her are markedly different. When he enters her house, for example, he comfortably settles on the floor in the traditional living room, which has no seating furniture. Here he does not struggle to fit awkwardly on a small piece of European furniture that does not fit his stature. Azam serves him tea as he waits for her father, and although she stands while he sits, we did not see her from his perspective, so she does not tower over the viewer like Soheila does. Later Qeysar watches Azam through a window as she prepares the *qaliyān* (hookah) for the men, and his attraction to her is evident. In this more traditional scheme, the gender roles are clear: she serves him, and he admires her from afar. As a result, Azam does not prompt the same level of anxiety from Qeysar as Soheila does. The female characters in the film thus demonstrate the changing roles of women in society but at the same time provide an opportunity for the film to reflect on how those changes affect tough guys.

Of course, as Eve Kosofsky Sedgwick reminds us, any study of gender would be incomplete without consideration of sexuality, and in *Qeysar* anxieties about gender and sexuality converge and redirect the ideals of masculinity toward violence.[28] The character of Soheila, in addition to representing the new, modern woman, hints at changing notions of sexuality as well. When she first approaches Qeysar in the café, we see him eating and only hear her voice as she tries to get his attention. She says, "Pst. Pst. Sir? Mister?" Her voice is so deep that the viewer assumes it belongs to a man, and when she finally refers to Qeysar as *mamani*—a derivative of the word "mom" that means "cutie"— the viewer is struck by the gender at play, as a very masculine voice says a word that usually women use. At this very moment, the viewer finally sees the speaker, Soheila, and realizes that the voice belongs to a woman. It is a confounding experience, because Soheila's preceding performance demonstrates her sex appeal, but at the same time she is masculine. That she carries herself in a simultaneously masculine yet sexual way reinforces the changing gender roles during this period while also hinting at new orders of sexuality and the subsequent anxieties surrounding these changing orders.

Historians and literary scholars have extensively documented premodern sexual practices in Iran, and they have established that homoerotic relationships between men were an important part of society during the premodern period.[29] However, beginning in the nineteenth century, the watchful gaze of European imperialist forces shamed Iranian society into consolidating its diverse sexual practices, and only heterosexual relations were normalized. As Afsaneh Najmabadi has shown, although the official rhetoric regarding homosexuality changed rather suddenly, Iranian society and culture grappled with this new order more gradually.[30] By the time we arrive at the mid-twentieth century and *Qeysar*, art is continuing to negotiate these changes, and one can see remnants of the former systems of homoeroticism. These negotiations were particularly forceful at this time because the encounter with modernity—of which the consolidation of sexuality is an important part—was particularly traumatic during this period, as Mohammad Reza Pahlavi's White Revolution policies sought to modernize the country rapidly. In *Qeysar* these negotiations expose the violence that grew out of anxieties about sexuality during this particular historical moment.

No scene captures the collapse of sexual anxiety and violence more powerfully than the bathhouse murder in *Qeysar*. One of the most recognizable moments in Iran's film history, this scene follows Qeysar into a traditional bathhouse, or *hamām*, as he seeks revenge on the first Ab-Mangol brother, Karim. Golestan criticizes this scene for its "Orientalist" perspective and for its unrealistic representation of the bathhouse, including the lack of steam and the overpowering sound of water during the murder scene.[31] However, Golestan's expectation that the scene be realistic overlooks the film's modernist, surreal mode. Kimiai and the film's cinematographer, Maziar Partow, often regarded as Iran's first cinematographer, created an environment in the bathhouse that reflects the anxieties of both Qeysar and a changing society. The scene's slow pace, with long shots that provide sweeping views of the *hamām*'s various chambers and rituals, echoes Qeysar's uncertainty as he struggles to come to terms with the murder he is about to commit. Without steam, the scene seems sterile and educational, a quality that speaks to the film's intentional construction of an Iran that seems foreign to local audiences in order to convey the rapid social changes.

One absence that Golestan does not mention, but that is perhaps most perplexing of all, is the lack of body hair on the male characters in the bathhouse, and the many close-ups of the actor Behruz Vosuqi's bare, hairless chest highlight this strange feature of the scene. Certainly, these hairless bodies address changing standards of male beauty, perhaps inspired by European or American ideals. At the same time, the issue of body hair in Iran has also historically been tied to sexuality, and in particular homosexuality. Premodern sexual relations between men often involved an older man and a young boy, and the lack of body hair of young men helped draw the boundaries of this system. Once a man reached sexual maturity, he was no longer a suitable object of sexual desire. In medieval poetry, a boy reached the height of his desirability when he grew a *khatt-e sabz*, or green line, the first traces of a mustache. After his facial hair filled out, he was no longer sought after in this sexual practice. The hairless adult male bodies in *Qeysar* confound this traditional way of categorizing both sexual maturity and desire, especially at a time when sexual mores were changing.

Qeysar eventually follows Karim into a shower stall, where they seem to struggle before Qeysar finally kills him with a straight razor. However, during this scene the shower's running water drowns out all of the other sounds so that we hear only water while watching two naked, hairless bodies embrace, and in fact their first move is a long hug. Without the sounds of their struggle, the various poses of the men's brawl seem intimate and impassioned. The movement ends with a close-up of Karim's hand sliding down the shower wall, followed by a shot of Qeysar stepping back, leaning against the shower door, out of breath. Both of these gestures could signal either the end of a fight or the end of a sexual encounter (figures 4.2 and 4.3). It is not until Qeysar sets the razor down and we see blood in the drain that the events that just transpired become clear. That this scene simultaneously captures intimacy and murder suggests the extent to which violence is wrapped up in sexuality.

And, indeed, it is the unrelenting and unchecked violence of this scene that connects the film to the fervor that fueled the revolution of 1978–1979. Scholars see this shower scene as a clear citation of Alfred Hitchcock's *Psycho* and the murder of Marion. In *Qeysar* Karim's hand on the tiled shower wall recalls Marion's final moment in *Psycho*, and this shot reflects Kimiai's knowledge of international film at this time.[32] And yet there is an important difference between these two films' respective shower scenes that has thus far gone unacknowledged. A series of cinematic cuts in *Psycho* correspond to Norman's knife; each new shot cues for the viewer a different stab. As Kaja Silverman has noted, the rapid succession of violent cuts, both physical and cinematic, leaves us with "no choice but [to] identify with Marion in the shower."[33] In other words, the film's editing and cinematography force us to empathize with her as a victim. *Qeysar*, however, resists this kind of identification with the victim, Karim. As the scene begins, we occupy a vantage point far above the shower stall, a distance that does not favor one character over the other. Our perspective then moves to within the shower, amid the fighting bodies, but a steady series of shot–reverse shots refuse to privilege either Karim or Qeysar. And, unlike in *Psycho*, in which we are forced to look at Marion's tiny,

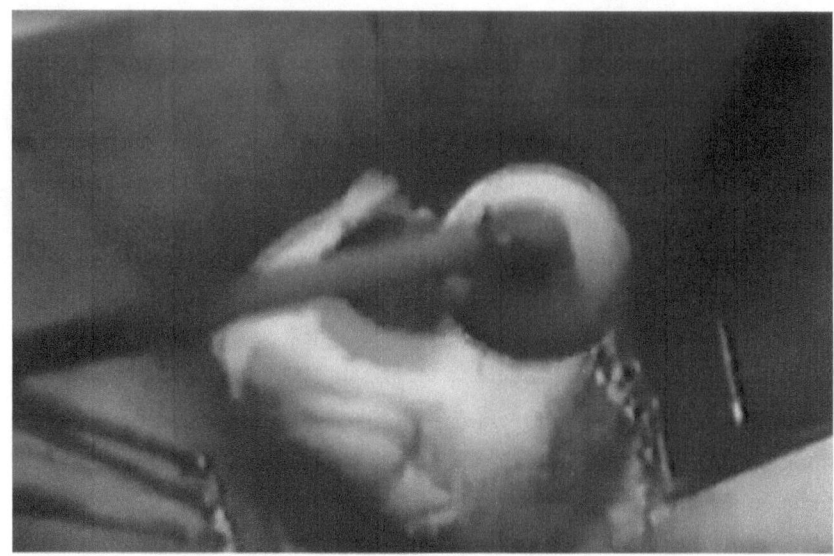

FIGURE 4.2. Aerial view of the shower fight. Frame enlargement from *Qeysar*.

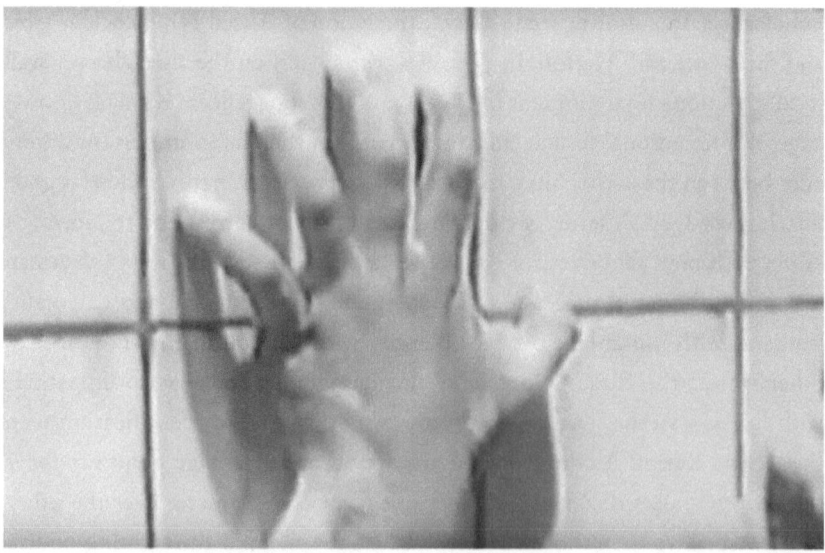

FIGURE 4.3. This shot of a hand on the shower tile recalls the shower scene in Alfred Hitchcock's *Psycho*. Frame enlargement from *Qeysar*.

dead body, in *Qeysar* we never see Karim's corpse. After the murder we only see Qeysar's relief, so if any act of identification occurs, it is with the murderer and not the victim. At the very least, the shower scene in *Qeysar* does not evoke sympathy for the victim.

The film's danger rests in the absence of this act of identification. *Qeysar* is a film that does not condemn its own violence, which, in turn, opens up a space for condoning violence, especially in the name of honor, the nebulous force that drives the character of Qeysar. Throughout the film, the police pursue Qeysar, which establishes tension between the rule of law and vigilante justice. That Kimiai refuses to show Qeysar's apprehension in the end is a testament to the film's ambivalence about operating outside of the law, when such actions are in the name of a higher moral code not covered by the modern legal system. This ambivalence ultimately led to the government's decision to ban the film.

Mohammad Reza Pahlavi had a private screening of the film in his home and initially praised the film, but later the government banned it. This abrupt change in policy presents a puzzle. Why would the shah support a film but later allow it to be banned? Reports of young men in south Tehran violently acting out immediately after seeing the film help us understand the effect that it had on the class it represented, and these reactions are often cited as the reason for the film's ban from theaters.[34] However, this is only part of the full picture. That the film inspired violence was not nearly as dangerous as the fact that the film was being received as a call to violence and that it defied and even confronted the police presence on which the Pahlavi regime depended in order to maintain its power. The government's ambivalence and, ultimately, its rejection of the film make more sense when one considers the critical work on Kimiai's film that was published shortly after the revolution. These essays, time and time again, liken the film to a rallying cry for the revolution,[35] in the same way that literary scholars and historians look to the works of Jalal Al-e Ahmad and Ali Shariati as indicators of the fervor that would fuel the revolution. *Qeysar* captured the frustrations of a generation of men caught in the throes of tremendous social change, which left them with very little social, economic, and political power. But the film did more than simply represent an increasingly disenfranchised group; it also offered a way out through violence and the reinstatement of traditional values, a rhetoric that would emerge more fully ten years later, during the revolution.

THE HERO REDEFINED

Released thirty years after *Qeysar*, *Protest* begins with the same celebration of violence. The film opens with Amir confronting Reza's fiancée. Amir explains that he found her lover's house easily, and he scolds her for not cutting off relations with him. He reminds her that he warned her the last time he discovered her infidelity that he would kill her the next time. He repeatedly tells her that she will not see her lover, Ahmad, again, and he insists that she not speak. Initially, we only hear Amir's voice laid over a black screen, and when an image does appear, the camera focuses squarely on Amir, so that the viewer cannot see his addressee. Finally, the camera shuffles to the right and reveals the silhouette of a woman, but even in the closeup shots of her, the light coming from the window behind her prevents us from seeing her face. As Amir grows angrier, he hits a table, and the woman's hand awkwardly falls to the side. He bitingly asks, "Who named you Sharifeh?"—a question that plays with the meaning of her name, which translates as "noble." In the next shot, Amir picks up the phone and calls Reza. As he explains about Sharifeh's infidelity, the camera pans back to Sharifeh and settles on the floor, where a pool of blood gathers under her seat. It is in this moment that we recognize what we already knew: that Amir had already killed Sharifeh and has been speaking to her corpse the entire time.

This scene gives way to a montage that shows Amir aging behind bars, and unlike in *Qeysar*, in which we never see the main character held accountable to the law, in *Protest* Amir suffers the legal repercussions of his actions. However, in the opening scenes of *Protest*, the rule of law still does not win over personal moral codes. When Amir is released twelve years later, a fellow prisoner delivers a speech in his honor. He lauds Amir's crime and describes it in terms of *nāmus*, or honor. He reminds Amir and the other prisoners that God is the true judge of crimes and implies that God would not deem Amir's murder a crime. The prisoner says, "Today a *man* will be set free," and his stress on the word "man" emphasizes Amir's manliness and links his honorable crime to his sense of masculinity. As Amir leaves the prison, the other prisoners cheer for him and donate money to his life as a free man. At the time of the murder and in prison, he is considered a hero for the crime he has committed, and he encapsulates the revolutionary violence that we also see in *Qeysar*.

The opening two scenes of *Protest* recall *Qeysar* in a number of ways. Family honor and female chastity drive the murder in *Protest* just as they fuel the violence in *Qeysar*. In both films, the characters recognize that they are operating outside of the law but believe that their moral code is more important than the rule of law. When Amir calls Reza to tell him what he has done, he says, "If I hadn't done it, you would have." This sentence directly recalls *Qeysar*, when Farman claims, "If I don't do it [go after Mansour Ab-Mangol], then Qeysar will slaughter the entire bazar." In both instances, the elder brother believes that the younger shares the same commitment to protecting the family's honor. Of course, in *Qeysar* Farman's prophecy comes true, and Qeysar goes on a murdering spree. However, in *Protest*, Reza, with the benefit of twelve years to think it over, claims that he would not have made the same decision that Amir made. My interest in *Protest* rests precisely in this claim. Why does this chain of violence, which extends over thirty years from Farman to Qeysar to Amir, come to an end with Reza at this particular moment in 1999? The film destabilizes the place of the traditional luti tough guy through Amir and replaces him with a new hero through the character of Reza. Political reform, although heavily criticized in the film, ultimately opens a space for this new hero to prevail in the end.

As Amir leaves prison, he dons a hat similar to the fedoras popular among lutis of the mid-twentieth century, including Farman in *Qeysar*. He wears the hat throughout the film and only takes it off in his final moments as he slowly bleeds out. The hat both marks Amir as a traditional tough guy and singles him out; no other character outside of prison wears a hat. Indeed, once Amir leaves prison, he discovers that the traditional tough guy represented by the hat no longer has a place in society, and we see Amir struggle to find space in two different places: the home and the city. After his family picks him up from the prison gate, Amir discovers that they have sold their previous home and currently rent a place that builders are preparing to destroy in order to construct a skyscraper. When he arrives at the house, Amir boldly states that although the rest of the family may be comfortable in the house, he is not. Later we see his large body sprawled on a small couch. He tries to sleep while his mother talks on the phone and the silhouettes of his sister and brother-in-law angrily move behind a glass door. The claustrophobia of this scene overwhelms both Amir and the viewer. In this house he literally has no space, which reflects his standing in the family. Although Amir is the eldest son and should step into the role of the head of the household following his father's death, his mother announces to him that his brother-in-law Farhad is in charge in this house. The family whose honor Amir defended with his crime not only refuses to valorize him but also denies him a meaningful role in the family structure.

Amir's lack of space extends beyond the home and into the street, as he fails to secure a place for himself anywhere in the city and, by extension, anywhere in society. Reza likens his brother to a "stranger wandering the streets," claims that Amir "lives by his own laws," and finally concludes, "There is no one like him left in Tehran." This pointed description grounds the scenes we see of Amir interacting with the city. He wanders deserted stockyards, lurks in the shadows, and at one point we see him emerge from a highway tunnel, walking in the middle of the road in broad daylight. Both the desolate street and Amir's decision to walk in the middle of it would be striking to anyone familiar with traffic in Tehran. This scene has no bearing on the film's plot. The preceding and subsequent scenes do indicate a point of origin or a destination, and this brief scene ultimately only serves to remind the viewer of the dislocation between Amir, on the one hand, and the city and its rules, on the other. Amir's physical relationship with Tehran underscores his position in society. Because of his status as a criminal, he never finds honest work and must resort to running errands for a bookie. When Farhad asserts that Amir does not scare him, because "the days of outlaws are long over," the viewer recognizes that Amir has no social currency and no power. The violent qualities that once demanded respect now preclude him from being a meaningful member of society.

Amir's struggle to locate a place in society forces him into the underworld of cockfighting, a place where traditional luti ideals still hold true. Cockfighting was historically a popular luti pastime, so it is no coincidence that Amir finds a home within this circle. *Protest* casts Amir as the inheritor of traditional luti values but also relocates those values underground and represents them as inhumane. The viewer's first encounter with cockfighting reveals its cruel violence. As crowds of men circle around two roosters and wave money to place their bets, slow-motion shots establish the primitive violence between the two birds. They attack to kill, and the law of the jungle reigns supreme, but it is human intervention that ultimately lends this scene its brutality. During a short time-out, men forcefully push a rag down the cock's throat to absorb the blood so that he can continue fighting. Slow motion again heightens the inhumanity of this act, and Amir, whose eyes mediate this scene for the viewer, looks away. Despite Amir's obvious disgust for the fight that unfolds, he nevertheless stays and eventually becomes part of that world.

The underground world that provides Amir with a job and some semblance of a life kills him in the end. One night as he leaves the cockfight, he knows that Ahmad, Sharifeh's former lover, is following him. Amir pulls Ahmad into a dark alley and, as it begins to rain, tells him to "be a man" and kill him, to seek revenge for the murder that Amir committed against his lover and his unborn child. Ahmad quietly stabs Amir and runs away as Amir slowly bleeds out in the rain. Whereas at the beginning of the film Amir proudly claims that he would kill Sharifeh again if he had the chance, near the end of the film he declares that "the shame of the murder I committed chokes me more and more every day." Amir's values do not necessarily change throughout the course of the film. After all, he uses the same rhetoric of revenge to incite Ahmad to murder him. Although he does not undergo any sort of teleological change, Amir does recognize that his values no longer have a place in society. His quiet death hails the death of those traditional tough-guy values at the same time that it marks the end of the cycles of celebrated violence that determined the Islamic Republic during its early history.

As Amir bleeds out, the scene fades and returns to the pizza shop, where Reza sulks. He has just inadvertently delivered pizza to a wedding party for the woman he loves, Ladan. Although she returns his love, he refuses to marry her because Amir's release from jail unsettles him and makes him aware of his own disadvantaged background. As Reza's friends try to console him, Ladan suddenly appears in the rain in her wedding dress. A meaningful glance between Reza and Ladan confirms that she has left her groom to be with him, and a frozen frame of a closeup shot of Ladan smiling at Reza closes the film. By the standards of popular Iranian cinema, getting the girl identifies a film's hero, and in this case, Reza clearly emerges victorious. So in the same moment and under the same rain in which the tough guy, who previously represented the ideals of masculinity, bleeds to death, a very new kind of heroic masculinity is born.

Reza's character fixes the terms of this new, idealized masculinity. He is thoughtful, intellectual, sensitive, and—above all—rational. Although underemployed as a pizza delivery boy, he has a master's degree and spends most of the film discussing politics and philosophy with his friends. During all of these conversations, he demands their respect with his ideas and talks more than any of the other characters. At one point in the film, he gently helps his friend overcome an addiction to opium, and later he carefully tends to Ladan after she is attacked during a protest. His condemnation of violence, though, contrasts most sharply with the tough-guy masculinity of yesterday. During a conversation with Amir, he explains, "If I had known Sharifeh was still involved with Ahmad, I would have acted differently. I would have satisfied my conscience, as you say, without ruining other people's lives as well. Keeping your dignity is good, but ruining another person's life is taking it too far." He balances a sense of honor with pacifism, and he takes it a step further when he declares, "Sharifeh's child could have been a good citizen of this country." This description of the unborn child, which Amir refers to as a "sin within a sin," attests to Reza's logic and to his optimism. He not only forgives Sharifeh but also sees hope in her mistakes. Reza's kind, rational masculinity looks beyond the dynamics of family honor and seeks what is best for society as a whole.

The violent masculinity venerated by characters like Qeysar and Amir responds to the emasculating experience of modernity, and one must wonder what kind of rupture gives rise to the gentle, logical masculinity embodied in the character of Reza. *Protest* clearly positions itself in a moment of profound social change. From Amir's observation about the new public discourse to Reza's insistence that "the days of such reactions [i.e., honor killings] have passed," *Protest* suggests that Iranian society has undergone significant transformation in the twelve years since Amir went to prison. Amir finds these changes so disorienting that he declares, "I am sick of this freedom," a play on not only Reza's repeated claim that society is free now but also Amir's new status as a free man. He continues, "Such reactions might have no place in your lives anymore, but I won't just bow to the change of time." His desire to die at the end of the film confirms the fact that these changes are not fleeting but rather constitute a rupture in traditional social values.

In *Protest*, these changes bounce in the wave of political reform that had swept the country at the turn of the century. Many of the references to reform and social change occur in dialogue, but the film also uses music to establish reform as the impetus for this new kind of masculinity. Reform and the reformists serve as the main talking points during discussions among the young students in the pizza shop, and reformist newspapers like *Khordād* and *Neshāt* cover the table. Similarly, during Amir and Reza's heated discussion, Reza says, "I am talking about today's sense of reason in society . . . a progressive society." His choice of words here clearly references "civil society," one of Khatami's most important political platforms. During this same conversation, as a piano player sings pop music in the background, Amir explodes, "Is that guy singing or whining?" Reza shakes his head disapprovingly, and the shot switches to a close-up of the piano player, whose presence is also very much wrapped up in the cultural environment fostered by Khatami and the reformists. Before Khatami's presidency, this kind of live pop music would not have been allowed in a restaurant.[36] This song, along with Amir's reaction to it, suggests a small change in society at the same time that it points to the political atmosphere that engendered the change. Throughout the film, references to how much society has changed are often punctuated with references to Khatami. So reform is clearly the rupture that puts an end to the old, violent masculinity and clears way for a new, rational masculinity.

Like Rakhshan Bani-Etemad's *Under the Skin of the City*, *Protest* criticizes reform at the same time that it performs it. Although pulled from theaters after only one week, the film was wildly popular because of its direct political commentary, and this commentary would not have made it through Ministry of Culture and Islamic Guidance had it not been for Khatami's presidency.

Toward the end, the film becomes particularly pointed in its critique of Khatami and the reformist movement. Reza says:

> Philosophy can't run the country. You need power, law, and freedom together. One side has the law while the other side has the power. . . . I, for one, haven't read a convincing definition of civil society. . . . Khatami once said, "I am everyone's president." We're all part of the nation, which is a liberal stand. But who will implement it? Those who have the power do not agree with Khatami.

In a rather concise manner, Reza echoes the major criticisms launched against Khatami at this time, even among his staunchest supporters. These criticisms included Khatami's unwillingness to pin down certain philosophical terms, like "civil society," and his inaction and inability to enact many of the changes he promised during his campaign. As Reza speaks, he suddenly breaks the fourth wall and directly addresses the audience, implicating the viewer in everything he says. As a result, when one of the characters says, "This isn't politics; it's everyday talk," the viewer understands and has even experienced cinematically the all-encompassing experience of Khatami's presidency, which helps explain why, as various characters insist that society has changed, it is easy to understand reform as the impetus for this change.

Protest dramatizes the tension between revolution and reform by casting them as two brothers. When Kimiai kills Amir, he essentially kills Qeysar and with him the entire tough-guy genre. During the period of reform, space was made for a new kind of masculinity, and as a result, the tough-guy genre, just like Amir, no longer had a place in society. Although the revolution of 1978–1979 altered the tough-guy genre by Islamizing it, the real structural change to the genre (i.e., its demise) came during Khatami's presidency, because the moderate political and cultural environment he fostered refigured what it meant to be a man, and it eliminated the need for and desire to have an idealized, violent tough guy. This pattern is visible throughout the history of Iranian cinema. The establishment of the Islamic Republic enacted a number of surface changes to cinema, especially through censorship, but discussions of reform actually created some of the most profound changes to the industry.

WHO KILLED THE TOUGH GUY?

MOHAMMAD KHATAMI: PRESIDENT, INVISIBLE MOVIE STAR

Protest marks Khatami's entrance into popular cinema and proves that it was not just art-house filmmakers invested in his philosophical contributions who sought to situate his presidency in a larger system of cinematic representation. Abulhosssein Davudi's *Nān o 'eshq o mutur-e hezar* (Bread, love, and a 1000cc motorcycle, 2001) powerfully attests to Khatami's larger place in popular cinema and uses the tropes of the *filmfārsi* franchise in order to criticize factionalist politics during Khatami's presidency at the same time that it undercuts its own heritage as a *filmfārsi* film. In other words, *Bread, Love, and a 1000cc Motorcycle* functions simultaneously as parody and satire, poking fun of its own form in order to make a larger social critique. The film stages political factionalism by way of dramatic haircuts: members of the *basij* cut the hair of those people they believe to be reformists, to whom they refer as *mozdur-e estekbār*, or "hired by the arrogant" (i.e., the United States). They ironically start with the local hairdresser and then speed off on their newly converted 1000cc motorcycle. Of course, these bad haircuts do not even approach the actual violence that occurred between conservative *basij*s and reformists during this period, and these hair attacks may even refer to the infamous serial murders of reformists during Khatami's presidency.

The political narrative in *Bread, Love, and a 1000cc Motorcycle* plays out against a melodramatic love story typical of *filmfārsi*, as orphaned Baran must find a suitable husband in three days or her guardian uncle will give away her inheritance. In the midst of an exaggerated courtship, Baran watches a scene from James Cameron's *Titanic* (1997); as Rose says her final goodbye to Jack, and her emotional reaction to this scene reminds the viewer that melodramas construct romance to elicit a response. Throughout the film, *Bread, Love, and a 1000cc Motorcycle* overperforms and overdetermines its own *filmfārsi*-ness, with over-the-top characters and storylines, and this tactic makes its political reality slippery for the viewer and perhaps also for the censors. Indeed, the opening moments of the film obscure the line between reality and fiction (and *filmfārsi* melodrama, at that). As the title flies onto the screen, a voiceover reminds us, "This is a true story. A story that is very similar to a film. Although there are a number of unemployed bums who believe that this tale is a lie, you should believe that everything you see and hear is exactly the truth." Locating the very serious political message among the heightened and often hilarious melodrama proves challenging. *Bread, Love, and a 1000cc Motorcycle* unabashedly makes fun of everything—from intellectualism to politics to *filmfārsi* itself—with little discernment.

There is no doubt that *Bread, Love, and a 1000cc Motorcycle* deals directly with *filmfārsi*. The title screen and voiceover warning give way to a scene showing the famous actor Fardin in his role of Ali in *Ganj-e Qarun* (Qarun's treasure, 1965), a quintessential *filmfārsi* film. And much of the film's humor depends on the viewer's knowledge of *filmfārsi* conventions; the exaggerations only make sense if one understands what the film exaggerates. As is typical of *filmfārsi*, *Bread, Love, and a 1000cc Motorcycle* neatly ties up its loose ends, and the film ends with a brief report on what each of the characters has been up to, and this report is accompanied by stills of photographs, a common technique that lets the viewer know that the future of these characters has been determined. Just when the film should be over, a coda appears, and the voiceover announces that two of the characters, one a reformist and the other a *basiji*, never make it to the wedding because something "interesting" happened to them. We see them stranded in a desert, when suddenly a motorcade drives by and pulls over to offer them a ride. When Arashak, the reformist, opens the door, we see his surprise, and he says, "Mr. Khatami." His *basiji* companion, Dariush, at first refuses to get into the car but is ultimately persuaded to get in, and the scene comes to a close as the two men pile into Khatami's car and the narrator says, "And this is another story altogether." The political message here is explicit: these two competing groups need to come together and move forward with Khatami.

However, this coda also raises an important question about reform and popular film. Why would a film so invested in its own status as a *filmfārsi* unravel its neat ending to include this scene with an invisible Khatami as its star? Ultimately, such a scene positions Khatami and reform—as much as melodrama and happy endings—as inseparable parts of popular cinema. Khatami's presence in popular film at this time was inevitable. Khatami's early engagement with film, during his tenure as minister of culture and Islamic guidance, revealed the fact that his reformist ideas constituted part of a much larger philosophical and intellectual movement taking place in Iran in the early 1990s. His greatest achievement as president was to bring these abstract concepts to a popular audience, where they became "everyday talk." It is only natural, then, that Khatami as a character and his reformist policies did not remain stagnant in art-house cinema but also made their way to popular cinema.

5

FILM ARCHIVES AND ONLINE VIDEOS

The Search for Reform in Post-Khatami Iran

The 2005 elections effectively closed the moderate atmosphere cultivated by Khatami's presidency and marked the rise of the neoconservative movement in Iran.[1] During his presidency, Khatami had positioned himself as a populist champion. Now, with Khatami precluded from seeking reelection in 2005 due to Iran's consecutive two-term limit, a new self-styled "populist" rose to take his place. Although Mahmoud Ahmadinejad's hardline conservative platform radically differed from Khatami's moderate policies, Ahmadinejad also chose to position himself as a populist during the election, in stark contrast to his main rival, Akbar Hashemi Rafsanjani, a cleric and member of the ruling elite. With the support of Supreme Leader Khamenei, Ahmadinejad promised to address the country's economic problems, especially its alarming unemployment rates, a promise that helped him garner more than 60 percent of the vote and solidify his position as the people's voice.[2]

Mahmoud Ahmadinejad's election reflected the country's frustration with the reformist movement and Khatami's broader failure to liberalize the government during his eight-year presidency.[3] Almost immediately, Ahmadinejad and his newly formed cabinet began codifying more conservative cultural policies. The newly appointed minister of culture, Hossein Saffar-Harandi, banned the distribution and exhibition of films that promoted "secularism" and "feminism."[4] However, this ban was not enough for conservative members of the Majles. In early 2006, the Majles sharply criticized Ahmadinejad for his failure to better regulate the film industry. Specifically, the Majles claimed that the films released during Ahmadinejad's first year as president were "not significantly different" from "Khatami-era" films, did not meet the "higher values of the Islamic regime," and thus needed tighter control. This criticism brings into focus two important features of Iranian cinema after Khatami's presidency. First, a shift toward neoconservatism created new conflict within Iran's film industry. Second, the reformist aesthetic project, initiated under Khatami's presidency, remained relevant during Ahmadinejad's first term.

The previous chapters have thus far examined the ways in which cinema and political reform came together at various points in Mohammad Khatami's political career, and how these intersections created a reformist aesthetic that continued to develop and transform even after the reformist movement, as a political entity determined by Khatami's presidency, ended. Cinema continued to seek the relevance of Khatami's popular discourse, and specifically it attempted to evaluate the terms of his political platform after the reformist movement failed to create the changes that it promised. Although the films released after Khatami's presidency do not benefit practically from his political leadership, these films are nevertheless invested in a reformist aesthetic. And, should we narrowly define the reformist movement's impact on cinema only in terms of its ability to foster a culturally liberal political atmosphere, these films might otherwise be overlooked.

Massoud Bakhshi's *Tehrān anār nadārad* (Tehran has no more pomegranates, 2007), an experimental documentary, and the music video "'Eshq-e sor'at" (Love of speed, 2007), performed by the underground band Kiosk and directed by Ahmad Kiarostami, demonstrate that reform as a media event functioned outside of the temporal limits of its political antecedent. Although both works were released two years after Khatami's presidency ended and did not benefit directly from his cultural liberalism, the experimental documentary and music video are still central to the reformist debates. Specifically, they question the legacy of Khatami's political platform, which included concepts like "civil society" and "religious democracy." The films' experimentation with form further suggests that the reformist aesthetic possesses a momentum that permits it to develop and transform without explicit contact with the political movement that inspired it. Analyzing a film alongside a music video connects cinema innovations to trends in social media and youth culture, introducing a new model for studying media ecology in contemporary Iran.

CELLULOID REFORM

Tehran Has No More Pomegranates is a self-described "musical, historical, comedy, docu-drama, love story, experimental film," and although relatively short (68 minutes), it succeeds in encompassing all of the styles and genres to which it lays claim. Playing with fact and fiction is a common stylistic device in Iranian cinema. Massoud Bakhshi's experimental film takes this interplay and Eisenstein's notion of cinematic montage to new extremes. The film changes mediums, switches narratives, and makes disorienting jumps in space and time. In doing so, *Tehran Has No More Pomegranates* forces disparate images to collide across distant temporal and social boundaries, much as the city itself exists in a constant state of flux and perpetual evolution.

Because the film actively resists the informing logic that often determines the documentary genre, some critics have questioned whether Bakhshi's creation can even be categorized as a documentary. Other critics take a more extreme view and argue that the film is better classified as *zed-e mostanad* (antidocumentary) because of its willingness to defy the argument-based conventions of the documentary genre.[5] By viewing the film through the lens of reform, however, we may approach the question of categorization from a different vantage point. Reform is both a point of entry into the narrative and a strand to be traced throughout the film. *Tehran Has No More Pomegranates*'s composite style makes a profound statement about the history and legacy of reform in Iran. Significantly, because the film is also about the process of documentary filmmaking in the country, it theorizes reform as an aesthetic possibility.

As we begin our analysis of *Tehran Has No More Pomegranates*, it is useful to consider the film in comparison to Kamran Shirdel's *Un shab keh bārun umad* (The night it rained, 1967), discussed in chapter 2. Although the two plots may differ substantially, both films ultimately offer a self-reflexive critique of the "real." Shirdel's *The Night It Rained* plays with the disconnection created by contradictory images and sounds. This approach to filmmaking challenges the formation of truth, prompting the viewer to question truth as an epistemological category. Similarly, Bakhshi's *Tehran Has No More Pomegranates* creates tension between image and sound within the film's first minute. In the opening scene, wild images of Tehran's nighttime traffic fill the screen. Simultaneously, a voice reads from Zakariya Qazvini's thirteenth-century text *Āthār al-bilād wa-akhbār al-'ibād* (Monuments of the countries and the history of their inhabitants): "Tehran is a large village near the city of Rey, full of gardens and fruit trees.[6] Its inhabitants live in anthill-like underground holes. The village's several districts are constantly at war." The images of a modern, chaotic metropolis in perpetual motion directly clash with this aural description.

This audiovisual collision foreshadows the entire viewing experience: one must prepare to reconcile this collision by neglecting either the audio or the visual *or* by reaching a conclusion about why the difference exists. By forcing viewers to contemplate how film constructs an "accurate" portrait of Tehran, the reliability of the film itself (including the specific medium of film) is brought into question. Five minutes into the film, just as we are coming to terms with this basic premise, a warning flashes on the screen: *shabāhat-e ādam-hā va havādes-e film bā namuneh-hā-ye vāqe'i dar besiyāri az mavāred ettefāqist* (similarities between the people and events of this film and *real* cases are, in many cases, coincidental).[7]

The statement's tentativeness is what makes it so important. The film is neither purely factual nor fictitious. A kernel of truth is embedded in all the events, more evident in some than others, and it is up the viewer to discern fact from fiction. Bakhshi reminds the viewer of this tension between fact and fiction, reality and perception, throughout the film. For example, Bakhshi overlays his "found footage" with a narrative voice that reminds viewers, "Owing to problems in verifying facts, this film is probably full of mistakes." Nosrat Karimi, who provides the voiceover in this section, repeats his warning twice, because he intentionally misspeaks the first time. The film's initial onscreen warning and subsequent voiceover mistake challenge the viewer to determine which people and events merely bear a fleeting resemblance to historical fact and which people and events are truly grounded in historical fact, thus calling into question the very nature of "history" and "truth." This intentional obfuscation makes latching onto specific arguments within the documentary a near impossibility.

Despite these challenges, Bakhshi establishes reform as an important theme early in the film, starting with the film's narrative premise. This premise—a production report presented as a written letter from Bakhshi to the president of the Documentary Center within the Ministry of Culture and Islamic Guidance—underscores reform's importance as a central theme. Throughout the film, Bakhshi's voice functions as the narrative voiceover, describing the filmmaking process and claiming that the film he set out to make is incomplete. Bakhshi starts the film by identifying himself using details such as his name, birthplace, marriage status, and employee number at the Documentary Center. He explains how writing the film script five years earlier, and the subsequent five-year journey to obtain the necessary permits, has rendered the original script obsolete. The permit Bakhshi (finally) obtained flashes onto the screen, along with other official documents, including his ID card and contract. Bakhshi argues that because "Tehran is constantly in a state of reform," the five-year-old script bears no relevance to Tehran today. Accordingly, the director and his crew decided to produce a different film, one that compares an old found documentary with images of contemporary Tehran. This statement also forces viewers to contemplate the bigger reality that even if Bakhshi had filmed the original script shortly after he wrote it, the natural passage of time between writing, filming, producing, and distributing would have meant that the Tehran that Bakhshi filmed would have already evolved in new directions and would no longer exist as it did on film. Throughout the film Bakhshi skillfully layers these multiple messages, which continually push the viewer toward unexpected examination.

Bakhshi's description of the film's production locates reform temporally, geographically, and structurally within the film's text and context. *Tehran Has No More Pomegranates* premiered at the twenty-fifth Fajr Film Festival in February 2007. Thus the five-year window Bakhshi references in his letter positions the film's genesis well within Khatami's presidency and the reformist movement. As minister of culture, Khatami played an important role in forming the institutions that oversee filmmaking in the Islamic Republic to this day. Repeated references to permits, both in Bakhshi's voiceover and visually as evidence onscreen, together with direct references to the Ministry of Culture and Islamic Guidance bring Khatami's reforms—and the very state of Tehran—to the film's forefront.

In *Tehran Has No More Pomegranates*, Bakhshi suggests that Tehran is in a constant state of physical, political, and social reform. The constant cycles of construction and physical transformation mirror the city's ongoing cultural and spiritual evolution. Like Rakhshan Bani-Etemad in her film *Zir-e pust-e shahr* (Under the skin of the city, 2000), Bakhshi uses the city of Tehran to signal reform. At the same time, the atmosphere of reform literally reshapes Bakhshi's project and determines a new direction for the film, and as a result, we see reform affecting his filmmaking methods and aesthetics. The connection between *Tehran Has No More Pomegranates* and reform, which Bakhshi introduces early in the film, becomes increasingly complex as the film proceeds. Although at times these complexities appear to obscure Bakhshi's central message, together they constitute a convoluted but cogent statement about the legacy of reform in the post-Khatami period.

Tehran Has No More Pomegranates's basic narrative structure comprises two main sections. In the first section, the director and his film crew compare images of contemporary Tehran to images of the city from the old "documentary" that they allegedly find in the archives of the Ministry of Culture and Islamic Guidance. In this part, the film evaluates the effectiveness of reform as a historical process and considers its late nineteenth- and early twentieth-century iterations. In the second section, the film crew focuses on the institutions that define Tehran, in an attempt to construct a "realistic" image of the city. Here, the film questions how reform, with its roots in the nineteenth century, plays out in contemporary Tehran, a sprawling megametropolis.

The message from both film components is clear: Tehran, Bakhshi tells us, is a city defined by foreigners with preconceived agendas and by Iranians who stretch the truth. There is no singular, realistic contemporary or historical image, and it is futile to attempt to create one. The film's methodology engenders a comparative and cross historical perspective, and *Tehran Has No*

More Pomegranates ultimately guides us to the conclusion that reform—as an alternative to revolution—is an ineffective instrument for enacting true social and political change in Iran.

Tehran Has No More Pomegranates formally introduces the theme of reform when the voiceover for the found documentary declares that Naser al-Din Shah, on returning to Iran from Europe, declared himself an *eslāhtalab*, or reformist. The Qajar ruler of Iran from 1848 to 1896, Naser al-Din is also the first king in Iran's modern history to travel to Europe. Fascinated by Western technology during his trips abroad, Naser al-Din published his travel diaries and is credited with initiating early reforms in Iran. Significantly, he also brought the first filmmaking technology to Iran. In *Tehran Has No More Pomegranates*, Bakhshi equates Naser al-Din's early reforms to Westernization or the "Europeanization" of everything. For example, the film discusses Naser al-Din's attempts to reform the gardens of Iran by introducing new produce. This discussion is followed by sounds from the bazaar: *tut-e farangi* ("strawberry," literally "European berry"), *gujeh farangi* ("tomato," literally "European plum"), *hamash farangiyeh!* (all of it is European!). Is "reforming" gardens true reform?

With the Europeanization of everything in mind, the film ultimately questions the effectiveness of the changes that Naser al-Din Shah made by comparing them with similar phenomena in contemporary Tehran. Although modern Iran has been in a constant state of transformation, including several waves of reform driven by at least two revolutions, *Tehran Has No More Pomegranates* demonstrates that Tehran faces the same struggles in the twenty-first century that it faced in the nineteenth. The film utilizes such points of comparison to introduce this argument to the viewer and in the process emphasizes it through the use of humor, which ultimately strengthens rather than tempers the director's critique of reform. The beginning of the found documentary introduces old Tehran as a place of "clay huts, grand gardens and narrow alleys," and Tehranis of that time as "illiterate, stupid, and vulgar people." In contrast, Bakhshi, the narrator of contemporary Tehran, states, "By the grace of God, today we have wide highways and wise citizens." However, the images that the film presents as visual evidence refute rather than support this statement.

A wide highway is made narrow by an expansive traffic jam. The narrator describes "wise citizens" as onscreen images depict a *zurkhāneh* (traditional

Iranian gym). The carnivalesque music and slow motion that accompany the images from the *zurkhāneh* make a mockery of the athlete's movements, which do not seem to be the pursuit of a wise individual. The camera abruptly cuts to a wide-angle shot of a supermarket that emphasizes the narrow aisles, a contemporary rendering of old Tehran's narrow alleys. This scene, in contrast to the preceding one, is in fast motion, which emphasizes the narrowness of the aisles that people are quickly navigating. Although the highway, the *zurkhāneh*, and the grocery store are initially onscreen for less than 60 seconds, these exact images are repeated again and again throughout the film. Superficially, these shots attest to the technological experiences of modernity and progress: they are colorful, industrial, and in motion. Fundamentally, however, they signal the absence—rather than the presence—of reform. The technology may have changed, but the underlying challenges Tehran residents face remain the same.

Tehran Has No More Pomegranates continues its examination of historical reforms through Amir Kabir, a nineteenth-century reformist whom Naser al-Din Shah appointed as prime minister in 1848. The film introduces Amir Kabir, like the other nineteenth- and twentieth-century figures, through the found documentary. A voiceover declares, "The Shah appointed the reformist Amir Kabir as prime minster. He opposed court bribery and corruption. He condemned all kinds of crimes: stabbing and lewdness." Often considered Iran's first reformist, Kabir sought to modernize and Westernize the country while working within the existing monarchal framework. Massoud Bakhshi uses his discovery of Amir Kabir's reformist efforts in the found documentary as a springboard for investigating reforms in contemporary Tehran. The results of his investigation, Bakhshi states, are as follows: "I discovered that reforms are still widespread in Tehran. Today the state reforms trees, grass, parks, and male facial hair." This statement, though humorous, functions as a biting critique. The contemporary Iranian government is only interested in superficial changes that fall far short of the systematic reforms promised by Mohammad Khatami, such as rule of law, civil society, and religious democracy.

The film's references to Amir Kabir and to Tehran's superficial reforms contextualize the reformist movement of Khatami's presidency within a broader conversation about reform in Iran. In particular, these references evoke Khatami's predecessor, Akbar Hashemi Rafsanjani, who served as president between 1989 and 1997, a period popularly known as the "Period of Construction," following the country's devastating losses during the eight-year Iran-Iraq War. Consequently, many of Hashemi Rafsanjani's efforts focused on the privatization of Iran's economy in an effort to spur development. Although his platform was "economically liberal," his noneconomic reforms were philosophically traditional.[8] He attempted to control bodily surfaces, including facial hair and women's dress. Despite intensifying, rather than lessening, state control over freedom of expression, Hashemi Rafsanjani believed that his policies continued the legacy of Amir Kabir's earlier reformist efforts. As an avid supporter of Amir Kabir, Hashemi Rafsanjani even wrote a biography, entitled *Amir Kabir yā qehremān-e mobārezeh bā este'mār* (Amir Kabir or the hero of the battle with imperialism, 1968). By drawing on the elements of Hashemi Rafsanjani's political career, Bakhshi intentionally positions Khatami's reformist efforts as a continuation of the previous presidency. In doing so, Bakhshi creates the same sense of untimeliness that haunts Bani-Etemad's *Ruzegār-e mā*... (Our times..., 2002).

As *Tehran Has No More Pomegranates* cuts from this critique of Khatami and Hashemi Rafsanjani back to the found documentary, the voiceover notes, "But Amir's reforms didn't satisfy the corrupted court so they killed him." At this moment, the pseudodocumentary film breaks, the magnetic film spins meaninglessly in its projector, and the viewer is left with the jarring sound of the flapping film—an eerie meditation on both Amir's death and the failure of reform. By juxtaposing nineteenth-century reform with the stark absence of true contemporary reform, Massoud Bakhshi establishes reform in Iranian history as a cyclical process that arguably produces no deeper impact than superficial appearances. Facial hair growth is policed and highways are widened, but meaningful change remains elusive.

Despite being more or less a complete history of modern Iran, Bakhshi's film mentions the revolutions that radically altered the country's political systems but does not develop a true discussion of any of them. For example, the found documentary that forms the basis of the film's first section ends right as the revolution of 1978–1979 is happening. Bakhshi's choice to acknowledge but never analyze the revolutions instead positions reform as the true system of change around which Iran's modern history *revolves*. At the same time, the film's representation of the lack of progress of nineteenth-century reform and its ultimate collapse suggests reform as an unsustainable and ineffective means of enacting change. Furthermore, the film's juxtaposition of two of the cycles of reform prompts viewers to reflect on the fate of contemporary reforms, positing that these reforms are also doomed.

The film's critique of progress, especially within the context of historical reform, continues into the twentieth century. The documentary voice notes the rise of Reza Khan, his overthrow of the Qajar Dynasty in 1925, and the subsequent establishment of the Pahlavi regime. Images of the Pahlavi military rigidly marching accompany this narrative and are interspersed with images of the Qajar military in procession, which the viewer has already seen.

Splicing together these chronologically disparate images forces the viewer to note the similarities between them. The technology of the Pahlavi military may be more advanced, but the basic structure of the two military processions remains strikingly similar. In the Iranian context, nineteenth-century reforms are aligned with Westernization, and in the twentieth century Westernization means modernization and access to new technologies. However, with scenes like this one, *Tehran Has No More Pomegranates* questions the impact of this technology on Iran, especially in the context of structural change.

This discussion of nineteenth-, twentieth-, and twenty-first-century reform efforts also allows viewers to better understand the film's alternative title. During the opening sequence, the film first introduces itself as طهران/تهران, or *Teheran/Tehran*, and moments later offers تهران انار ندارد, or *Tehran Has No More Pomegranates*, as its title. Although the director ultimately favors the latter, the former is in some ways more provocative and instructive. By capturing the tension between the nineteenth and twenty-first centuries, the alternate title acts as a metaphor for reform both during and between these periods. The title *Teheran/Tehran* (طهران/تهران) plays with the spelling of the capital city. Although both spellings are pronounced exactly the same in Persian, the first spelling (طهران) is an older spelling with Arabic origins. The newer spelling (تهران) gained wider acceptance in the late nineteenth century, during roughly the same period as the Qajar reforms.[9]

The film posits the orthographical change as analogous to the reforms of both the nineteenth and the twentieth/twenty-first centuries: a superficial spelling change has no impact on pronunciation or meaning. This change on the surface brings to mind the film's critique of contemporary reform: trees are planted, the grass is greener, and facial hair is policed, but nothing truly changes. Later in the film Bakhshi describes contemporary Tehran as the "age of *false* construction," underscoring the futility of these surface reforms. Bakhshi's description also positions the current era in stark contrast to the era of mass construction that followed increased oil revenues in the 1960s and 1970s. This statement is followed by images of half-completed buildings and bulldozers aimlessly pushing around dirt piles. These shots recall similar images in both Bani-Etemad's *Under the Skin of the City* and Kiarostami's *Ta'm-e gilās* (Taste of cherry, 1997). Once again we see that the reformist aesthetic is invested in the city of Tehran as a dynamic space that accommodates and represents the sense of futility against which the reformist movement initially reacted and to which it would ultimately fall powerless.

The first portion of the film ends as the revolution of 1978–1979 unfolds at the end of the found documentary. The film crew of *Tehran Has No More Pomegranates* decides to shoot a "realistic" image of contemporary Tehran. Establishing a fair vantage point for shooting this realistic image, however, proves challenging for the crew. As Bakhshi notes, tongue in cheek, "Tehran has thousands of extraordinary subjects, each worthy of an entire film!" Following careful consideration, the film crew determines that the two most important institutions in Tehran today are the law and the motorcycle phenomenon (*padideh-ye motorsiklet*). Law is particularly relevant to the discussion of reform in the film. Viewers, especially at the time of *Tehran Has No More Pomegranates*'s release in 2007, would immediately recognize the film's reference to the law as a gesture toward Mohammad Khatami's promise to follow the "rule of law" (*hokumat-e qānun*) in Iran. Bakhshi states, "Tehran is much more law and democracy abiding than ever before," but his stress on the word *besiyār* (much) adds a hint of sarcasm to his claim. A song plays in the background: its lyrics, "Here, everything is shaking, trembling, shaking," underscore the ironic sentiment in Bakhshi's statement. At this point in the film, the soundtrack—both the narrative voice and the music—destabilizes the effectiveness of Khatami's promise to bring the rule of law to Iran.

Bakhshi continues to call into question Iran's contentious relationship with democratic reforms through his continued documentation of the filmmaking process. In the second portion of the film, the cameraman suggests that the crew film the Tehran cityscape. In response to this suggestion Bakhshi replies with glib, tongue in cheek humor, "I, as a respecter of democracy, had to accept this idea." The cameraman's request is followed by one from "the young photographer," who uses "democracy as a pretext" to request permission to shoot portraits of Tehran's citizens; once again, Bakhshi must "acquiesce" to this demand. The images that follow both of these requests—presumably images captured by the cameraman and the photographer—reflect the paradoxes of contemporary Tehran. Shots of wild traffic in Tehran appear alongside scenes from the *zurkhāneh*. An old man uses a stick and mallet to gin cotton as a bright yellow train passes behind him, drawing the viewer's attention to the tension between modern and traditional forces in Iranian society. Bakhshi makes a significant statement by citing his "respect for democracy" as the driving force for producing these images of modernization and tradition in direct conflict. In doing so, *Tehran Has No More Pomegranates* questions the place of democracy in this polarized system. Is Khatami's construct of democracy capable of reconciling these disparate forces? Does it even attempt to do so? Whereas *Tehran Has No More Pomegranates* merely alludes to these questions, as we will see in a later section, Kiosk's music video "Speed of Love" forcefully answers them.

By critiquing the terms that Mohammad Khatami introduced into popular discourse in Iran, *Tehran Has No More Pomegranates* directly challenges Khatami's reformist movement. Abstractions developed by Khatami, such as civil society, are shown to be out of touch with the concrete problems plaguing the contemporary megalopolis of Tehran. In this sense, *Tehran Has No More Pomegranates* applies a methodology that is similar to the methodology used in Rakhshan Bani-Etemad's *Under the Skin of the City*. In both films, the city of Tehran offers sociopolitical, economic, and geographic problems that the reformist movement is either unable or unwilling to address. Whereas Bani-Etemad's film focuses on Tehran's north-south divide and the subsequent socioeconomic problems this divide creates, Bakhshi's film spotlights Tehran's epic density dilemma. Specifically, Bakhshi draws our attention to the earthquake experts predict will devastate Tehran at some point in the near future. Bakhshi examines both Tehran's density dilemma and the earthquake predictions within the context of Khatami's terminology. In doing so, Bakhshi applies the basic mechanisms of the montage theory that determines the film's visuality in order to encourage the viewer to question the expansive reach of Khatami's proposed reforms.

Massoud Bakhshi and his film crew conclude that Tehran's most pressing concern, "alongside of civil society, democracy, and these kinds of things" is the problem of density. The film defines density as "the space that one occupies in Tehran!" and it determines that this distribution of space differs for every citizen in the city. To illustrate this difference, the film returns to an earlier example that compares a citizen from north Tehran to a citizen from south Tehran. Babak *jān* is a London-born construction manager living with his wife in a 600-square-meter apartment in north Tehran. Thus, according to the film's density definition, Babak and his wife each have a density of 300 square meters. In contrast, *Āqā* Jafar, a Kurdish employee at a brick factory, lives in south Tehran with his wife and two children in a 25-square-meter apartment, so accordingly each member in his family has a density of 5 square meters. This comparison suggests that special distribution disparities are geographically predetermined, a conclusion supported by Bakhshi's claim that "truths about south and north Tehran" are revealed "just by changing the location of the camera." The accompanying shots demonstrate the differences in density that distinguish Tehran's cityscape as determined by the city's north-south divide.

Bakhshi slyly interweaves his analysis of Tehran's density problem within the context of Khatami's reformist movement. He configures the uneven distribution of space alongside of Khatami's terminology (civil society and democracy), and this formulation initially appears to lend credence to the abstract ideas of the reformist movement. However, by delivering compelling visual evidence and materiality to fully develop the problem of density, Bakhshi decisively elevates this problem above such abstractions as civil society and democracy. Bakhshi further renders these issues inaccessible to the viewer throughout the film, while concretely reinforcing Tehran's physical and spatial problems (i.e., density). Bakhshi further trivializes the reformist terminology by following "civil society" and "democracy" with *va in harf-hā* (and such words). This dismissive term marginalizes Khatami's political agenda. Placing density alongside civil society and democracy forces us to reflect on the impact, or lack thereof, that the reformist movement has had on the physicality of Tehran and the true day-to-day life of its citizens.

When Massoud Bakhshi announces that civil society and democracy are among Tehran's most pressing concerns, it is with a deep sense of irony. Bakhshi has intentionally structured his film around the social and economic disparities that are, for most Tehranis, far more urgent. One of the film's most persistent characters is a man named Jafar *khān*, a recent immigrant to Tehran, who replies *nārāzi* (unsatisfied) during all of the film's polls about the city's current state. Eventually, as the film nears its conclusion, the crew asks Jafar *khān* why he is dissatisfied with everything. Significantly, Bakhshi visually anchors the scene around a trashcan on which the motto *shahr-e mā, khāneh-ye mā* (Our city, our home) has ironically been stenciled. In one of the film's most lucid moments, Jafar *khān* explains:

> I have been in Tehran for three months. I have seen what happens in the parks and on the streets. I have seen the poor. They are without money and homeless. The homeless are forced to sleep in parks. They have nowhere else to go. But the policemen attack them and beat them, which they don't even do to dogs. These are human beings. . . . Everyone is human. Yes, we are hungry and homeless, but we are humans.

As Jafar *khān* makes this plea, the film switches to scenes from a Qajar-era film that play first forward and then backward. Jafar *khān*'s speech, juxtaposed with the Qajar images (forward and reverse), suggests that Tehran's urban problems are historically grounded and have been overlooked and unattended by successive regimes and political movements, including the reformist movement, and that no resolution to these problems is forthcoming.

The film's final critique of reform is similarly related to Tehran's physical problems; however, in this case, *Tehran Has No More Pomegranates* examines the geological (rather than socioeconomic) structures of the city. Bakhshi claims that his crew "peered under the surface of the city" and discovered a "menace... a horrible threat." According to the film, experts predict that an earthquake will devastate Tehran in the near future, destroying 65 percent of the city's buildings. The film casts this predicted earthquake into a historical cycle, likening it to the earthquakes that devastated the city of Rudbar in 1990 and Bam in 2003.[10] By citing "past mistakes" as the reason for the forecasted earthquake's vast destruction, the film powerfully positions the cyclical nature of the country's geological history as a metaphor for the country's cyclical socioeconomic history. To further this comparison, Bakhshi intentionally chooses language that mimics a thirteenth-century quotation by Qazvini about Tehran. Bakhshi says that postearthquake Tehran will "return to its origins." The film's finale epitomizes this idea of stripping away the façade of modernity in order to reconnect with the city's true roots. The last scene depicts the discovery of a tiny pomegranate—the kind of pomegranate that Tehran no longer has—outside of the city.

Tehran Has No More Pomegranates ties the predicted earthquake to the reformist movement when it concludes: "After the earthquake, democracy, reformist movements (*jonbesh-e eslāhāt*), and civil society will no longer exist." The powerful, jarring still images that follow this statement depict the vast human suffering that followed the 2003 Bam earthquake. In the context of such suffering, abstract concepts like democracy, civil society, and reform are out of touch with humanity's most basic survival needs. The reformist movement's philosophical promises will thus hold little relevancy or urgency in a postapocalyptic Tehran. At first, the incongruous placement of the reformist movement in this world can be viewed as humorous and even amusing; on closer inspection, however, the incongruities force the viewer to consider seriously the reformist movement's inability to address the foundational (and even geological) issues teeming just beneath Tehran's surface. Significantly, the earthquake ends the film's history of Tehran at the same time that it ends the film's critique of the reformist movement. Just as the film begins with reform, so too does it end with reform, and this fact is crucial to establishing reform as an informing logic within the film's structure.

FILM ARCHIVES AND ONLINE VIDEOS

At the same time that the film concerns itself with the history and legacy of political reform, it is also acutely aware of the reforms and transformations that are born from the relationship between certain films and the reformist movement. *Tehran Has No More Pomegranates* is a metadocumentary: a documentary about documentary filmmaking. The director, Massoud Bakhshi, narrates the film as production notes for an incomplete film, and in the process creates the film that we are watching. *Tehran Has No More Pomegranates* constantly refers to its own creativity and its technological processes. Throughout the film, we see shots of the crew organizing their equipment or watch the crew in the very act of filming. Bakhshi employs the same method of juxtaposing contradicting sounds and images to draw attention, often ironically, to the film crew's onscreen presence as he does to draw attention to the contradictions between reformist agendas and the reality of these reforms. For example, in one scene, we hear a sound bite of the modernist poet Forugh Farrokhzad reading a famous line of her poetry: "va in manam / zani tanhā / dar āstāneh-ye fasl-e sard" (And this is I / a lonely woman / at the threshold of a cold season). As Farrokhzad reads her lines, a woman appears alone onscreen, peering out of a window. However, the bright sunlight is casting a shadow on the wall below her window, creating a perfect silhouette of the film crew (figure 5.1). With the film crew and the bright sunshine, the woman is neither alone nor at the threshold of a cold season; the visual images effectively contradict the stated reality.

In addition to showing crewmembers on film, *Tehran Has No More Pomegranates* often shows the technology that it uses, including frequent allusions to 35 mm film. Film is loaded, repaired, watched, played back, and transported in canisters. All of these images serve as reminders that *Tehran Has No More Pomegranates* is in fact a *film*, created and preserved in celluloid. *Tehran Has No More Pomegranates* also readily identifies itself as a film that is composed, in part, by other films. Massoud Bakhshi's composite film is achieved through the inclusion of a "documentary" that the film crew allegedly finds in the archives of the Ministry of Culture and Islamic Guidance. Bakhshi's use of this kind of archival material positions the film within the global tradition of found footage, an avant-garde trend that initially gained momentum in the 1960s.

FILM ARCHIVES AND ONLINE VIDEOS

FIGURE 5.1. The film crew is visible in a shot from Massoud Bakhshi's *Tehran Has No More Pomegranates*. Frame enlargement.

Although the found documentary in Bakhshi's film is overlaid with a narrative voice that lends it authority, authenticity, and continuity, the informed viewer quickly identifies the images that establish the documentary as visual traces of Iran's cinematic history. The film features scenes from Mirza Ebrahim Akkasbashi Sani al-Saltaneh's early camerawork with the Qajar court (1900), Ardeshir Irani and Abdolhossein Sepanta's *Dokhtar-e Lor* (The Lor girl, 1933), Ahmad Faruqi Qajar's *Tehrān-e emruz* (Iran today, 1962), Kamran Shirdel's *Tehrān pāytakht-e Iran ast* (Tehran is the capital of Iran, 1966), Bahram Beyzaie's *Kalāgh* (The crow, 1976), and others. Meanwhile, the voice that narrates the documentary belongs to Nosrat Karimi, a famous actor and filmmaker. Karimi played Aqa Jun on the popular 1976 television show *Dāyi jān Nāpol'on* (My Uncle Napoleon, 1977–1979), which means the sound of his voice is immediately recognizable for Iranian viewers. Therefore, as quickly as the film creates the illusion of a coherent found documentary, it just as quickly destabilizes the unity of these documentary components.

FILM ARCHIVES AND ONLINE VIDEOS

On the topic of found footage, William C. Wees observes that whether films that use archival images "preserve the footage in its original form or present it in new and different ways, they invite us to recognize it *as* found footage, *as* recycled images." He categorizes trends in found footage as constitutive of "collage," a practice separate from mere appropriation. Collage, the use of montage in the context of found footage, "probes, highlights, contrasts," while "appropriation accepts, levels, homogenizes."[11] By assembling disparate archival images and sounds under the auspices of a single documentary, *Tehran Has No More Pomegranates* initially seems to approximate the latter, which creates a sense of leveling or homogenization. However, by splicing the found documentary with contemporary shots of Tehran, the film ultimately achieves Wees's notion of collage. This technique, creating filmic unity and then tearing it apart, demonstrates how celluloid film is constantly being reformed and reshaped within *Tehran Has No More Pomegranates*. Significantly, Bakhshi shows the process of film being cut and manipulated onscreen, reminding us that film can be formed and reformed, and old images can therefore be preserved and at the same time generate new meanings in different contexts.

The particular sounds and images that Bakhshi preserves in his film are especially important because they establish a trajectory within which the director positions his own film. The two scenes that Bakhshi repeats most often in *Tehran Has No More Pomegranates* come from Mirza Ebrahim Akkasbashi Sani al-Saltaneh's early camerawork with the Qajar court (1900) and Ardeshir Irani and Abdolhossein Sepanta's *The Lor Girl*. These two films represent two of the most significant moments in Iran's early cinematic history. The grainy moving images shot by Akkasbashi depict Mozaffar al-Din Shah's visit to Belgium in 1900, and scholars generally agree that they are the first moving images shot by an Iranian. Akkasbashi, whose name references the fact that he was a photographer for the Qajar court, was responsible for bringing film technology to Iran, with the support and encouragement of Mozaffar al-Din Shah, the son of Naser al-Din Shah. Mozaffar al-Din Shah shared his father's interest in technology and reform. Negar Mottahedeh argues that these images, which were taken during a flower ceremony, emphasize the exchange of glances between the Iranian men of the Qajar court and European women. Since its inception, Iranian cinema has been grounded in the tension between engendered gazes.[12] But these images also reinforce the idea that late Qajar reform efforts were grounded in Western technology.

The second film to which *Tehran Has No More Pomegranates* devotes significant screen time is the 1932 film *The Lor Girl*. This film is significant as the first Persian-language talkie film. As such, it marked the first time that Iranian audiences could relate to the characters on a linguistic level and hear them speak Persian.[13] *Tehran Has No More Pomegranates* makes ready use of *The Lor Girl*'s sound capabilities. Multiple times during his film, Bakhshi plays a sound bite of *The Lor Girl*'s main female character, Golnar, screaming "Jafar," layering this cry over a diverse set of images from contemporary Tehran. The film's politicized content was also an innovation at the time. *The Lor Girl* tells the story of Jafar, a young bureaucrat who is sent to Lorestan, a particularly unyielding province at the time. He falls in love with a teahouse attendant named Golnar, who is held captive by a band of thieves. Jafar defeats the bandits, and he and Golnar escape to India, fleeing the chaos of Iran. On learning of Reza Shah's efforts to modernize the country, the couple returns to Tehran. Hamid Reza Sadr argues that *The Lor Girl*, through its plot, location, and characters, encompasses many of Reza Shah's reforms. For example, Jafar's challenges in Lorestan parallel those of Reza Shah, whose first course of action was to centralize power and break up the tribal system that governed much of Iran. Similarly, Sadr views Golnar's arrival into the city as an echo of Reza Shah's "attempt to bring modernity through secularization, industrialization, and the nuclearization of the family."[14]

By referencing Akkasbashi's early moving images and *The Lor Girl*, *Tehran Has No More Pomegranates* positions itself within a tradition of innovation. At the same time, the film makes an important observation about the relationship between sociopolitical reform and cinematic reform. The advent of Iranian cinema and the invention of talkie technology in the Iranian context occurred alongside two of the most significant reform efforts of the early twentieth century. Although scholars have argued that revolution, and specifically the revolution of 1978–1979, has radically altered the course of Iranian cinema, it is reform, a more subtle discourse, that catalyzed some of the most profound changes in Iranian cinema. *Tehran Has No More Pomegranates* focuses on reform and reconfigures the history of Iranian cinema to favor a reformist orientation.

Tehran Has No More Pomegranates places itself at this juncture between cinematic and political reform movements. It focuses on the history of political reform at the same time that it plays with the possibilities that come with restructuring actual film. Significantly, despite the rise of video and digital film, 35 mm film remains Bakhshi's medium of choice.[15] With *Tehran Has No More Pomegranates*, Bakhshi offers an alternative to the digital push, and he revives old-fashioned celluloid film as young and experimental. Specifically, by combining archival footage with new footage, the film creates new contexts and, as a result, new meanings. Bakhshi literally re-forms old films, a process that we witness playing out before us throughout the film. This methodology accords with Mohammad Khatami's reformist movement, which similarly sought to recontextualize (i.e., within the Islamic Republic) the historical cycles of reform that began in the nineteenth century.

The film's far-reaching appeal is one of its most significant contributions to documentary filmmaking in Iran. As the first documentary to be shown widely in theaters since the revolution of 1978–1979, the film performed surprisingly well at the box office.[16] The film's successful showing coupled with its attempt to reshape the previously restrictive limits of documentary filmmaking opens the genre up to possibilities that filmmakers like Rakhshan Bani-Etemad never saw. Whereas Bani-Etemad attempts overcome the limited reach of documentary films by bringing elements of documentary filmmaking to narrative film, Bakhshi physically reshapes the conventions of the genre by juxtaposing a sundry set of contemporary and archival images and laying them alongside an equally diverse soundtrack. The effect of this methodology is an aesthetic that is as humorous as it is critical, and one that actively resists the informing logics that normally define documentary filmmaking. The success of *Tehran Has No More Pomegranates* in 2007 ultimately speaks to the momentum that the reformist aesthetic possessed even after Khatami's presidency and its corresponding liberal cultural policies came to an end.

The reformist movement might have been over, but its impact on Iranian cinema was not.

FILM ARCHIVES AND ONLINE VIDEOS

POLITICAL PIZZA

The historical-political context that *Tehran Has No More Pomegranates* examines and the methodologies it creates developed coevally with certain innovations in Iran's media ecology. Specifically, the music video "Love of Speed," performed by the underground band Kiosk, directed by Ahmad Kiarostami, and released on YouTube in 2007, shares the film's aesthetic concerns and its critique of Mohammad Khatami's reformist movement. Whereas *Tehran Has No More Pomegranates* self-reflexively draws attention to the tangible canisters of celluloid film that preserve its images, "Love of Speed" is a digital video whose images and sounds formlessly wander through infinite Internet space, tagged and shared on various social networking sites and available to nearly everyone. Despite these differences in form and access, a real, if unexpected, relationship exists between the two works. Elements of the reformist aesthetic that I have described throughout this book inextricably bind them together. By closely examining the music video "Love of Speed," one can more precisely delineate the nature of this relationship, and it becomes clear that reform as an aesthetic movement continues to evolve even though Khatami's presidency has ended. Further, this relationship between philosophical film and the products of youth culture establishes reform, rather than revolution, as a new model for the analysis of cultural productivity in the Islamic Republic over the last twenty years.

Despite scholars' increased willingness to consider music videos as a medium worthy of serious analysis, the existing framework for this study is limited in scope.[17] These works draw almost exclusively on the American music video tradition, and the critical questions that they ask about race, class, and gender privilege American and Western European values. These studies often position themselves vis-à-vis capitalism and suggest that they are reacting against the idea that music videos are just by-products of capitalism, and they offer the possibility that music videos can resist capitalist models. They work under the assumption that music videos are tied to the music industry, and that the transmission of music videos goes in tandem with the exchange of capital. Kiosk's "Love of Speed" allows for the expansion this scholarly

FILM ARCHIVES AND ONLINE VIDEOS

frame by accounting for music videos that draw on non-Western traditions and that function as products in a global transmission. At the same time, an analysis of "Love of Speed" enables a preliminary theorization on those music videos that emerge from nonindustrialized underground and repressed music scenes that are not tied to the same capitalist models that dominate the American popular music industry. Like the examples in many of the scholarly accounts of music videos, Kiosk's video is deeply political, but the marriage of lyrical and visual elements in the video requires the contextualization of trends within Iran's modern cultural and intellectual history.

"Love of Speed" was the first single off of Kiosk's second album by the same title, released in 2007, a year after the band members left Iran and settled in the United States and Canada. Kiosk formed underground in 2003 at a time when the underground music scene in Iran was reaching its height. However, Mahmoud Ahmadinejad's election in 2005 marked the end of Khatami's moderate era, and the band left the country a year later to pursue their music with fewer restrictions, which in turn allowed them to pursue greater social and political critique in their music. The underground music scene in Iran, like the film industry, is very much tied to notions of reform and Khatami's reforms in particular. The policies that emerged after the revolution of 1978–1979 drastically restructured the music industry in Iran. Female singers were banned from performing in public, and all forms of music deemed "Western" were similarly forbidden. These policies were based on statements by Ayatollah Khomeini but were codified and implemented by Khatami's Ministry of Culture and Islamic Guidance during the Islamic Republic's first decade. Just as with Khatami's beliefs regarding cinema, one can detect a significant transformation in Khatami's beliefs about music between his tenure as minister of culture and his presidency.

Music, like film, benefited from the liberal cultural policies that emerged following Khatami's 1997 election. In 1998, the ban on Western-style pop music was lifted, and Laudan Nooshin argues that one can trace the origins of the current underground music scene in Iran to that moment when the ban was lifted.[18] This policy change profoundly restructured how Iranian society interacted with music. Most significantly, the ban's end marks the demarcation point at which Iranians went from only being consumers of Western pop music to also being producers of this music in their own right. Legalizing

Western music production significantly increased the number of bands in Iran. Nooshin credits the rise of active musicians to the liberal cultural atmosphere fostered by Khatami's presidency and the resulting discourses of civil society.[19] All of these factors have created "an unregulated grass-roots popular music movement," a new phenomenon for a country where pop music had previously been limited to government or foreign sources.[20]

However, like filmmakers, musicians in Iran need permits (*mojavvez*) from the Ministry of Culture and Islamic Guidance in order to distribute their music or perform it in public. Although the new policies in 1998 meant that groups that performed certain kinds of Western music could conceivably receive permits, the reality was that few did, and that fact remains true today.[21] Generally, the pop bands that have succeeded in obtaining permits from the Ministry of Culture and Islamic Guidance perform songs that are almost indistinguishable *musically* from their counterparts in the Los Angeles–based Iranian expatriate pop music industry but are, *lyrically*, deeply religious and draw on traditional Shi'i motifs and images. As a result, Iran's underground music scene is inherently political, because bands engage in "musical acts of resistance" every time they publicly perform music that is unsanctioned by the government, regardless of whether their lyrics contain a social or political critique. At the same time, the current underground music scene and its many frustrations are tied to Khatami. As Nooshin notes, his election created momentum for the creation of a popular music industry in Iran, founded on the hope that Khatami's reforms would allow music that had begun underground to come to the surface. However, that possibility was never realized, and by 2007, when "Love for Speed" was released, the underground music scene in Iran had come to a head and had nowhere to go.

The music video "Love of Speed" powerfully captures both the personal frustrations of underground musicians and the disillusionment of Iranian society as a whole as it comes to terms with the end of both Khatami's presidency and moderate reform in the country. As a form, music videos must reconcile the various layers (musical, lyrical, and visual) that they comprise, making them especially well-suited to representing the various levels of concern about the reformist movement's legacy after Khatami's presidency. In her groundbreaking study of music video as a distinct genre, Carol Vernallis explains that music videos create a multitude of complex meanings by establishing give-and-take between sound and image. Music videos are relatively short, because at the time of their inception they were in competition with one another for airtime on limited venues, like specialized television stations.[22] Consequently, these temporal limitations, together with the interplay of sound and image, profoundly affect a music video's narrative abilities.

Vernallis identifies debates in the field about whether music videos function according to narrative, like some movies or television shows, or whether they act as "postmodern pastiche that actually gains energy from defying narrative conventions." Vernallis argues that attempting to examine music videos through the lenses of other forms and genres fails to capture the rich meanings that emerge from the collision of the various elements that form the basis of a music video. Instead, Vernallis argues that videos take shape according to the song's form, which favors "episodic" or "cyclical" rather than sequential direction.[23]

Vernallis's model is a useful tool in the comprehensive analysis of Kiosk's music video "Love of Speed." The video cohesively critiques the reformist movement, a critique that defies the conventions of narrative, but not in a self-reflexive, postmodern way. Instead, the video's lyrics and images generate a system of contradictions and playful suspense that positions Khatami's reformist movement in the context of a larger set of contradictions that define urban life in Iran. By positioning reform as just another urban problem, Kiosk's music video operates in a manner similar to Massoud Bakhshi's *Tehran Has No More Pomegranates*.

Through its lyrics and images, "Love of Speed" establishes Iran, and Tehran specifically, as a site of paradox, a place where contradictions live in a functional—if somewhat unsettling—harmony. The video's first few moments capture the unique tension between opposing forces in contemporary Tehran, at the same time that the opening scene demonstrates the profound connection between word and image in the video. The song's countdown, *seh, do, yek, boro* (three, two, one, go), coincides with a counter on a traffic light, and traffic, which is an important motif throughout the video, begins as the song begins. The framing of this opening scene depends on the traffic coming from the right side of the frame and a mosque that fills the left side of the frame (figure 5.2).

FIGURE 5.2. The opening shot of Kiosk's music video "Love of Speed" balances the tensions of modern urban life. Frame enlargement.

The video visually achieves balance by creating tension between the traditional and contemporary elements that create the Tehran cityscape. Whereas the mosque architecturally and religiously represents tradition, traffic is one of the quintessential markers of life in a contemporary metropolis, and traffic lights operate as the mechanism that systemizes and regulates vehicular movement. The tradition-modernity theme is picked up and repeated as the video continues. We see shots of different kinds of city traffic, including busy streets, narrow alleys, and big highways. The video creates visual interest as it pans from undistinguished highway traffic (that could exist anywhere) to a bright digital billboard advertising BMWs, before finally settling on a huge neon, hillside side that resembles the Hollywood sign but reads *yā Hossein*.[24] Once again, we see the juxtaposition of tradition and modernity in these iconic symbols of religious and urban life. .

The song's first words, which begin after the instrumental introduction that ends with the *yā Hossein* sign, underscore the juxtaposition of tradition and modernity as a central theme for the song and video: "qodrat-e 'eshq o 'eshq-e qodrat / modernitiyeh yā sonnat" (the power of love and the love of power / modernity or tradition). The arrival of sung words also introduces the video's unique way of performing its lyrics. Throughout the music video, the lyrics are lip-synched by people on the streets of Tehran, rather than by the band, Kiosk.[25] Lip-synching is a standard, though not uniform, convention in the music video genre. In its most basic form, lip-synching seeks to create (or underscore) a relationship between word and image. Lip-synching is also a means through which the performer visualizes the production of voice and claims authorship of the work. Kiosk's video subverts this convention and plays off of viewer expectation, using this subversion to heighten the relationship between word and image. Because the body does not match the voice, we are more aware of the image and thus better able to sense the disconnection between the individual we see and the voice we hear.

The video's lip-synching technique, drawing on the relationship between the lyrics and the people on the streets of Tehran, positions the person who performs the lyrics as representative of the lyrics being performed. Like the montage in *Tehran Has No More Pomegranates*, the mismatched lip-synching in "Love of Speed" forces the viewer to confront these disjointed mash-ups and to consider further their layers of meaning. The delivery of the song's first lyrics, mentioned previously, establishes this system through a particularly significant juxtaposition. The song opens with a man who is clearly not Arash Sobhani, the lead singer of Kiosk, performing the words "qodrat-e 'eshq o 'eshq-e qodrat / modernitiyeh yā sonnat" (the power of love and the love of power / modernity or tradition). Instead of Sobhani, it is a cleric, standing on the street with a huge work of graffiti behind him, who sings these words. The cleric's performance instantly brings a new layer of meaning to the lyrics. The lyrical structure takes "the power of love" and inverts it into the "love of power." The cleric's onscreen presence emphasizes the powerful role religious institutions play in Iran, with the lyrics ("the love of power") calling into question the motivation and legitimacy of the Islamic Republic.

By asking, "modernity or tradition?" the opening couplet's second line propels the discussion of power into a temporal dimension The cleric's onscreen performance suggests, perhaps somewhat ironically, that tradition and modernity exist side by side in the Islamic Republic. The cleric represents a traditional force in Iranian society, but in the video he is singing along to an underground rock song and standing next to graffiti. Nevertheless, there is uneasiness in his performance, which makes it especially jarring and introduces the idea that perhaps tradition and modernity cannot comfortably coexist in Iranian society—an idea that is repeated in the song's refrain and its critique of the reformist movement.

Throughout the music video, just as in the first performance, the interplay between word and image is as playful and humorous as it is critical. For example, at one point in the video, Kiosk claims, "doktor-e qalb nemikhāim, jarāh-e fak o bini" (we don't want cardiologist, just facelifts and nose jobs). On the surface, this lyric pokes fun at the fact Iran that has become a world capital for cosmetic surgery, with young, upper-class Iranian women increasingly opting for nose jobs.[26] The two women who perform these lyrics epitomize the type of Tehrani woman who puts a lot of effort into her appearance. This moment in the video is representative of the humor that runs throughout the work but also contains a serious critique. The lyric highlights the fact that Iranian society favors superficial transformations (plastic surgery) rather than addressing the heart of the problem (cardiology). This preference is inscribed onto the bodies of women, both within the video and on the actual streets of Tehran.[27]

The lip-synching methodology created in "Love of Speed" establishes a relationship between word and image that is central to the video's successful critique of the reformist movement. Carol Vernallis argues that lip-synching participates in a "history of articulations" that every music video contains.[28] Professionally produced music videos typically feature a vast number of articulation points. First, for the song's production, singers and musicians lay separate vocal and instrumental tracks; sound engineers mix and add new layers; and producers and editors cut and reorganize. As the music video is filmed, the song is played on set and performers react to it and add new interpretations. Then the video footage is edited and reorganized before the song is laid on top of the images. In effect, the song is synthesized and reinterpreted multiple times through multiple layers.

The most important point in this history for "Love of Speed" is the moment at which performers react to and interpret the song's lyrics while on the set of the music video. With everyday people—rather than the band members—performing the song lyrics, we witness a wide range of reactions and interpretations that do not necessarily belong to the band. This feature of the video is most apparent during the song's refrain: "demukrāsi-ye dini, pitzā-ye qormeh sabzi" (religious democracy, *qormeh sabzi* pizza).[29] Several times in the video, the performers break into laughter when they say this line.

The performers are reacting to the idea of a "pitzā-ye qormeh sabzi" (*qormeh sabzi* pizza), which combines a traditional Iranian dish and pizza, and the inability of the nonprofessional actors to maintain a straight face marks the incongruity of these two dishes. The ridiculousness of *qormeh sabzi* pizza punctuates and accentuates the incongruity of the couplet's first line: "demukrāsi-ye dini" (religious democracy), a more serious concept being evaluated by the song's refrain. The song's lyrical structure recalls the structure of certain genres in the classical Persian poetic tradition, in which the two *mesra*s that form a *bayt*, or couplet, generate unity. In "Love of Speed," there is an equational or analogous relationship between the two terms of the couplet. In the case of the song's refrain, the coupling of religious democracy and *qormeh sabzi* pizza renders the former just as implausible (and undesirable) as the latter. With four simple words, Kiosk destabilizes the notion on which the reformist movement was premised. Khatami's efforts sought to create a religious democracy and introduce democratic ideals into the Islamic Republic's governance. His promise was that Islamic democracy could be created in Iran and that it would be the country's ultimate solution. However, "Love of Speed" casts doubt on that possibility by making a joke of it, and by bringing it down to the same level as a ridiculous food combination.

Released two years after Khatami's presidency ended, the music video's critique of the reformist movement's most basic tenets benefits from the hindsight that allows it to evaluate the effectiveness of Khatami's efforts. In between the lip-synching performances, the music video for "Love of Speed" features shots from the streets of Tehran. Many of these images establish the contradictions that determine contemporary life in Tehran. For example, we see a group of women in *chādor*s entering a mosque, a huge billboard for Dolce and Gabbana, a verse of Nezami's poetry, posters of Jack Nicholson and

Marlon Brando, and a car with an ornate Fatimah sticker in its rear window parked next to a car with the popular "peeing Calvin" decal on its bumper.

However, another category of images depicts Tehran as a troubled and problematic city. There are shots of dilapidated buildings, street violence, poverty, and pollution that echo the images from *Tehran Has No More Pomegranates*. Because the criticism of religious democracy is repeated several times—it is in fact the only lyric repeated in the song—"Love of Speed" situates the reformist movement in the context of Tehran's contradictions and problems. Like *Tehran Has No More Pomegranates* and Rakhshan Bani-Etemad's films, "Love of Speed" positions Tehran as a space where the country's lack of reform is especially visible.

The video's final scene, at twenty seconds long, is significantly longer than any other shot. It shows a man spraying a pile of wet trash with a hose, kicking it, stomping on it, doing anything he can to get it to go down a wired drain in the street. Because the scene stays onscreen for an uncomfortable amount of time, especially after the video has trained the viewer to become accustomed to rapid visual changes, the futility of the man's actions is especially salient. The length of the scene also gives rise to questions about the practicality of the man's efforts. Would it not be easier to pick up the small pile and throw it away? Is a pile of trash even supposed to go down a street drain? This scene is particularly interesting because an almost identical scene exists in Massoud Bakhshi's *Tehran Has No More Pomegranates* (figures 5.3 and 5.4). In both instances, this act functions as a metaphor for what the reformist movement was able to achieve—or not achieve, as the case may be. Two years after Khatami's presidency ended, both the film and the music video posit that the reformist movement achieved very little. Furthermore, the film and music video both posit that these minor achievements could have been more easily accomplished through other means, critiquing Khatami's futile expenditure of energy and resources. As "Love of Speed" and *Tehran Has No More Pomegranates* demonstrate, post-Khatami Iran has been marked by the same sense of futility and hopelessness that afflicted the intellectual classes in the early and mid-1990s.

As the final scene in the music video "Love of Speed" demonstrates, the city of Tehran is a dynamic space that conforms to the contours of the

FIGURE 5.3. AND FIGURE 5.4. Similar shots from Kiosk's music video "Love of Speed" and Bakhshi's *Tehran Has No More Pomegranates*. Frame enlargements.

successes and failures of the reformist movement. The metaphorical and transformational powers of Tehran represent one of the definitive features of the reformist aesthetic, especially in those works created during and after Khatami's election in 1997. "Love of Speed" also furthers our understanding of the relationship between visual media and Tehran, because the music video makes evident the ways in which urban locality can be transmitted globally. Although the music video is visually grounded in the physical streets of Tehran and the national and sociopolitical concerns of post-Khatami Iranian society, the video is also very much a transnational product.

A Los Angeles–based, Iranian-born videographer filmed "Love of Speed." Local Iranians performed the song. The song is the product of an Iranian band whose members currently live in the United States and Canada. Most importantly, the music video was released and continues to be transmitted and accessed on the Internet. In her study of the role of the Internet in the development of Iranian national identity among individuals in exile, Janet Alexanian argues that new media have allowed the Iranian nation "to be imagined as a transnational entity."[30] The "Love of Speed" music video proves that the reformist aesthetic has indeed entered this transnational public sphere. Because Khatami ostensibly sought to free Iran from its global isolation and to initiate global dialogue, the video's Internet location—YouTube—is a fitting place for the artistic responses to the reformist movement. The video "Love for Speed" creates a critical but also complicated and visually exciting picture of contemporary life in Iran that is open and accessible to the world.

Conclusion
IRAN'S CINEMA MUSEUM AND POLITICAL UNREST

Just steps away from the sycamore-lined northern stretches of Vali'asr Street, near the wealthy Tajrish district, the Cinema Museum (Muzeh-ye sinemā) stands impressive in Tehran's historic Ferdows Garden (Bāgh-e ferdaws), among some of the city's most stylish boutiques and cafés. A placard at the entrance informs visitors about the historical significance of the museum's context and surroundings: a garden that dates back to the reign of Mohammad Shah Qajar (1834–1848); the establishment of a school during Reza Khan's rule in the 1930s; efforts to turn the space into an artistic and cultural center in the 1950s; and the Ministry of Culture and Islamic Guidance's control of the building after the revolution of 1978–1979. The museum's location in Ferdows Garden and its description of the site attest to the cultural value of cinema in Iran, or at least to the museum's ambitions for cinema as high art, a designation wherein the film industry is an elite cultural institution that has helped to write the Iranian national narrative. I visited the Cinema Museum during the summer of 2014, and despite the ways in which the museum positions itself with regard to this narrative, the experience of navigating through the building's various hallways and corridors reveals the museum as a distinctly reformist institution.

The placard at the garden's entrance betrays the urgency of situating the museum—and by extension cinema as a whole—historically, an urgency that

CONCLUSION

grows out of the museum's relative youth. The Cinema Museum, the only one of its kind in Iran, was formally established in 1998 and opened its doors to the public in its current location in 2002. Whereas the Ministry of Culture and Islamic Guidance and other government offices house film and video archives in Iran, the Cinema Museum is unique as a public research institution that exhibits the history of the film industry and that archives documents related to Iranian cinema. On entering the museum building, visitors do not encounter an old camera, a film canister, or even a movie poster but, rather, run into another placard, one that describes the circumstances surrounding the founding of the Cinema Museum. The description establishes a cast of characters who helped bring the museum to fruition. These include Mohammad Beheshti, the first director of the Farabi Cinema Foundation, cited as the impetus for the museum's establishment; the deputy of cinematic affairs (Seyfollah Dad); and Mohammad Khatami, who was present at the museum's opening in Ferdows Garden. These three men, in addition to their work supporting the film industry in Iran, are reformist politicians, and the emphasis on their contributions to the museum's establishment positions it as a reformist effort.

The Cinema Museum began its work in 1998, and a ceremony in honor of the museum's establishment was held on May 25, 1998. Just two days earlier, on the one-year anniversary of Khatami's election, celebrations among his supporters had swept through the country. The date of the museum's founding therefore takes on special significance; holding the ceremony almost exactly one year after Khatami's election situated the museum politically within reform, part of the changing cultural sphere. The way in which the museum's founders imagined it also spoke to this positioning. Seyfollah Dad, who had directed Mohammad Khatami's campaign movie just a year earlier, was serving as the deputy for cinematic affairs at this time. At the museum's inauguration Dad stated that "the opening of the museum is an instrumental step in advancing and distinguishing Iranian cinema, and it is an effort to preserve the works, masterpieces, and relics of the history of Iranian cinema."[1] To this end, the museum's founders envisioned not only exhibits that display the material history of Iranian cinema but also a library that preserves its rich textual history. At the time of its founding, the museum had already amassed

CONCLUSION

a collection of 4,000 publications related to Iranian cinema, and one of the chief aims of the museum at this time was to publish reports on these archival materials. The museum endeavored to publish these reports in other languages as well so non-Iranians could also use them.[2] The museum thus envisioned Iranian cinema as a barometer for the success of the Islamic Republic and as a means of diplomacy. This vision of Iranian cinema was radically different from a revolutionary cinema that privileged ideology over aesthetics and anti-imperialism over diplomacy. Within the Cinema Museum, Iranian cinema is not simply at the service of the Islamic Republic as an instrument for propaganda but is, rather, a discursive feature of Iranian culture, battling for authority in art, politics, and ideology.

The Cinema Museum, as a reformist institution, reaffirms reform cinema as a distinct period within the history of Iranian film, one that tracked aesthetic and political changes but also witnessed new institutional support, like the museum. Reform cinema, the inheritor to revolutionary cinema, marked legal changes and new discursive operations within and with regard to the film industry. New laws regulated the oversight of video technology, looser interpretations of censorship codes prevailed, and filmmakers developed new aesthetic strategies to contribute to the discourse of political reform. At the same time, the rise of reformist politics in Iran also facilitated new institutional support for the film industry, including the Cinema Museum. We can see traces of this institutional support in the country's cinema-related periodicals as well. For example, in the first twenty-five years of the Islamic Republic there were forty-four film journals, and seventeen of them (or more than one-third) were established during Khatami's presidency. Similarly, in the eighteen years between the revolution and Khatami's election, 520 books related to cinema were published; in contrast, during the first seven years of Khatami's presidency a staggering 676 books on the topic of cinema were published, more than the total sum of books published in the prior period.[3] The surge in cinema-related publishing during Khatami's presidency was part of the reformist push to foster a free press within the country.[4] The institutional support of cinema that developed in tandem with the rise of political reform, such as new publications and venues for scholarship and the Cinema Museum, reminds us that reform cinema fostered not just aesthetic

CONCLUSION

changes but also the centralization and stabilization of the film industry. The establishment of the multifaceted film culture that we associate with cinema within the Islamic Republic thus grew out of reformist politics and not just the initial enthusiasm of the revolution.

Central to the Cinema Museum's vision of Iranian cinema is the film industry's role as a diplomat, a cultural interlocutor that responds to Mohammad Khatami's call for a "dialogue among civilizations." To this end, the museum's third and largest hall is devoted specifically to displaying the awards that filmmakers have won at international film festivals, including Abbas Kiarostami's Palme d'Or. Iranian film posters from around the world adorn the walls and displays of this hall, which makes it one of the most visually exciting spaces within the museum. Tucked away deep inside the building, this hall is also full of surprises, and when visitors enter, they are immediately greeted by a large poster for *In film nist* (This is not a film, 2011), a movie directed by Jafar Panahi and Mojtaba Mirtahmasb (figure C.1). On this poster, a black-and-white sketch of Panahi holds an iPhone pointed directly at the onlooker, and he seems to be recording us, tracking our every move, and implicating us in some larger project of witnessing. The poster captures the movie's dizzying convergence of technology, politics, and storytelling, and its prominent place within the Cinema Museum is shocking because *This Is Not a Film* was produced underground, without any permits, and it defiantly pushes back on the twenty-year ban on filmmaking (*mahrumiyat az filmsāzi*) that the Islamic Republic's Revolutionary Court issued Panahi in December 2010.

The story of *This Is Not a Film*'s arrival at the 2011 Cannes Film Festival, where it received a special out-of-competition screening, has all the trappings of a Hollywood action movie. *This Is Not a Film* arrived in France on a USB stick that had been hidden in a cake that was sent from Iran to Paris.[5] Mirtahmasb, who had previously served as Panahi's cameraman, shot *This Is Not a Film* on an iPhone as well as the more traditional digital video camera. The movie, filmed over just four days, purportedly examines a day in the life of Panahi in his home as he anxiously awaits the start of his six-year jail sentence. In December 2010 Tehran's Revolutionary Court convicted him of conspiring to commit crimes against national security and of spreading propaganda against the Islamic Republic, charges typically filed against dissident

CONCLUSION

FIGURE C.1   The poster for Jafar Panahi's *This Is Not a Film* in the Cinema Museum in Tehran. Photograph by the author.

artists. He was sentenced to six years in prison and was issued a twenty-year ban on making films, leaving the country, and talking to foreign media. Many people, however, speculate that Panahi's real crime was supporting the efforts of Jonbesh-e sabz (the Green movement), a grassroots initiative calling into question the legitimacy of the 2009 electoral results that guaranteed Mahmoud Ahmadinejad's second term as president.

The Green movement began as a series of mass demonstrations following the announcement of Ahmadinejad's victory, and these demonstrations marked the largest protests in Iran since the revolution thirty years earlier.

CONCLUSION

Supporters of the movement rallied around Mir-Hossein Mousavi and Mehdi Karoubi, the two reformist candidates who had challenged Ahmadinejad. Mohammad Khatami was also originally on the ballot, but he withdrew his candidacy during the campaigning period and endorsed Mousavi in an effort not to split the reformist vote. Following the initial wave of protests, at a time when it seemed like the country was once again on the verge of revolution, Mousavi, Karoubi, and Khatami became the ex post facto leaders of a movement that sought to reform the political system in Iran, especially in light of Ahmadinejad's neoconservative politics and Ayatollah Khamenei's unilateral support of Ahmadinejad's election. Although the Green movement ultimately failed to unite around a single set of goals and eventually broke down, especially after Mousavi and Karoubi were placed under house arrest, the Green movement enjoyed widespread support during the year that followed the 2009 elections, especially among Iran's youth.

Iranian filmmakers, both those based in Iran and those based outside of the country—including Marjane Satrapi, Mohsen Makhmalbaf, Jafar Panahi, and Mohammad Rasoulof—voiced their support of the young protestors. In spring 2010, Panahi and Rasoulof were arrested while shooting a fictional film they were codirecting about the devastating effects of the government's crackdown on personal liberties following the rise of the Green movement. Prior to his arrest, in September 2009, Panahi convinced all of the jurists at the Montreal Film Festival to wear green scarves in support of the Green movement in Iran, and this defiant move, along with the unpermitted movie, was added to the list of charges launched against him during his sentencing. Following his initial sentencing, Panahi was released from jail, but since that time he has been subject to a policy in Iran known as *habs-e ta'ziri* (suspended sentence). This policy means that although Panahi is not currently serving his six-year jail sentence, the courts could send him to prison at any time.

Despite the tenuousness of his situation, Panahi has refused to stay quiet, and he has continued to make movies and conduct interviews with foreign media outlets. *This Is Not a Film* was the first movie that he made following his sentencing, and its arrival at Cannes surprised those familiar with the politics of culture in Iran. Many film critics have been distracted by its unconventional submission to Cannes and the details of Panahi's arrest; however,

CONCLUSION

the movie is ultimately a complicated exploration into what it means to make a film in Iran and how reformist politics have refashioned filmmaking in the country. The title, *This Is Not a Film*, calls film as a category into question, a designation that is particularly important in Iran because Persian does not have a platform-neutral word like "movie." Instead, in Persian all movies are films, even if they only exist in a digital format, like *This Is Not a Film*, which arrived at Cannes on a flash drive rather than in a film canister. The movie's title gestures toward the epistemological limitations of "film" in Persian, and Mirtahmasb and Panahi capitalize on these limitations by suggesting that their movie is not a film and thus not covered in the terms of Panahi's ban on filmmaking. The use of video, and iPhone video footage in particular, allows Mirtahmasb and Panahi to sidestep the governmental approval process, even as they challenge the democratic vision of video that reform cinema helped establish. *This Is Not a Film* is replete with tricks that reveal that as much as digital video technology frees the director, as Kiarostami claimed, video footage in turn deceives the viewer. At one point, Panahi even directly addresses the camera and declares, "I feel like what we are doing here is also a lie."

In *This Is Not a Film*, Mirtahmasb and Panahi use medium as a launching point for a larger inquiry into the nature of filmmaking, accountability, and authority. Storytelling is central to this inquiry, and Panahi devotes a large portion of *This Is Not a Film* to a script that had recently been rejected by the Ministry of Culture and Islamic Guidance. In this script, a young woman has been accepted to study art at university, but her parents, who disapprove of her plans, lock her in their house instead. Of course, the similarities to Panahi's captivity in *This Is Not a Film* are not meant to go unnoticed, and this is one way that Mirtahmasb and Panahi misguide us. Despite the fact that Panahi has never been placed under house arrest, the sense of captivity that Panahi creates with the claustrophobic video shots and the references to house arrest in the rejected script have caused film critics to assume erroneously that Panahi was under house arrest when *This Is Not a Film* was shot, and even the movie's description on Amazon.com claims that the film takes place "during his house arrest in Tehran." At one point, Panahi reads from the rejected script and constructs the interior space of the young woman's home-jail using masking tape on his carpet. He abruptly stops in the middle

CONCLUSION

of constructing the imaginary floor plan, however, and asks the camera, "If we could tell a film, why make a film? Or, indeed, why write about one?" These questions return to the movie's title. *This Is Not a Film* does not attempt to tell a story or advance a plot, and by this measure it is not a film, according to the definition that Panahi introduces.

Although it claims not to be a film at all, *This Is Not a Film* builds off the concerns that Panahi raised in his previous three films: *Dāyereh* (The circle, 2000), *Talā-ye sorkh* (Crimson gold, 2003), and *Āfsāyd* (Offside, 2006). These three films examine individuals who push the legal limits in Iran and often suffer the consequences. Rather than condemning these criminals, however, Panahi's camera sympathetically positions them as victims of social disparity and an unfair legal system. In *This Is Not a Film*, Panahi is the criminal who is represented sympathetically onscreen. *This Is Not a Film* thereby inverts many of the normative features of film, and it creates a space in which the director becomes a character; the cameraman becomes the director; scripts are read rather than performed; iPhones replace 35 mm film cameras; three-dimensional spaces (like houses) are reduced to two-dimensional masking tape lines; and a film is not even a film. In light of the political events surrounding this project, *This Is Not a Film* ultimately demonstrates how the cry for reform in the Islamic Republic has affected filmmaking and has refashioned many of its conventions.

The poster for *This Is Not a Film* in the Cinema Museum thus testifies to the ways in which reform cinema has reorganized what it means to make a film in Iran, and how certain film institutions have been implicated in this process. But the poster's presence is more than just a relic of reform cinema. It is also a statement of protest, and its position within the Panahi display case appears to be a sleight of hand on the part of the museum's curators. On October 20, 2010, Panahi appeared in court to face his sentencing, and he read aloud a statement outlining his defense, which was later published online. In this statement, he asked, "Is there anyone in this court who recalls that the display case for Jafar Panahi's awards at the Cinema Museum is much bigger than his prison cell was during his arrest?"[6] Of all of Panahi's internationally successful films, *This Is Not a Film* is the only one to feature an image of

CONCLUSION

Panahi on its poster. To see Panahi held captive in this display reminds us of just how political filmmaking had become, especially in Ahmadinejad's Iran.

To this end, *This Is Not a Film* and its prominent place in the Cinema Museum unearth one of the most important implications of reform cinema in Iran. Beginning with its rise in the early 1990s, reform cinema marked the exact point at which revolutionary politics were no longer radical but rather represented the old order. Political reform became the dominant progressive ideology in Iran, whereas revolutionary rhetoric became the domain of the conservative guard. Whereas Massoud Bakhshi's *Tehran Has No More Pomegranates* captured the tension between revolution and reform and the instability of both of these terms, *This Is Not a Film*, which grew out of the political uprisings of 2009, shows us that reform cinema might easily give way to another radical revolutionary cinema. Revolutions, we are wont to remember, revolve. They circle back as reform reaches its limits.

NOTES

INTRODUCTION: REVOLUTIONARY CINEMA AND THE LOGIC OF REFORM

1. Ellie Violet Bramley, "Behind the Scenes with Syria's 'Emergency Cinema,'" *Guardian*, March 26, 2014, http://www.theguardian.com/film/filmblog/2014/mar/26/abounaddara-collective-syria-cinema.
2. Ruhollah Khomeini, *Islam and Revolution: Writing and Declarations of Imam Khomeini*, trans. Hamid Algar (London: Routledge and Paul Kegan, 1981), 258.
3. Khomeini, *Islam and Revolution*, 258.
4. Hamid Naficy, *A Social History of Iranian Cinema*, vol. 3: *The Islamicate Period, 1978–1984* (Durham, NC: Duke University Press, 2012), 34.
5. Hamid Naficy, "Islamizing Film Culture in Iran: A Post-Khatami Update," in *The New Iranian Cinema: Politics, Representation and Identity*, ed. Richard Tapper (London: I. B. Tauris, 2002), 28.
6. Naficy, "Islamizing Film Culture in Iran," 26–58.
7. Naficy, "Islamizing Film Culture in Iran," 29.
8. Naficy, *A Social History of Iranian Cinema*, vol. 3; and Negar Mottahedeh, *Displaced Allegories: Post-Revolutionary Iranian Cinema* (Durham, NC: Duke University Press, 2008).
9. For more, see Lary May, *Out the Past: The Birth of Mass Culture and the Motion Picture Industry* (Chicago: University of Chicago Press, 1983); Nancy J. Rosenbloom, "Between Reform and Regulation: The Struggle Over Film Censorship in Progressive America, 1909–1922," *Film History* 1, no. 4 (1987): 307–25; Scott Simmon, "Movies, Reform, and New Women," in *American Cinema in the 1910s: Themes and Variations*, ed. Charlie Keil and Ben Singer (New Brunswick, NJ: Rutgers University Press, 2009).
10. Rosenbloom, "Between Reform and Regulation, 309.

INTRODUCTION

11. Simmon, "Movies, Reform, and New Women," 26–47.
12. Brigit Beumers, *A History of Russian Cinema* (Oxford: Berg, 2009), 40; and Denise J. Youngblood, *Soviet Cinema in the Silent Era, 1918–1935* (Austin: University of Texas Press, 1991), Kindle Edition, chap. 1, "Beginnings (1918–23)."
13. Youngblood, *Soviet Cinema in the Silent Era*, chap. 1.
14. Youngblood, *Soviet Cinema in the Silent Era*, introduction.
15. Vance Kepley Jr., "Soviet Cinema and State Control: Lenin's Nationalization Decree Reconsidered," *Journal of Film and Video* 42, no. 2 (Summer 1990): 3.
16. Youngblood, *Soviet Cinema in the Silent Era*, chap. 2.
17. Kepley, "Soviet Cinema and State Control," 12.
18. Youngblood, *Soviet Cinema in the Silent Era*, introduction.
19. Youngblood, *Soviet Cinema in the Silent Era*, introduction.
20. Kepley, "Soviet Cinema and State Control," 12.
21. Frantz Fanon, *The Wretched of the Earth*, trans. Richard Philcox (New York: Grove City Press, 2005).
22. Teshome H. Gabriel, *Third Cinema in the Third World: The Aesthetics of Liberation* (Ann Arbor, MI: UMI Research Press, 1982), 2.
23. See, for example, Hamid Naficy, *An Accented Cinema: Exilic and Diasporic Filmmaking* (Princeton, NJ: Princeton University Press, 2001); Robert Stam, "Beyond Third Cinema: The Aesthetics of Hybridity," in *Rethinking Third Cinema*, ed. Anthony R. Guneratne (London: Routledge, 2003), 32–47.
24. Robert Lang, *New Tunisian Cinema: Allegories of Resistance* (New York: Columbia University Press, 2014).
25. Anthony R. Guneratne, introduction to *Rethinking Third Cinema*, ed. Guneratne (London: Routledge, 2003), 6.
26. For a compelling discussion of the unique filmic grammar that has developed in the Islamic Republic and its relationship to the Persian language, see Mottahedeh, *Displaced Allegories*, 62–65.
27. For more, see Naficy, "Islamizing Film Culture in Iran"; and Naficy, *A Social History of Iranian Cinema*, vol. 3. For a detailed study of the economics of the film industry during the first decade and a half of the Islamic Republic, see Hossein Ghazian, "The Crisis in the Iranian Film Industry and the Role of Government," in *The New Iranian Cinema: Politics, Representation and Identity*, ed. Richard Tapper (London: I. B. Tauris, 2002), 77–84.
28. Hamid Naficy, *A Social History of Iranian Cinema*, vol. 4, *The Globalizing Era, 1984–2010* (Durham, NC: Duke University Press, 2012), 140.
29. See, for example, John Haglund, "Last Night's Best Speech," *Slate*, February 27, 2012, http://www.slate.com/blogs/browbeat/2012/02/27/asghar_farhadi_s_oscar_speech_the_best_of_the_night.html.
30. For more on factionalism in Iran, see Daniel Brumberg, *Reinventing Khomeini: The Struggle for Reform in Iran* (Chicago: University of Chicago Press, 2001); and Mehdi Moslem, *Factional Politics in Post-Khomeini Iran* (Syracuse, NY: Syracuse University Press, 2002).

INTRODUCTION

31. See, for example, Abdolkarim Soroush, *Qabz va bast-e te'urik-e shari'at: nazarieh-ye takāmol-e ma'refat-e dini* [The theoretical contraction and expansion of religious law: The concept of the evolution of religious knowledge] (Tehran: Mo'aseseh-ye farhang-e sarāt, 1999).
32. Nima Hassaninasab, "Zhānr-e dovom-e Khordād" [The genre of the Second of Khordād], *Film* 19, no. 270 (2001): 10.
33. For more, see Naficy, "Islamizing Film Culture in Iran"; and Saeed Zeydabadi-nejad, *The Politics of Iranian Cinema: Film and Society in the Islamic Republic* (London: Routledge, 2010), 37–38.
34. Zeydabadi-nejad, *The Politics of Iranian Cinema*, 37.
35. "Nezārat bar nemāyesh-e film va eslāyd va vidiyu va sodur-e parvaneh namāyesh-e ānhā" [Supervision over the exhibition of films, slides, and video and issuing their exhibition permits], *Markez-e pazhuhesh-hā-ye majles-e shurā-ye eslāmi* [Islamic Parliament Research Center], July 3, 1982, http://rc.majlis.ir/fa/law/show/106928. A number of scholars have examined the effects of these censorship policies on the aesthetic and structural practices of Iranian cinema. See, for example, Mottahedeh, *Displaced Allegories*; Naficy, "Islamizing Film Culture in Iran," and *A Social History of Iranian Cinema*, vol. 3; and Zeydabadi-nejad, *The Politics of Iranian Cinema*.
36. See, for example, Sussan Siavoshi, "Cultural Policies and the Islamic Republic: Cinema and Book Production," *International Journal of Middle Eastern Studies* 29, no. 4 (1997): 517; and Zeydabadi-nejad, *The Politics of Iranian Cinema*, 47.
37. "Matn-e este'fānāmeh hojjat al-eslām va al-moslamin doktor Khatami montashar shod" [The text of his excellency Doctor Khatami's resignation letter was published], *Ettelā'āt*, 4 Khordād 1371 / May 25, 1992.
38. Babak Dad, *Sad ruz bā Khatami: matn-e kāmel* [A hundred days with Khatami: The complete text] (Tehran: Ministry of Culture and Guidance, 1998), 54–55.
39. Ervand Abrahamian, *A History of Modern Iran* (Cambridge: Cambridge University Press, 2008), 186.
40. Amy Motlagh, *Burying the Beloved: Marriage, Realism, and Reform in Modern Iran* (Stanford, CA: Stanford University Press, 2011), 113–14.
41. Mohsen Kadivar, *Salām*, 26 Mordād 1376 / August 17, 1997.
42. Mohammad Khatami, address to the UNESCO Roundtable on Dialogue Among Civilizations, September 5, 2000, http://www.unesco.org/dialogue/en/khatami.htm.
43. Azadeh Farahmand, "Perspectives on Recent (International Acclaim for) Iranian Cinema," in *The New Iranian Cinema: Politics, Representation and Identity*, ed. Richard Tapper (London: I. B. Tauris, 2002), 97.
44. For a compelling discussion of civil society, the discourse of reform, and their relationship to literature, see Motlagh, *Burying the Beloved*, 112–28.
45. Jean Noh, "Mohsen Makhmalbaf, *The President*," *Screen Daily*, October 5, 2014, http://www.screendaily.com/features/interviews/mohsen-makhmalbaf-the-president/5078286.article.

1. WHEN LOVE ENTERED CINEMA: MYSTICISM AND THE EMERGING POETICS OF REFORM

1. "Matn-e este'fānāmeh hojjat al-eslām va al-moslamin doktor Khatami montashar shod" [The text of his excellency Doctor Khatami's resignation letter was published], *Ettelā'āt*, 4 Khordād 1371 / May 25, 1992.
2. Hamid Naficy, *A Social History of Iranian Cinema*, vol. 3: *The Islamicate Period, 1978–1984* (Durham, NC: Duke University Press, 2012), 141.
3. "'Eshq-e mobtazal dar jashnvāreh-ye fajr" [Cheap love at the Fajr Film Festival], *Jomhuri-ye Eslāmi*, 12 Esfand 1369 / March 3, 1991.
4. Hossein Ghazian, "The Crisis in the Iranian Film Industry and the Role of Government," in *The New Iranian Cinema: Politics, Representation and Identity*, ed. Richard Tapper (London: I. B. Tauris, 2002), 77.
5. Ghazian, "The Crisis in the Iranian Film Industry and the Role of Government," 77–84.
6. M. Shushtari, "Jashnvāreh-ye Fajr-e 1369" [The 1369/1991 Fajr Film Festival], *Resālat*, 2 Esfand 1369 / February 21, 1991.
7. Hamid Dabashi, *Makhmalbaf at Large: The Making of a Rebel Filmmaker* (London: I. B. Tauris, 2008), 17.
8. A. Nasrabadi, "Jashnvāreh-ye film-e 69: mosalleh-e 'eshq v nafi-ye ārmān-hā" [The film festival of 1991: Armed with love and the negation of desire], *Keyhān*, 8 Esfand 1369 / February 27, 1991.
9. Shahrnush Parsipur, *Khāterāt-e zendān* [Prison memoirs] (Stockholm: Baran, 1996), 396–405; Nasrin Rahimieh, "Overcoming the Orientalist Legacy of Iranian Modernity: Women's Post-Revolutionary Film and Literary Production," *Thamyris/Intersecting* 10 (2003): 149.
10. Abu Sabra, "Mosallas-e bi-'effati dar Nowbat-e 'āsheqi" [The impure triangle in Time for love], *Jomhuri-ye Eslāmi* [The Islamic Republic], 15 Esfand 1369 / March 6, 1991. The term *gharbzade* might be translated as "West-stricken" or "Westoxicated." This concept became popular in Iran following the publication of Jalal Al-e Ahmad's *Gharbzadegi* (Westoxification, 1962). In this essay, Al-e Ahmad expands Ahmad Farid's term *gharbzadegi* and argues that an infatuation with the West is like a plague from which Iran suffers. He offers Shi'i Islam, a source of unaffected locality, as a possible cure to this disease. For more, see Jalal Al-e Ahmad, *Plagued by the West*, trans. Paul Sprachman (Delmar, NY: Caravan Books, 1982).
11. Abdolkarim Soroush, "Nowbat-e 'āsheqi" [Time for love], *Omid*, 12 Esfand 1369 / March 3, 1991.
12. I distinguish here between the Islamic Republic's ethical system and Iranian society's ethical system, because the Islamic Republic, as a religious government, purports a certain interpretation of Islam and holds its citizens to the moral code born of that interpretation. Makhmalbaf's film and the reactions it incited allow us to discern the tension between how the Islamic Republic, as a system of governance, perceives what is ethical and how certain segments of Iranian society perceived themselves and their institutions as ethical or nonethical entities.
13. Morteza Razavi, "Nowbat-e Nawbeh," *Abrār*, 6 Farvardin 1370 / March 26, 1991.

1. WHEN LOVE ENTERED CINEMA

14. Ali Motahhari, "Tekrār-e tārikh va ebtezāl-e farhangi" [The repetition of history and the cheapening of culture], *Ettelāʾāt*, 27 Esfand 1369 / March 18, 1991. Motahhari is the son of Morteza Motahhari, a conservative cleric who was killed less than a year after the revolution. Ali Motahhari was a professor of theology at Tehran University and has a long history of antireform beliefs. He currently serves as a member of the Majles and was elected on a pro-Ahmadinejad and antireformist platform.
15. Negar Mottahedeh, *Displaced Allegories: Post-Revolutionary Iranian Cinema* (Durham, NC: Duke University Press, 2008), 8.
16. Sabra Kowsari, *Keyhān*, 12 Esfand 1369 / March 3, 1991.
17. "ʿEshq-e mobtabzel dar jashnvāreh-ye fajr" [Cheap love at the Fajr Film Festival].
18. "Cheshmandāz-e yek bahs" [An overview of one debate], *Film* 108 (Tir 1370 / July 1991): 86–94.
19. N. Mahdiar, "Naqd-e maʿlul qalat ast bāyad beh risheh-hā pardākht" [Defective criticism is wrong: We should go after the roots], *Keyhān*, 23 Esfand 1369 / March 14, 1991.
20. Said Motamedi, *Resālat*, 25 Esfand 1369 / March 16, 1991.
21. A. Darai, *Resālat*, 14 Esfand 1369 / March 7, 1991.
22. Ahmad Jannati, "Sokhanāni az namāz-e jomʿeh-ye Qom" [Words from the Friday prayer of Qom], *Ettelāʾāt*, 16 Esfand 1369 / March 6, 1991.
23. Jannati, "Sokhanāni az namāz-e jomʿeh-ye Qom" [Words from the Friday prayer of Qom].
24. Mohammad Khatami, "Pāsokh-e vazir-e farhang va ershād-e eslāmi beh sokhanān-e matrah shodeh dar namāz-e jomʿeh-ye Qom" [The minister of culture and Islamic guidance's answer to the words posited at the Friday prayer of Qom], *Ettelāʾāt* [Information], 21 Esfand 1369 / March 12, 1991.
25. Mehdi Moslem, *Factional Politics in Post-Khomeini Iran* (Syracuse, NY: Syracuse University Press, 2002), 167.
26. Fakhreddin Anvar, "Sinemā-ye Iran beh cheh zarurat-hāʾi pasokh midahad?" [To what needs does Iran's cinema respond?], *Ettelāʾāt*, 16 Esfand 1369 / March 6, 1991.
27. Seyfollah Dad, "Hoviyyat-e sinemā va sinemāgar-e Irāni" [The identity of Iranian cinema and filmmakers], *Resālat*, 7 Farvardin 1370 / 27 March 1991.
28. The original Persian reads: ... و خانه‌نشین و عروس شد که باشیم جنگلی کوچک ناراحت و نگران ما. شست سینما‌ی وسیله‌ی به اسلامی انقلاب و اسلام تاریخ معرفی برای خود مبارزات از دست. The author played with the titles of films and is referencing another downward trend (in his opinion) that is similar to the course that led from *Towbeh-ye Nasuh* to *Nowbat-e ʿāsheqi*. Rahim Rahimipur, "Sinemā va jarayān-e roshanfekri-ye qarbzade" [Cinema and the course of West-stricken intellectualism], *Keyhān*, 1 Ordibehesht 1370 / April 21, 1991.
29. Rahimipur, "Sinemā va jarayān-e roshanfekri-ye qarbzade" [Cinema and the course of West-stricken intellectualism].
30. Dabashi, *Makhmalbaf at Large*, 47–48.
31. Mohsen Makhmalbaf, "Vaqt fara resid ..." [The time has come ...], *Omid*, 19 Esfand 1369 / March 10, 1991.
32. Mohsen Makhmalbaf, "Nāmeh-ye sargoshādeh" [An open letter], *Omid*, 10 Farvardin 1369 / March 30, 1991.

1. WHEN LOVE ENTERED CINEMA

33. Makhmalbaf, "Nāmeh-ye sargoshādeh" [An open letter].
34. Khatami, "Pāsokh-e vazir-e farhang va ershād-e eslāmi beh sokhanān-e matrah shodeh dar namāz-e jom'eh-ye Qom" [The minister of culture and Islamic guidance's answer to the words posited at the Friday prayer of Qom].
35. Khatami, "Pāsokh-e vazir-e farhang va ershād-e eslāmi beh sokhanān-e matrah shodeh dar namāz-e jom'eh-ye Qom" [The minister of culture and Islamic guidance's answer to the words posited at the Friday prayer of Qom].
36. Scholars have drawn comparisons between Makhmalbaf and Soroush, but these analyses do not consider material interactions between these two intellectuals. Previous attempts to consider these two intellectuals together have not engaged Soroush's commentary on Makhmalbaf's films or any other tangible exchange between them. Instead, this body of scholarship compares broad trends in these two individuals' philosophical and intellectual works and their shared experiences within the Islamic Republic. In his comprehensive study of Makhmalbaf, Eric Egan argues in general that Soroush undertook the intellectual work of justifying religiously Mohammad Khatami's notion of civil society through "attacks" on the "religio-political manifestations of the Islamic Republic." This act, which in part permitted the rise of civil society in popular and public discourse, "meant a relaxation of the censorship laws" for filmmakers such as Makhmalbaf. See Eric Egan, *The Films of Makhmalbaf: Cinema, Politics, and Culture in Iran* (Washington, DC: Mage, 2005), 172. Hamid Dabashi sees both Makhmalbaf and Soroush as "moral and intellectual by-products" of an Islamic revolution intended to overturn a monarchy with deep imperial ties and interests. As such, Soroush and Makhmalbaf, respectively, add "metaphysical (other-worldly)" and "artistic (aesthetically emancipatory)" dimensions to the "political resistance to the classical colonialization of Iranians." See Dabashi, *Makhmalbaf at Large*, 20. Yet for Dabashi these two thinkers are separated by differing "modes of creative emancipation . . . from the colonial trappings of agential de-subjection." Whereas he sees Soroush as "epistemicly trapped" in the "dialectical paradoxes of Enlightenment modernity in its colonial shadows," Dabashi envisions Makhmalbaf's "creative outbursts" as offering "a far more emancipatory track out of that cul-de-sac." The difference crucially emerges from their respective methodologies. Soroush seeks "moral and political agency" by staging a "hermeneutic encounter . . . between Islam and Enlightenment modernity." Makhmalbaf, on the other hand, navigates this terrain "artistically," which renders his work less vulnerable to colonial subjugation. Although Dabashi astutely notes a historical and intellectual connection between Makhmalbaf and Soroush, his anti-imperialist agenda overshadows the creative and aesthetic ruptures that unite these two thinkers. In particular, mysticism acts as a force that marries Soroush's and Makhmalbaf's philosophical and creative efforts. Because mysticism and Sufism share long, historical ties with Persian poetry and Iranian culture, they are less susceptible to "epistemic trappings" and therefore allow me to move beyond the postcolonial discourse that limits—and even traps—Dabashi's own analysis of this important relationship. See Dabashi, *Makhmalbaf at Large*, 19–20.
37. Gilda Boffa, "A Study of Mohsen Makhmalbaf's 'Time of Love's' Intertextual References to Maulana Jalal al-Din Rumi's Poem 'The Three Fish,'" *Offscreen* 10, no. 7 (2006); Boffa

1. WHEN LOVE ENTERED CINEMA

also considers the film in mystic terms. Her analysis of the mystic elements in *Love's Turn* is based on a comparison she stages between Makhmalbaf's film and Rumi's famous poem "The Three Fish," which she claims is the inspiration for the film. Although her reading is productive in that she establishes some similarities between the poem and the film, Boffa overstates her suggestion that the poem directly informs the film. Her argument is, in fact, based on a misreading of the main character's name. She writes, "Countless elements in the film provide hints that Makhmalbaf was deeply influenced by mystic poetry in the making of *Time for Love*. The name of the main female character for example, is Ghazal." She goes on to connect this name to the ghazal, a traditional poetic form employed by Rumi. However, the main character's name is actually Güzel, a Turkish name meaning "beauty." In the film's Persian *filmnāmeh*, the character's name is written گُزل, which should not be confused with غزل, the word for the poetic form. In *The Films of Makhmalbaf*, Eric Egan also connects *Time for Love* to poetry and focuses on particular symbols that he sees as poetic; see Eric Egan, *The Films of Makhmalbaf: Cinema, Politics and Culture in Iran* (Washington, DC: Mage, 2005), 132–35. However, he fails to connect these symbols to any mystic tradition.

38. For more on the relationship between Rumi and Soroush, see Franklin D. Lewis, *Rumi: Past and Present, East and West: Life, Teaching, and Poetry Jalāl al-Din Rumi* (Oxford: Oneworld, 2000), 493–95.
39. Lewis, *Rumi*, 24.
40. Annemarie Schimmel, *As Though a Veil: Mystical Poetry in Islam* (New York: Columbia University Press, 1982), 64.
41. Schimmel, *As Through a Veil*, 67.
42. Hamid Naficy, "Veiled Vision/Powerful Presences: Women in Post-Revolutionary Iranian Cinema," in *In the Eye of the Storm: Women in Post-Revolutionary Iran*, ed. Mahnaz Afkhami and Erika Friedl (Syracuse, NY: Syracuse University Press, 1994), 148.
43. Soroush, "Nowbat-e 'āsheqi" [Time for love].
44. Abdolkarim Soroush, "Moshkel hekāyati ast keh taqrir mikonand," in *Gong-e khābideh: montakhab-e maqāleh-hā, goftogu-hā, va barrasi-hā* [Muted dreams: A selection of articles, interviews, and reviews], vol. 3, ed. Mohsen Makhmalbaf (Tehran: Nashr-e nay, 1372), 326.
45. Mohsen Makhmalbaf, "Nowbat-e 'āsheqi: yāddāsht-e kārgardān" [Time for love: Director's notes], in *Gong-e khābideh* [Muted dreams], vol. 3, ed. Mohsen Makhmalbaf (Tehran: Nashr-e nay, 1372), 306.
46. Makhmalbaf, "Nowbat-e 'āsheqi: yāddāsht-e kārgardān" [Time for love: Director's notes], 307.
47. Makhmalbaf, "Nowbat-e 'āsheqi: yāddāsht-e kārgardān" [Time for love: Director's notes], 308.
48. Makhmalbaf, "Nowbat-e 'āsheqi: yāddāsht-e kārgardān" [Time for love: Director's notes], 312–13.
49. Shahla Haeri, "Sacred Canopy: Love and Sex Under the Veil," *Iranian Studies* 42, no. 1 (2009): 114.
50. Since the late 1970s intellectuals in Iran have used term *nasbiyat-e akhlāq* (moral relativism), but it does not imply the same "suspension of moral judgement" that it does in a European

1. WHEN LOVE ENTERED CINEMA

context. Rather, it is synonymous with what Soroush calls "pluralism." In 2000, the newspaper *Ettelā'āt* reprinted a series of articles entitled "Moral relativism," originally written in the late 1970s by Ayatollah Motahhari, who was a revolutionary Islamic philosopher and a contemporary of Khomeini. Motahhari, like Makhmalbaf in the late 1980s and early 1990s, was interested in the religious dimensions of morality but pushed for a more pluralist approach through the term "moral relativism." That these articles were reprinted during Khatami's presidency points to the fact that *nasbiyat-e akhlāq*, or moral relativism, became important to the reformist discourse as well.

51. Makhmalbaf, "Nowbat-e 'āsheqi: yāddāsht-e kārgardān" [Time for love: Director's notes], 299–300.
52. Hamid Dabashi, *Close Up: Iranian Cinema, Past, Present, and Future* (London and New York: Verso Books, 2001), 212. In an interview with Heike Hurst, Makhmalbaf claims that in *Time for Love* he tried to approximate cinematically the ideas conveyed in that Rumi anecdote. For more, see Heike Hurst, "Makhmalbaf questionne le pouvoir," *Jeune Cinéma* 247 (May–June 1996): 19.
53. Makhmalbaf, "Nowbat-e 'āsheqi: yāddāsht-e kārgardān" [Time for love: Director's notes], 300–301.
54. Soroush, "Moshkel hekāyati ast keh taqrir mikonand," 325.
55. Soroush, "Moshkel hekāyati ast keh taqrir mikonand," 325–26.
56. Makhmalbaf, *Gong-e khābideh* [Muted dreams], vol. 3, 305.
57. Makhmalbaf, *Gong-e khābideh* [Muted dreams], vol. 3, 303.
58. Makhmalbaf, *Gong-e khābideh* [Muted dreams], vol. 3, 304.
59. Makhmalbaf, *Gong-e khābideh* [Muted dreams], vol. 3, 303.
60. Hamid Reza Sadr, *Iranian Cinema: A Political History* (London: I. B. Tauris, 2006), 254.
61. Sadr, *Iranian Cinema*, 254.
62. This statement follows several lines from Ahmad Shamlu's famous modernist poem "Pariā" (Fairies): "Fire! Fire! So Pretty! Wow! / And it's almost sunset now / Jumping up and jumping down / Jumping into the silver pond." Hamun references Shamlu's poetry several times throughout the film. As Ahmad Karimi-Hakkak has noted, Shamlu had mystical tendencies himself, particularly in the poem "Dar in bon bast" (In this dead end), in which the perfect revolution is presented as a kind of beloved, dreamt and fantasized but never realized. For more, see Ahmad Karimi-Hakkak, "Of Hial and Hounds: The Image of the Iranian Revolution in Recent Persian Literature," *State, Culture, and Society* 1, no. 3 (1985): 148–80. Shamlu's poetry is also significant to the film because Hamun's thesis topic, the love and faith of Abraham—an exploration into mysticism in its own right—is also the subject of one of Shamlu's famous poems, "Sorud-e Ebrāhim dar ātash" (The song of Abraham in the fire). More generally, Shamlu was the archetypal poet, the very kind of intellectual figure that the film critiques.
63. Hamun's use of Ali's surname crucially distinguishes him from Ali, the rightful successor of Mohammad according to Shi'i belief and the father of Hussein. Without this reference to his last name, Hamun's question "Have you seen Ali?" might be misinterpreted in the context of the *'āshurā* ceremonies.

1. WHEN LOVE ENTERED CINEMA

64. Dabashi, *Makhmalbaf at Large*, 29.
65. Dabashi, *Makhmalbaf at Large*, 29.
66. Dabashi, "Dead Certainties: The Early Makhmalbaf," in *The New Iranian Cinema: Politics, Representation and Identity*, ed. Richard Tapper (London and New York: I. B. Tauris, 2002), 134–35. Although Dabashi does not explicitly refer to Derrida, his description of Makhmalbaf's early films as both the illness and the disease recalls "Plato's Pharmacy," in which Derrida argues that writing is both a poison and a remedy. Whereas Derrida sees the space created by the collapse of this binary as wrought with potential and productivity, Dabashi considers it a barrier that must be overcome, which he calls the "decisive moment," and thereby establishes a new limiting binary between Makhmalbaf's early films and his later films. For more, see Jacques Derrida, "Plato's Pharmacy," in *Dissemination*, trans. Barbara Johnson (New York and London: Continuum Books, 2004), 67–154.
67. Dabashi, *Makhmalbaf at Large*, 20.
68. Dabashi, "Dead Certainties," 135.
69. Afshin Matin-asgari, "Abdolkarim Sorush and the Secularization of Islamic Thought in Iran," *Iranian Studies* 30, nos.1–2 (Winter/Spring 1997), 102.
70. Matin-asgari, "Abdolkarim Sorush and the Secularization of Islamic Thought in Iran," 103.
71. Matin-asgari, "Abdolkarim Sorush and the Secularization of Islamic Thought in Iran," 103.
72. John Cooper, "The Limits of the Sacred: The Epistemology of Abd al-Karim Soroush," in *Islam and Modernity: Muslim Intellectuals Respond*, ed. John Cooper, Ronald L. Nettler, and Mohamed Mahmoud (London and New York: I. B. Tauris, 1998), 43.
73. Abdolkarim Soroush, "Islamic Revival and Reform: Theological Approaches," in *Reason, Freedom and Democracy in Islam: Essential Writings of 'Abdolkarim Soroush*, trans. and ed. Mahmoud Sadri and Ahmad Sadri (New York: Oxford University Press, 2000), 30.
74. Soroush, "Islamic Revival and Reform," 31.
75. Soroush, "Islamic Revival and Reform," 31.
76. Soroush, "Islamic Revival and Reform," 31.
77. Soroush, "Islamic Revival and Reform," 31.
78. Soroush, "Islamic Revival and Reform," 32.
79. Soroush, "Islamic Revival and Reform," 34.
80. Ashkan P. Dahlén, *Islamic Law, Epistemology and Modernity: Legal Philosophy in Contemporary Iran* (London: Routledge, 2003), 255.
81. Abdolkarim Soroush, "Tolerance and Governance: A Discourse on Religion and Democracy," in *Reason, Freedom and Democracy in Islam: Essential Writings of 'Abdolkarim Soroush*, trans. and ed. Mahmoud Sadri and Ahmad Sadri (New York: Oxford University Press, 2000), 145.
82. Soroush's challenge of the political system has resulted in serious backlash. Soroush was initially a close ally of Khomeini and served on the Culture Revolution Institute, an organization whose seven members were handpicked by Khomeini to restructure higher education curricula to favor a more Islamic orientation. However, in the 1990s, he became increasingly critical of the clergy and their role in politics, falling out of favor with the government. Since 2000 he has lived in exile in the United States.

1. WHEN LOVE ENTERED CINEMA

83. For more, see Daniel Brumberg, "Ascetic Mysticism and the Roots of Khomeini's Charisma," in *Reinventing Khomeini: The Struggle for Reform in Iran* (Chicago: University of Chicago Press, 2001), 39–54.
84. Oliver Roy, "The Crisis of Religious Legitimacy in Iran," *Middle East Journal* 87, no. 2 (Spring 1999): 215.
85. See, for example, Mangol Bayat, *Mysticism and Dissent: Socioreligious Thought in Qajar Iran* (Syracuse, NY: Syracuse University Press, 1982), 29.
86. The term "clash of civilizations" was first used by Bernard Lewis in "The Roots of Muslim Rage," *Atlantic Monthly* 266, no. 3 (September 1990): 47–60. The concept, which is rooted the colonial term "clash of cultures," was picked up and expanded by Huntington, first in the article "Clash of Civilizations?" *Foreign Affairs* 72, no. 3 (Summer 1993): 22–49 and later in *The Clash of Civilizations and the Remaking of World Order* (New York: Touchstone, 1997).
87. Mohammad Khatami, "Round Table: Dialogue Among Civilizations," UNESCO, September 5, 2000, accessed December 27, 2014, http://www.unesco.org/dialogue/en/khatami.htm.
88. Khatami, "Round Table: Dialogue Among Civilizations."

2. SCREENING REFORM: CAMPAIGN MOVIES, DOCUMENTARIES, AND URBAN TEHRAN

1. Majid Maafi, "Siyāsat dar keluz āp" [Politics in close-up], *Sorush* 27 (28 Khordād 1384 / June 18, 2005): 54.
2. Scott Mcleod, "The Vote in Iran," *Time*, February 13, 2000, accessed December 29, 2014, http://content.time.com/time/magazine/article/0,9171,39214,00.html.
3. Maafi, "Siyāsat dar keluz āp" [Politics in close-up], 54.
4. Hadani Ditmars, "Rakhshan Bani-Etemad Talks to Hadani Ditmars About Bending the Rules in 'May Lady,'" *Sight and Sound* 20 (January 1999): 20.
5. Rakhshan Bani-Etemad, "Ghamkhār-e bi edde'ā-ye zanān-e darmānde: goftogu bā Rakhshan Bani-Etemad" [Sympathy without the pretense of distressed women: A conversation with Rakhshan Bani-Etemad], *Zanān* [Women] 25 (Mordād/Shahrivār 1374/1995): 44.
6. See, for example, Hamid Naficy, "Veiled Voice and Vision in Iranian Cinema: The Evolution of Rakhshan Banietemad's Films," in *Ladies and Gentlemen, Boys and Girls: Gender in the Film at the End of the Twentieth Century*, ed. Murray Pomerance (Albany, NY: SUNY Press, 2001). Naficy seeks to chart the increasing presence of women in post-revolution cinema, to position Bani-Etemad's films in the trajectory, and to examine the ways in which the director confronts or conforms to certain policies regulating onscreen modesty.
7. Rahul Hamid, "Review: Under the Skin of the City," *Cineaste* 51 (2003): 50.
8. Massoud Mehrabi, "Commitment, Cinema, Construction: An Interview with Rakhshan Bani-Etemad," *Film International* 13, nos. 52–53 (2007): 83.
9. Hamid Naficy, "Kiarostami's *Close-Up*: Questioning Reality, Realism, and Neorealism," in *Film Analysis: A Norton Reader*, ed. Jeffrey Geiger and R. L. Rutsky (New York: W. W. Norton, 2005), 804.

2. SCREENING REFORM

10. Bill Nichols, *Introduction to Documentary* (Bloomington and Indianapolis: Indiana University Press, 2001), 20.
11. Bill Nichols, *Representing Reality: Issues and Concepts in Documentary* (Bloomington: Indiana University Press, 1991), 5.
12. See Nichols, *Introduction to Documentary*; Bill Nichols, *Blurred Boundaries: Questions of Meaning in Contemporary Culture* (Bloomington: Indiana University Press, 1994); and Nichols, *Representing Reality*.
13. Nichols, *Representing Reality*, 3–4.
14. For more see, Massoud Mehrabi, *Farhang-e film-hā-ye mostanad-e sinemā-ye Irān: az āghāz tā sāl-e 1375* [A guide to Iranian documentary films: From the beginning to 1997] (Tehran: Daftar-e Pezhuhesh-hā-ye farhangi, 1375/1997); and Hamid Naficy, *A Social History of Iranian Cinema*, vol. 2: *The Industrializing Years, 1941–1978* (Durham, NC: Duke University Press, 2011), 49–146. Nichols, *Blurred Boundaries*, 1.
15. Nichols, *Blurred Boundaries*, 1.
16. Ditmars, "Rakhshan Bani-Etemad Talks to Hadani Ditmars About Bending the Rules in 'May Lady,'" 20.
17. Rakhshan Bani-Etemad, "Man filmsāz-e herfeh-i nistam: harf-hāi az Rakhshan Bani-Etemad" [I am not a professional filmmaker: A few words from Rakhshan Bani-Etemad], *Film* 19, no. 263 (2001): 124.
18. Bani-Etemad, "Man filmsāz-e herfeh-i nistam" [I am not a professional filmmaker], 124.
19. Hamid Naficy, "Islamizing Film Culture in Iran: A Post-Khatami Update," in *The New Iranian Cinema: Politics, Representation and Identity*, ed. Richard Tapper (London: I. B. Tauris, 2002), 41–44.
20. Bani-Etemad, "Man filmsāz-e herfeh-i nistam" [I am not a professional filmmaker], 123.
21. Slavoj Žižek, *The Fright of Real Tears: Kryztof Kieslowski Between Theory and Post-Theory* (London: British Film Institute, 2001), 52.
22. Hamid, "Review," 51.
23. Stephen Winberger, "Neorealism, Iranian Style," *Iranian Studies* 40, no.1 (2007): 5–16; and Shohini Chaudhuri and Howard Finn, "The Open Image: Poetic Realism and the New Iranian Cinema," *Screen* 44, no. 1 (Spring 2004): 38–57.
24. Hamed Safaee and Vahid Parsa, "Tehrān; shahr-e bi-hāfezeh" [Tehran: The city that forgets], *Tehran Avenue* (May 2007), http://www.tehranavenue.com/article.php?id=693.
25. For a thorough account of the luti and his political role in Iran's modern history, see Willem M. Floor, "The Political Role of Lutis in Iran," in *Modern Iran: The Dialectics of Continuity and Change*, ed. Michael E. Bonine and Nikki R. Keddie (Albany: State University of New York Press, 1981), 83–95.
26. For an analysis of one of these films, *Dash Akol* (1971), directed by Masud Kimiai, see Hamid Naficy, "Iranian Writers, Iranian Cinema, and the Case of 'Dash Akol,'" *Iranian Studies* 18, nos. 2–4 (Spring–Autumn 1985): 231–51. This genre of film is examined further in chapter 4.
27. Hamid Reza Sadr, *Iranian Cinema: A Political History* (London: I. B. Tauris, 2006), 115.
28. Other urban films that feature gritty and unflinching representations of Tehran include *Khesht va āyeneh* (Mudbrick and mirror, 1965), directed by Ebrahim Golestan; *Qeysar* (1969),

2. SCREENING REFORM

by Masud Kimiai; and *Zir-e pust-e shab* (Under the skin of the night, 1974), by Feridun Goleh.
29. Mohsen Kadivar, *Salām*, 26 Mordād 1376 / August 17, 1997.
30. Mehran Kamrava, "The Civil Society Discourse in Iran," *British Journal of Middle Eastern Studies* 28, no. 2 (2001): 170.
31. Saïd Arjomand, *After Khomeini: Iran Under His Successors* (Oxford and New York: Oxford University Press, 2009), 95–97. For a particularly compelling discussion of the ways in which the framework of the Islamic Republic is unable to accommodate the freedoms of civil society, see Bahram Rahmani, *Afsāneh-ye jāme'eh-ye madani* [The myth of civil society] (Köln: Forugh Books, 2001). This book, published around the time of Khatami's reelection, is representative of Iranians' disillusionment with their president. As a political/philosophical text it resonates with Rakhshan Bani-Etemad's cinematic effort in *Under the Skin of the City*.
32. Mehdi Moslem, *Factional Politics in Post-Khomeini Iran* (Syracuse, NY: Syracuse University Press, 2002), 257–65.
33. My assessment of the reformist movement is not an attempt to belittle the efforts of Mohammad Khatami or to devalue the appeal of his platform. Bani-Etemad's film *Our Times . . .* (2001), a documentary about the 2001 elections, demonstrates how strongly some people believed in these concepts. Rather, I am stressing that his big-picture ideas were unaware of the urgency of the economic hardships that most Iranians faced.
34. Michel de Certeau, *The Practice of Everyday Life*, trans. Steven Rendall (Berkeley and Los Angeles: University of California Press, 1984), 92–93.
35. Sergei Eisenstein, "A Dialectic Approach to Film Form," *Film Form: Essays in Film Theory*, trans. Jay Leyda (San Diego and New York: Harvest Books, 1969), 46, 49.
36. Walter Benjamin, "The Work of Art in the Age of Mechanical Reproduction," in *Illuminations: Essays and Reflections*, trans. Harry Zohn (New York: Pantheon, 1968), 250.
37. "Parvandeh-ye yek film: *Bu-ye kāfur, 'atr-e yās*" [The file on one film: *The Smell of Camphor, the Scent of Jasmine*], *Film* 264 (Bahman 1379 / February 2001): 79.
38. Hamid, "Review," 51.
39. Ali Madanipour, *Tehran: The Making of a Metropolis* (New York: John Wiley & Sons, 1998), 114.
40. Naghmeh Samini, "Rakhshan Bani-Etemad dar yek negāh" [Rakhshan Bani-Etemad at a glance]. *Film* 19, no. 263 (2001): 131–32.
41. Farzaneh Milani, *Veils and Words: The Emerging Voices of Iranian Women Writers* (Syracuse, NY: Syracuse University Press, 1992), 23.
42. Bani-Etemad has a precedent for naming her female characters after important literary figures. For example, the main character in *Bānu-ye ordibehesht* (*May Lady*, 1998) is a documentary filmmaker named Forugh, who is shooting a film about motherhood. She is a clear reference to the famous poet Forugh Farrokhzad—also a documentary filmmaker—who likewise struggled with motherhood, losing custody of her only biological son and later adopting a child from a leper colony that was the site of her famous film *Khāneh siāh ast* (The house is black, 1962).
43. For a more detailed discussion of this novel as a feminist statement, see Kamran Talattof,

3. VIDEO DEMOCRACIES

"Feminist Discourse in Postrevolutionary Women's Literature," *The Politics of Writing in Iran: A History of Modern Persian Literature* (Syracuse, NY: Syracuse University Press, 2000), 135–72. See also Amy Motlagh, *Burying the Beloved: Marriage, Realism, and Reform in Modern Iran* (Stanford, CA: Stanford University Press, 2011), 104–7.

44. *Khabargozāri-ye Mehr* estimates that 80 percent of runaway girls fall victim to illegal activities, mainly in the form of prostitution and drug smuggling, within their first twenty-four hours on the street (http://www.mehrnews.com/fa/NewsDetail.aspx?NewsID=112382).
45. The feminist journal *Zanān* published an interview with Mohammad Khatami during the 1997 elections. Khatami's answers to the journal's questions about the status of women in Iran indicate that the reformist movement collapsed the solution to a variety of problems into the category of "civil society." For Khatami, adhering to the ideals of democracy and civil society would have a similar positive effect on the social and economic problems that plagued the country. For more, see "Khatami darbāreh-ye zanān che mi-guyad?" [What does Khatami say about women?], *Zanān* 34 (Ordibehesht 1376 / May 1997): 2–5.
46. Ahmadreza Jalili, "Sinemāgarān dar entekhābāt: ruzegār-e mā ..." [Filmmakers in the elections: *Our Times* ...], *Film* 20, no. 283 (2002): 18.
47. Madanipour, *Tehran*, 114.
48. Madanipour, *Tehran*, 111.
49. Madanipour, *Tehran*, 113.
50. Madanipour, *Tehran*, 114.
51. Nichols, *Representing Reality*, 4.
52. Wendy Brown, *Edgework: Critical Essays on Knowledge and Politics* (Princeton, NJ: Princeton University Press, 2005), 15.
53. Brown, *Edgework*, 4.
54. Walter Benjamin, "Theses on the Philosophy of History," in *Illuminations: Essays and Reflections*, trans. Harry Zohn (New York: Pantheon, 1968), 257.

3. VIDEO DEMOCRACIES: OR, THE DEATH OF THE FILMMAKER

1. Hamid Dabashi, *Close Up: Iranian Cinema Past, Present, and Future* (London and New York: Verso, 2001), 268–69.
2. Nima Hassaninasab, "Zhānr-e dovom-e Khordād" [Genre of the Second of Khordād], *Film* 19, no. 270 (2001): 10.
3. Hassaninasab, "Zhānr-e dovom-e Khordād" [Genre of the Second of Khordād], 10.
4. Hassaninasab, "Zhānr-e dovom-e Khordād" [Genre of the Second of Khordād], 10–14.
5. Hassaninasab, "Zhānr-e dovom-e Khordād" [Genre of the Second of Khordād], 10.
6. Abbas Yari, "Noqteh-ye 'atf: goftegu bā Seyfollah Dad" [Turning point: A conversation with Seyfollah Dad], *Film* 205 (Khordād 1376 / June 1997): 40–41.
7. See, for example, Peter Chelkowski and Hamid Dabashi, *Staging a Revolution: The Art of Persuasion in the Islamic Republic of Iran* (New York: New York University Press, 1999); and

3. VIDEO DEMOCRACIES

Roxanne Varzi, *Warring Souls: Youth, Media, and Martyrdom in Post-Revolution Iran* (Durham, NC: Duke University Press, 2006).

8. "Vorud-e navār-e khām-e vid'eo mamnun shod" [The importing of blank video tapes is forbidden], *Film* 34 (Esfand 1364 / March 1986): 10.
9. "Āmār-e vaz'iyat-e sinemā, televiziyun va vid'eo dar 42 keshvar-e jahān" [Statistics on the status of cinema, television, and video in 42 countries around the world], *Film* 135 (Dey 1381 / January 1993): 8.
10. "Tahājom-e farhangi, 'azm-e melli: nokāti az gozāresh-e vazir-e farhang va ershād beh majles va amār-e vaz'iyat-e sinemā, televiziyun va vid'eo dar jahān" [The assault on culture and national resolve: Points from the Ministry of Islamic Culture and Guidance's report to Majles and a look at statistics on the status of cinema, television, and video in the world], *Film* 135 (Dey 1381 / January 1993): 6.
11. "Vazir-e farhangi va ershād-e eslāmi jāme'eh rā az gheflat nesbat beh pishrafteh-hā-ye teknuluzhik bar hazar dasht" [The minister of culture and Islamic guidance warned society about ignorance regarding technological advances], *Ettelā'āt*, 12 Ordibehesht 1372 / May 2, 1993.
12. "Hamchenān darbāreh-ye vid'eo" [Still about video], *Film* 125 (Tir 1371 / July 1992).
13. Ali Mohammad Fakharzadeh, "Cherā vid'eo . . . ?" [Why video . . . ?], *Ettelā'āt*, 15 Shahrivar 1372 / September 7, 1993.
14. "Siyāsat-hā-ye towlid-e film-hā-ye vid'eo 'elām shod" [The policies for the production of video were announced], *Ettelā'āt*, 6 Mehr 1372 / September 26, 1993.
15. "1000 vide'o kelub tā pāyān-e in māh dar keshvar rāhandāzi mishavad" [By the end of this month, 1000 video clubs will open], *Ettelā'āt*, 12 Abān 1372 / November 3, 1993.
16. "Siyāsat-e pardākht-e samiyeh be towlidegān-e film-hā-ye vid'eoii e'lām shod" [A policy about subsidizing video movie producers was announced], *Ettelā'āt*, 12 Mehr 1372 / October 4, 1993; "Avalin jashnvāreh-ye vid'eoii-ye sureh aghāz shod" [The first Sureh video festival began], *Ettelā'āt*, 4 Dey 1372 / December 25, 1993.
17. Michael Z. Newman, *Video Revolutions: On the History of a Medium* (New York: Columbia University Press, 2014), 102–4.
18. See, for example, *Film* 204 (Khordād 1376 / June 1997), *Film* 207 (Shahrivar 1376 / September 1997), *Film* 270 (Khordād 1380 / June 2001), *Film* 287 (Tir 1381 / July 2002), and *Film* 288 (Mordād 1381 / August 2002).
19. Sony, Advertisement, *Film* 262 (Āzar 1379 / November 2001); Mo'asseseh Āyat Film, Advertisement, *Film* 280 (Bahman 1380 / January 2002); Sony, Advertisement, *Film* 287 (Tir 1381 / July 2002).
20. Sanyo, Advertisement, *Film* 275 (Mehr 1380 / September 2001).
21. Newman, *Video Revolutions*, 61–71.
22. Adam Ganz and Lina Khatib, "Digital Cinema: The Transformation of Film Practices and Aesthetics," *New Cinemas: Journal of Contemporary Film* 4, no. 1 (May 2006): 29.
23. *10 on Ten*, directed by Abbas Kiarostami (New York: Zeitgeist Films, 2004), DVD.
24. Parviz Alavi, "Sokhanrāni darbāreh resāneh-hā va jāme'eh madani" [A speech about media and civil society], *Ettelā'āt*, 5 Khordād 1377 / May 26, 1998.

3. VIDEO DEMOCRACIES

25. "Aba'ād-e namāyesh-e gheyr-e qānuni-ye film-hā-ye irāni dar NITV va shekāyat 'aliyeh in shabkeh" [Dimensions to the illegal screening of Iranian films on NITV and complaints against the network], *Film* 272 (Mordād 1380 / August 2001): 37–40.
26. "Estefādeh az barnāmeh-hā-ye vid'eoii bedun-e mojavvez-e katabi-ye sāhebān-e film-hā mamnu' ast" [The use of video programming without written consent from the films' owners is prohibited], *Film* 288 (Mordād 1381 / August 2002): 16.
27. Roger Ebert, "Review: *Taste of Cherry*," *Chicago Sun-Times*, February 28, 1998.
28. Mehrnaz Saeed-Vafa and Jonathan Rosenbaum, *Abbas Kiarostami* (Urbana and Chicago: University of Illinois Press, 2003), 95.
29. Azadeh Farahmand, "Perspectives on Recent (International Acclaim for) Iranian Cinema," in *The New Iranian Cinema: Politics, Representation and Identity*, ed. Richard Tapper (London: I. B. Tauris, 2002), 95.
30. Hamid Reza Sadr, *Iranian Cinema: A Political History* (London: I. B. Tauris, 2006), 238–39. This open governmental policy, which encouraged Iran's presence at international film festivals, is in contrast to the early 1990s, when religious leaders like Ali Jannati severely criticized the Ministry of Culture and Islamic Guidance for allowing films to be shown at film festivals around the world. "Sokhanān az namāz-e jom'eh-ye Qom" [Words from the Friday prayer of Qom], *Ettelā'āt*, 16 Esfand 1369 / March 6, 1991.
31. Shahram Tabemohammadi, "Hargez film-e siāsi nakhvāham sākht: goft-o-gu bā Abbas Kiarostami" [I will never make a political film: A conversation with Abbas Kiarostami], *Film* 19, no. 254 (Tir 1380 / July 2001): 44.
32. See, for example, Godfrey Cheshire, "How to Read Kiarostami," *Cineaste* 25, no. 4 (2000): 8–15; Alberto Elena, *The Cinema of Abbas Kiarostami*, trans. Belinda Coombes (London: Saqi Books, 2005); Julian Graffy, "*Taste of Cherry/Ta'am-e gilas*," *Sight and Sound* 8, no. 6 (June 1998): 57; Jonathan Rosenbaum, "Fill in the Blanks," *Chicago Reader*, May 29, 1998; and Khatereh Sheibani, "Kiarostami and the Aesthetics of Modern Persian Poetry," *Iranian Studies* 39, no. 4 (2006): 509–37.
33. Saeed Zeydabadi-Nejad, *The Politics of Iranian Cinema: Film and Society in the Islamic Republic* (London and New York: Routledge, 2010), 149.
34. Laura Mulvey, "Kiarostami's Uncertainty Principle," *Sight and Sound* 8, no. 6 (June 1998): 25–26.
35. F. Rosenthal, "Intiḥār," in *Encyclopaedia of Islam*, 2nd ed., ed. P. Bearman, Th. Bianquis, C. E. Bosworth, E. van Donzel, and W. P. Heinrichs (Brill, 2011), http://www.brillonline.nl.ezproxy.lib.utexas.edu/subscriber/entry?entry=islam_SIM-3581.
36. Olivier Roy, "The Crisis of Religious Legitimacy in Iran," *Middle East Journal* 87, no. 2 (Spring 1999): 215, 202.
37. Keyvan Tabari, "The Rule of Law and the Politics of Reform in Post-Revolutionary Iran," *International Sociology* 18, no. 1 (March 2003): 112.
38. Roy, "The Crisis of Religious Legitimacy in Iran," 215; Abdolkarim Soroush, "Interview with Dariush Sajjadi," *Homa TV*, March 9, 2006, accessed December 19, 2014, http://www.drsoroush.com/English/Interviews/E-INT-HomaTV.html.
39. Even in his criticism, Soroush notes the hope that Khatami's election brought to Iranian

3. VIDEO DEMOCRACIES

society. In a letter to Khatami, he says, "The peaceful and democratic uprising of the Iranian people against religious dictatorship in May 1997 was a sweet experience.... But your failure to keep the vote and your wasting of opportunities put an end to it and disappointed the nation. Now, failures have turned into unrest." For more, see "Khatami Threatens Resignation Over Power Struggle with Hard-Liners," *Daily Star*, July 17, 2003, accessed December 19, 2014, http://www.drsoroush.com/English/News_Archive/E-NWS-20030714-Khatami_Threatens_Resignation-The_Daily_Star.html.

40. Cited in Elena, *The Cinema of Abbas Kiarostami*, 124.
41. See, for example, Geoff Andrews, *10* (London: British Film Institute, 2005); Godfrey Cheshire, "How to Read Kiarostami"; Edmund Hayes, "10 × Ten: Kiarostami's Journey Into Modern Iran," *openDemocracy*, 2002, http://www.opendemocracy.net/content/articles/PDF/815.pdf; Laura Mulvey, "Repetition and Return," *Third Text* 21, no. 1 (January 2007): 19–29; Mehrnaz Saeed-Vafa and Jonathan Rosenbaum, *Abbas Kiarostami* (Urbana and Chicago: University of Illinois Press, 2003), 18–19; and Sheibani, "Kiarostami and the Aesthetics of Modern Persian Poetry."
42. For more on the role of music in this video coda, see Michael Price, "Imagining Life: The Ending of Taste of Cherry," *Sense of Cinema* 17 (November 2001), accessed December 19, 2014, http://sensesofcinema.com/2001/abbas-kiarostami-17/cherry/.
43. Elena, *The Cinema of Abbas Kiarostami*, 254n97.
44. Kiarostami, *10 on Ten*.
45. Ganz and Khatib, "Digital Cinema," 31.
46. Elena, *The Cinema of Abbas Kiarostami*, 178.
47. Walter Benjamin, "The Work of Art in the Age of Mechanical Reproduction," in *Illuminations: Essays and Reflections*, trans. Harry Zohn (New York: Pantheon, 1968), 228–31.
48. Ganz and Khatib, "Digital Cinema," 31.
49. Susan Sontag, *Regarding the Pain of Others* (New York: Picador, 2004), 46.
50. Elena, *The Cinema of Abbas Kiarostami*, 176; Negar Mottahedeh, *Displaced Allegories: Post-Revolutionary Iranian Cinema* (Durham, NC: Duke University Press, 2008), 138; Zeydabadi-Nejad, *The Politics of Iranian Cinema*, 125.
51. Elena, *The Cinema of Abbas Kiarostami*, 176.
52. Ganz and Khatib, "Digital Cinema," 30.
53. Saeed-Vafa and Rosenbaum, *Abbas Kiarostami*, 68.
54. Farzin Vahdat, "Religious Modernity in Iran: Dilemmas of Islamic Democracy in the Discourses of Mohammad Khatami," *Comparative Studies of South Asia, Africa, and the Middle East* 25, no. 3 (2005): 660.
55. Mohammad Khatami, *Gozideh sokhanranihā-ye ra'is jomhur darbāreh-ye tos'eh-ye siāsi va eqtesād va ammniyat* [Selected speeches by the president about political and economic expansion and security] (Tehran: Tahr-e No, 1379/2000), 83, quoted in Vahdat, "Religious Modernity in Iran," 660.
56. Mohammad Khatami, "Women and Men Are Different, but Women Are Not the Second Sex and Men Are Not Superior," *Zan-e ruz* 143 (1997): 8–10.
57. Mohammad Khatami, *Zanān va javānān* [Women and youth] (Tehran: Tahr-e no, 2000), 40.

3. VIDEO DEMOCRACIES

58. Khatami, *Zanān va javānān* [Women and youth], 32, 33.
59. Vahdat, "Religious Modernity in Iran," 660.
60. There is a similar scene in Mohsen Makhmalbaf's *'Arusi-ye khubān* (Marriage of the blessed, 1989), which tells the story of an Iran-Iraq War veteran trying to reenter society after his traumatic experiences at the front. In one scene, Haji, who is trying to resume his career as a photographer, enters a room to do a photographic portrait, and a women takes off her veil to reveal a bald head; presumably she is undergoing chemotherapy. In the case of *Marriage of the Blessed*, the male character quickly exits the room before taking the photo, and we only see the woman's bald head for a few seconds. In *10*, on the other hand, the mounted camera provides us with no relief through cuts or edits, and we have no choice but to watch.
61. Hamid Naficy, "Veiled Vision/Powerful Presences: Women in Post-Revolutionary Iranian Cinema," in *In the Eye of the Storm: Women in Post-Revolutionary Iran*, ed. Mahnaz Afkhami and Erika Friedl (Syracuse, NY: Syracuse University Press, 1994), 138.
62. Mottahedeh, *Displaced Allegories*, 9.
63. Zeydabadi-Nejad, *The Politics of Iranian Cinema*, 125.
64. Tabemohammadi, "Hargez film-e siāsi nakhāham sākht" [I will never make a political film], 44.
65. Saeed-Vafa and Rosenbaum, *Abbas Kiarostami*, 100–101.
66. Kiarostami, *10 on Ten*.
67. Ganz and Khatib, "Digital Cinema," 26.
68. Kiarostami, *10 on Ten*.
69. Kiarostami, *10 on Ten*.
70. "Parvandeh-ye yek film: *Bu-ye kāfur, 'atr-e yās*" [The file on one film: *The Smell of Camphor, the Scent of Jasmine*], *Film* 264 (Bahman 1379 / February 2002), 79. As recently as 2009 news reports in Iran claim that Farmanara is finally going to make a film under this title. It is not clear whether or not this film is the same highly political project that he originally submitted with this title.
71. "Parvandeh-ye yek film" [The file on one film], 79.
72. Dabashi, *Close Up*, 124–29.
73. Dabashi, *Close Up*, 135.
74. "Parvandeh-ye yek film" [The file on one film], 79.
75. "Parvandeh-ye yek film" [The file on one film], 77.
76. Dabashi, *Close Up*, 249.
77. Dabashi, *Close Up*, 146.
78. Dabashi, *Close Up*, 153.
79. Dabashi, *Close Up*, 153.
80. Adam Tarock, "The Muzzling of the Liberal Press in Iran," *Third World Quarterly* 22, no. 4 (2001): 590, 585–602.
81. For more, see Shirin Ebadi, *Iran Awakening: A Memoir of Revolution and Hope*, with Azadeh Moaveni (New York: Random House, 2006), 128–41.
82. Douglas Jehl, "Killing of 3 Rebel Writers Turns Hope Into Fear," *New York Times*, December

3. VIDEO DEMOCRACIES

14, 1998, accessed December 19, 2014, http://www.nytimes.com/1998/12/14/world/killing-of-3-rebel-writers-turns-hope-to-fear-in-iran.html?src=pm.
83. Dabashi, *Close Up*, 146.

4. WHO KILLED THE TOUGH GUY? CONTINUITY AND RUPTURE IN THE *FILMFĀRSI* TRADITION

1. See, for example, Hamid Naficy, "Islamizing Film Culture in Iran: A Post-Khatami Update," in *The New Iranian Cinema: Politics, Representation and Identity*, ed. Richard Tapper (London: I. B. Tauris, 2002); Negar Mottahedeh, *Displaced Allegories: Post-Revolutionary Iranian Cinema* (Durham, NC: Duke University Press, 2008); Saeed Zeydabadi-Nejad, *The Politics of Iranian Cinema: Film and Society in the Islamic Republic* (London: Routledge, 2010).
2. Hamid Naficy, *A Social History of Iranian Cinema*, vol. 2: *The Industrializing Years, 1941–1978* (Durham, NC: Duke University Press, 2011), 295, 333.
3. Naficy, *A Social History of Iranian Cinema*, 2:301; and Hamid Reza Sadr, *Iranian Cinema: A Political History* (London, I. B. Tauris, 2006), 139.
4. Hamid Dabashi, *Close-Up: Iranian Cinema, Past, Present, and Future* (London and New York: Verso, 2001), 250–51.
5. Naficy, *A Social History of Iranian Cinema*, 2:149.
6. Naficy, *A Social History of Iranian Cinema*, 2:150.
7. Hamid Naficy, "Iranian Cinema Under the Islamic Republic," *American Anthropologist* 97, no. 3 (1995): 549.
8. Azadeh Farahmand, "Perspectives on Recent (International Acclaim for) Iranian Cinema," in *The New Iranian Cinema: Politics, Representation and Identity*, ed. Richard Tapper (London: I. B. Tauris, 2002), 86–108.
9. See, for example, Tejaswini Ganti, *Bollywood: A Guidebook to Popular Hindi Cinema* (London: Routledge, 2002); Onookome Okome, "Nollywood: Spectatorship, Audience and the Sites of Consumption," *Postcolonial Text* 3, no. 2 (2007): 1–21; Ching-Mei Esther Yau, *At Full Speed: Hong Kong Cinema in a Borderless World* (Minneapolis: University of Minnesota Press, 2001).
10. Walter Armbrust, "New Cinema, Commercial Cinema, and the Modernist Tradition in Egypt," *Alif: Journal of Comparative Poetics* 15 (1995): 83, 82.
11. William Brown, "Cease Fire: Rethinking Iranian Cinema Through Its Mainstream," *Third Text* 25, no. 3 (2011): 335, 340–341.
12. Naficy, *A Social History of Iranian Cinema*, 2:147–49.
13. Naficy, *A Social History of Iranian Cinema*, 2:149.
14. See, for example, Ervand Abrahamian, *Iran Between Two Revolutions* (Princeton, NJ: Princeton University Press, 1982).
15. Naficy, *A Social History of Iranian Cinema*, 2:265.
16. Naficy also deals with what happens to this genre in exile and explores how the ideals of masculinity promoted by these tough-guy types are maintained by Iranians abroad, espe-

4. WHO KILLED THE TOUGH GUY?

cially by those Iranians in Los Angeles.

17. Naficy, *A Social History of Iranian Cinema*, 2:269–94.
18. Naficy, *A Social History of Iranian Cinema*, 2:305.
19. For more, see Naficy, "Islamizing Film Culture in Iran," 26–65. Naficy, *A Social History of Iranian Cinema*, 2:311–12.
20. Naficy, *A Social History of Iranian Cinema*, 2:311.
21. See, for example, Camron Michael Amin, *The Making of the Modern Iranian Woman: Gender, State, Policy, and Popular Culture, 1865–1946* (Gainesville: University of Florida Press, 2002); and Afsaneh Najmabadi, *Women with Mustaches and Men Without Beards: Gender and Sexual Anxieties of Iranian Modernity* (Berkeley: University of California Press, 2008).
22. Quoted in Naficy, *A Social History of Iranian Cinema*, 2:300.
23. Ebrahim Golestan, "Qeysar: sar mashq-e kāmeli az Masud Kimiai barā-ye Masud Kimiai" [Qeysar: Completed homework by Masud Kimiai for Masud Kimiai], in *Majmu'eh-ye maqālāt dar naqd va barrasi-ye āsār-e Masud Kimiai* [A collection of critical articles and reviews of the works of Masud Kimiai], ed. Zavan Qukasian (Tehran: Entesharāt-e āgāh, 1364/1985), 121–25.
24. Quoted in François Penz, "From Topological Coherence to Creative Geography: Rohmer's *The Aviator's Wife* and Rivette's *Pont du Nord* in Cities in Transition," in *The Moving Image and the Modern Metropolis*, ed. Andrew Webber and Emma Wilson (London: Wallflower Press, 2008), 132.
25. Jamshid Arjmand, Mohammad Ali Sepanlu, Hushang Golshiri, and Zavan Qukasian, "Va yek begumagu-ye dustāneh" [A friendly disagreement], in *Majmu'eh-ye maqālāt dar naqd va barrasi-ye āsār-e Masud Kimiai* [A collection of critical articles and reviews of the works of Masud Kimiai], ed. Zavan Qukasian (Tehran: Entesharāt-e āgāh, 1364/1985), 50–51.
26. *Qeysar 40 sāl-e ba'd* [Qeysar 40 years later], directed by Masud Najafi, 2010, accessed September 1, 2014, https://www.youtube.com/watch?v=apVJPvPVlfo.
27. Hamid Naficy, *A Social History of Iranian Cinema*, vol. 1: *The Artisanal Era, 1897–1941* (Durham, NC: Duke University Press, 2011), 273.
28. Eve Kosofsky Sedgwick, *Epistemology of the Closet* (Berkeley: University of California Press, 1990), 1.
29. See, for example, Najmabadi, *Women with Mustaches and Men Without Beards*, 15–25; Willem Floor, *A Social History of Sexual Relations in Iran* (Washington, DC: Mage, 2008), 279–354; Amy Motlagh, *Burying the Beloved: Marriage, Realism, and Reform* (Stanford, CA: Stanford University Press, 2011), 36–38.
30. Najmabadi, *Women with Mustaches and Men Without Beards*, 15–25.
31. Golestan, "Qeysar," 122.
32. Naficy, *A Social History of Iranian Cinema*, 2:297.
33. Kaja Silverman, *The Subject of Semiotics* (New York: Oxford University Press, 1983), 211.
34. Naficy, *A Social History of Iranian Cinema*, 2:301, 300.
35. Zavan Qukasian, ed., *Majmu'eh-ye maqālāt dar naqd va barrasi-ye āsār-e Masud Kimiai* [A collection of critical articles and reviews of the works of Masud Kimiai] (Tehran: Entesharāt-e āgāh, 1364/1985).

4. WHO KILLED THE TOUGH GUY?

36. Laudan Nooshin, "Underground, Overground: Rock and Youth Discourses in Iran," *Iranian Studies* 38, no. 3 (2005): 462–94.

5. FILM ARCHIVES AND ONLINE VIDEOS: THE SEARCH FOR REFORM IN POST-KHATAMI IRAN

1. For more, see Anoushiravan Ehteshami and Mahjoob Zweiri, *Iran and the Rise of Its Neo-conservatives: The Politics of Tehran's Silent Revolution* (London and New York: I. B. Tauris, 2007).
2. Eva Patricia Rakel, "The Political Elite in the Islamic Republic: From Khomeini to Ahmadinejad," *Comparative Studies of South Asia, Africa, and the Middle East* 29, no.1 (2009): 121–23.
3. Michael Slackman, "Winner in Iran Calls for Unity; Reformists Reel," *New York Times*, June 26, 2005.
4. Saeed Zeydabadi-Nejad, *The Politics of Iranian Cinema: Film and Society in the Islamic Republic* (London: Routledge, 2010), 53.
5. Mohammad Said Mohassesi, "Futbāl bā qavānin-e handbāl" [Soccer according to the rules of handball], *Film* 361 (2007): 109.
6. For more, see T. Lewicki, "Al-Ḳazwīnī, zakariyyā' b. muḥammad b. maḥmūd Abū Yaḥyā," in *Encyclopaedia of Islam*, 2nd ed., ed. P. Bearman, Th. Bianquis, C. E. Bosworth, E. van Donzel, and W. P. Heinrichs (Brill, 2011), http://www.brillonline.nl.ezproxy.lib.utexas.edu/subscriber/entry?entry=islam_SIM-4093.
7. The emphasis is mine. It should be noted that in the English subtitles, this caution is translated as "All the characters and events in this film seemed to be real, but it's not true." Although this translation conveys the basic meaning, it fails to capture the complexity of the original.
8. Daniel Brumberg, *Reinventing Khomeini: The Struggle for Reform in Iran* (Chicago: University of Chicago Press, 2001), 153.
9. Nevertheless, it is important to note that the old spelling was still in use throughout the first half of the twentieth century, and as late as the 1950s the old spelling of "Tehran" was featured on license plates.
10. It is interesting to note that the earthquake in Rudbar inspired Kiarostami's film *Zendegi va digar hich* (Life and nothing more, 1992). Kiarostami goes in search of the actors who played in *Khāneh-ye dust kojāst?* (Where is the friend's house?, 1987). The film mimics reality and shows a director and his son who return to the village where one of his films was set and examine the earthquake's devastation.
11. William C. Wees, *Recycled Images: The Art and Politics of Found Footage Films* (New York: Anthology Film Archives, 1993), 11, 46–47.
12. Negar Mottahedeh, "Iranian Cinema in the Twentieth Century: A Sensory History," *Iranian Studies* 42, no. 4 (September 2009): 529–31.
13. Interestingly, Iranian cinema's first venture into filmmaking with dialogue proved challenging. *The Lor Girl* was produced and filmed in India, and producers Ardeshir Irani and

5. FILM ARCHIVES AND ONLINE VIDEOS

Abdolhossein Sepanta had to rely on Iranians living in India to serve as actors. However, the exile community in India was largely composed of Iranians from the province of Kerman; among this group was the actress Ruhangiz Saminezhad. Because Saminezhad had a thick Kerman accent, Sepanta had to adjust his script, and he made Golnar's character originally from Kerman. It is also worth noting that *The Lor Girl* was the first Iranian film, and one of the first films in the Middle East, to cast a woman in a main role.

14. Hamid Reza Sadr, *Iranian Cinema: A Political History* (New York: I. B. Tauris, 2006), 27–28.
15. Mohassesi, "Futbāl bā qavānin-e handbāl" [Soccer according to the rules of handball], 109.
16. Jaber Tavazoi, "Jafar va Golnar dar Tehran-e bi-anār: goftogu bā Massoud Bakhshi" [Jafar and Golnar in Tehran without pomegranates: A conversation with Massoud Bakhshi], *Jām-e jam*, 9 Tir 1388 / June 25, 2009, 7.
17. See, for example, Roger Bebee and Jason Middleton, eds., *Medium Cool: Music Videos from Soundies to Cell Phones* (Durham, NC: Duke University Press, 2007); Diane Railton and Paul Watson, *Music and the Politics of Representation* (Edinburgh: Edinburgh University Press, 2011); and Carol Vernallis, *Experiencing Music Video: Aesthetic and Cultural Context* (New York: Columbia University Press, 2004).
18. It should be noted that other Western styles, including rock, alternative, and heavy metal, were still banned. However, the line that separates all of these different styles is fluid; thus determining the nature of "pop" has been left to the interpretive powers of various governmental agents. Laudan Nooshin, "Underground, Overground: Rock and Youth Discourses in Iran," *Iranian Studies* 38, no. 3 (2005): 469.
19. Nooshin, "Underground, Overground," 469, 463.
20. Laudan Nooshin, "The Language of Rock: Iranian Youth, Popular Music, and National Identity," in *Media, Culture, and Society in Iran: Living with Globalization and the Islamic State*, ed. Mehdi Samati (London and New York: Routledge, 2008), 70.
21. For a fascinating look at the underground music scene, one that takes into consideration the distribution of permits and issues of form and style, see Bahman Ghobadi's underground film *Kasi az gorbeh-hā-ye Irāni khabar nadārad* (No one knows about Persian cats, 2009).
22. Currently, competition among music videos is no longer based on limited airtime. Although in the age of YouTube storage and access to music videos is almost unlimited, the genre still adheres for the most part to its original conventions. Moreover, the hyper-nature of the Internet puts music videos in a different kind of competition, wherein they are rivaling against other videos and sites for user attention.
23. Vernallis, *Experiencing Music Video*, 3.
24. This Arabic phrase is invoked by Shi'i Muslims to refer to Hossein, the martyr at the Battle of Karbala in 680, and it is used especially during the celebration of Moharram. It also has a political history and has been used during resistance movements in Iran and India. Interestingly, in Iran supporters of Mir-Hossein Mousavi used *yā Hossein* as a slogan after the results of the 2009 elections were announced.
25. Although the choice to recruit random people on the streets of Tehran to perform the song's lyrics has a subversive role in the video's aesthetic (as I shall demonstrate), the decision was also likely practical. When the song and the video were released, the members of Kiosk were

5. FILM ARCHIVES AND ONLINE VIDEOS

already living in exile because of their music. Returning to Iran to perform the song may not have been possible for them.

26. For more on the cosmetic surgery phenomenon in Iranian society, see Mehrdad Oskouei's film *Damāgh, beh sabk-e Irāni* (Nose Iranian style, 2006). The film's title plays off of the title of Kim Longinotto and Ziba Mir-Hosseini's famous documentary *Divorce Iranian Style* (1998).
27. It is significant that over the last thirty years, different governments within the Islamic Republic have marked their political atmosphere by readjusting women's clothing. Moderate leaders allow women more freedom with their dress, and with the *hejāb* in particular, whereas conservative leaders have announced their conservativeness by cracking down on women's dress.
28. Vernallis, *Experiencing Music Video*, 55.
29. *Qormeh sabzi* is a traditional Iranian stew. Both in terms of taste and execution, it would be very difficult to create a *qormeh sabzi* pizza. Nevertheless, several months after the "Love of Speed" music video premiered, there were reports that an Iranian team won third place at an international pizza competition with a *qormeh sabzi* pizza. However, I was unable to find confirmation of this victory in non-Iranian sources. It is also worth noting that even the phrase *pitzā-ye qormeh sabzi* is contradictory, because the word *pitzā* (pizza) is a loanword, and it is being combined with the name of a very traditional dish. The Islamic Republic has attempted to eliminate Western loanwords and encourages the word *kesh loqmeh* (stretchy snack) for pizza.
30. Janet Alexanian, "Poetry and Polemics: Iranian Literary Expression in the Digital Age," *Multi-Ethnic Literature in the United States* 33, no. 2 (2008): 146.

CONCLUSION: IRAN'S CINEMA MUSEUM AND POLITICAL UNREST

1. "Muzeh-ye sinemā, ganjineh-ye asnād va yādgār-hā" [The Cinema Museum, a repository of documents and relics], *Film* 221 (Tir 1377 / July 1998): 19.
2. "Muzeh-ye sinemā" [The Cinema Museum], 19.
3. Ali Reza Mahmudi, *Bist-o-panj sāl-e sinemā-ye Irān: nashriyāt va ketāb-hā-ye sinemāii* [Twenty-five years of Iranian cinema: Cinematic publications and books] (Muzeh-ye Sinemā: Tehran, 1382/2004).
4. For more, see Abdollah Gholamreza Kashi, *Matbu'āt dar 'asr-e Khatami* [Publications during the Khatami period] (Tehran: Salak, 2000).
5. Catherine Shoard, "Jafar Panahi Not in Cannes for *This Is Not a Film* Premier," *Guardian*, May 21, 2011, http://www.theguardian.com/film/2011/may/21/jafar-panahi-cannes-not-film-premiere.
6. Jafar Panahi, "Tārikh barkhord bā honarmand rā farāmush nemikonad" [History will not forget the encounter with the artist], *Rooz Online*, 2 Aban 1380 / October 24, 2010, http://www.roozonline.com/persian/archive/overall-archive/news/archive/2010/november/11/article/-a53b46133d.html.

BIBLIOGRAPHY

Abdelkhah, Fariba. *Being Modern in Iran*. New York: Columbia University Press, 2000.
Abrahamian, Ervand. *A History of Modern Iran*. Cambridge: Cambridge University Press, 2008.
——. *Iran Between Two Revolutions*. Princeton, NJ: Princeton University Press, 1982.
Aghaie, Kamran Scot. *The Martyrs of Karbala: Shi'i Symbols and Rituals in Modern Iran*. Seattle: University of Washington Press, 2004.
Al-e Ahmad, Jalal. *Plagued by the West*. Trans. Paul Sprachman. Delmar, NY: Caravan Books, 1982.
Alexanian, Janet. "Poetry and Polemics: Iranian Literary Expression in the Digital Age." *Multi-Ethnic Literature in the United States* 33, no. 2 (2008): 129–52.
Amin, Camron Michael. *The Making of the Modern Iranian Woman: Gender, State, Policy, and Popular Culture, 1865–1946*. Gainesville: University of Florida Press, 2002.
Andrews, Geoff. *10*. London: British Film Institute, 2005.
Arberry, John. *Sufism: An Account of the Mystics of Islam*. Mineola, NY: Dover, 2001.
Arjmand, Jamshid, Mohammad Ali Sepanlu, Hushang Golshiri, and Zavan Qukasian, "Va yek begumagu-ye dustāneh" [A friendly disagreement]. In *Majmu'eh-ye maqālāt dar naqd va barrasi-ye āsār-e Masud Kimiai* [A collection of critical articles and reviews of the works of Masud Kimiai], ed. Zavan Qukasian, 50–51. Tehran: Entesharāt-e āgāh, 1364/1985.
Arjomand, Saïd Amir. *After Khomeini: Iran Under His Successors*. Oxford and New York: Oxford University Press, 2009.
——. "Civil Society and the Rule of Law in the Constitutional Politics of Iran Under Khatami." *Social Research* 62, no. 2 (Summer 2000): 283–301.
——. "The Rise and Fall of Khatami and the Reformist Movement in Iran." *Constellations* 12 (Winter 2004): 502–20.
——. *The Shadow of God and the Hidden Imam: Religion, Political Order and Societal Change in Shi'ite Iran from the Beginning to 1890*. Chicago: University of Chicago Press, 1984.

BIBLIOGRAPHY

Armbrust, Walter. "New Cinema, Commercial Cinema, and the Modernist Tradition in Egypt." *Alif: Journal of Comparative Poetics* 15 (1995): 81–129.

Bani-Etemad, Rakhshan. "Ghamkhār-e bi edde'ā-ye zanān-e darmānde: goftogu bā Rakhshan Bani-Etemad" [Sympathy without the pretense of distressed women: A conversation with Rakhshan Bani-Etemad]. *Zanān* [Women] 25 (Mordād/Shahrivār 1374/1995): 44–50.

———. "Man filmsāz-e herfeh-i nistam: harf-hā-i az Rakhshan Bani-Etemad" [I am not a professional filmmaker: A few words from Rakhshan Bani-Etemad]. *Film* 19, no. 263 (2001): 120–24.

Bayat, Mangol. *Mysticism and Dissent: Socioreligious Thought in Qajar Iran*. Syracuse, NY: Syracuse University Press, 1982.

Bebee, Roger, and Jason Middleton, eds. *Medium Cool: Music Videos from Soundies to Cell Phones*. Durham, NC: Duke University Press, 2007.

Benjamin, Walter. *The Arcades Project*. Trans. Howard Eiland and Kevin McLaughlin. Cambridge, MA: Harvard University Press, 1999.

———. *Illuminations: Essays and Reflections*. Trans. Harry Zohn. New York: Pantheon, 1968.

Beumers, Brigit. *A History of Russian Cinema*. Oxford: Berg, 2009.

Boffa, Gilda. "A Study of Mohsen Makhmalbaf's 'Time of Love's' Intertextual References to Maulana Jalal al-Din Rumi's Poem 'The Three Fish.'" *Offscreen* 10, no. 7 (2006), accessed February 26, 2016, http://offscreen.com/view/time_of_love.

Bowering, Gerhard. "'Erfān.'" In *Encyclopedia Iranica*. Columbia University, 1982–. Article last updated January 19, 2012, http://www.iranicaonline.org/articles/erfan-1.

Bramley, Ellie Violet. "Behind the Scenes with Syria's 'Emergency Cinema.'" *Guardian*, March 26, 2014, http://www.theguardian.com/film/filmblog/2014/mar/26/abounaddara-collective-syria-cinema.

Brown, Wendy. *Edgework: Critical Essays in Knowledge and Politics*. Princeton, NJ: Princeton University Press, 2005.

Brown, William. "Cease Fire: Rethinking Iranian Cinema Through Its Mainstream." *Third Text* 25, no. 3 (2011): 335–41.

Brumberg, Daniel. *Reinventing Khomeini: The Struggle for Reform in Iran*. Chicago: University of Chicago Press, 2001.

Buck-Morss, Susan. *The Dialectics of Seeing: Walter Benjamin and the Arcades Project*. Cambridge, MA: MIT Press, 1989.

Chaudhuri, Shohini, and Howard Finn. "The Open Image: Poetic Realism and the New Iranian Cinema." *Screen* 44, no. 1 (Spring 2004): 38–57.

Chelkowski, Peter. "In Ritual and Revolution: The Image in the Transformation of Iranian Culture." *Views: The Journal of Photography of New England* 10 (Spring 1989): 7–11.

Chelkowski, Peter, and Hamid Dabashi. *Staging a Revolution: The Art of Persuasion in the Islamic Republic of Iran*. New York: New York University Press, 1999.

Cheshire, Godfrey. "How to Read Kiarostami." *Cineaste* 25, no. 4 (2000): 8–15.

Cooper, John. "The Limits of the Sacred: The Epistemology of Abd al-Karim Soroush." In *Islam and Modernity: Muslim Intellectuals Respond*, ed. John Cooper, Ronald L. Nettler, and Mohamed Mahmoud, 38–56. London and New York: I. B. Tauris, 1998.

BIBLIOGRAPHY

Dabashi, Hamid. *Close Up: Iranian Cinema, Past, Present, and Future.* London and New York: Verso, 2001.

———. "Dead Certainties: The Early Makhmalbaf." In *The New Iranian Cinema: Politics, Representation and Identity*, ed. Richard Tapper, 117–153. London and New York: I. B. Tauris, 2002.

———. *The Green Movement in Iran.* New Brunswick, NJ, and London: Transaction, 2011.

———. *Iran: A People Interrupted.* New York: The New Press, 2007.

———. *Makhmalbaf at Large: The Making of a Rebel Filmmaker.* London: I. B. Tauris, 2008.

———. *Masters and Masterpieces of Iranian Cinema.* Washington, DC: Mage, 2007.

———. *Theology of Discontent: The Ideological Foundations of the Islamic Revolution in Iran.* New York: New York University Press, 1993.

Dad, Babak. *Sad ruz bā Khatami: matn-e kāmel* [A hundred days with Khatami: The complete text]. Tehran: Ministry of Culture and Guidance, 1998.

Dahlén, Ashkan P. *Islamic Law, Epistemology and Modernity: Legal Philosophy in Contemporary Iran.* London: Routledge, 2003.

De Certeau, Michel. *The Practice of Everyday Life.* Trans. Steven Rendall. Berkeley and Los Angeles: University of California Press, 1984.

Derrida, Jacques. "Plato's Pharmacy." In *Dissemination*, 61–172. Trans. Barbara Johnson. New York and London: Continuum Books, 2004.

Ditmars, Hadani. "Rakhshan Bani-Etemad Talks to Hadani Ditmars About Bending the Rules in 'May Lady.'" *Sight and Sound* 20 (1999): 20.

Ebadi, Shirin. *Iran Awakening: A Memoir of Revolution and Hope.* With Azadeh Moaveni. New York: Random House, 2006.

Ebert, Roger. "Review: *Taste of Cherry.*" *Chicago Sun-Times*, February 28, 1998.

Egan, Eric. *The Films of Makhmalbaf: Cinema, Politics and Culture in Iran.* Washington, DC: Mage, 2005.

Ehteshami, Anoushiravan, and Mahjoob Zweiri. *Iran and the Rise of Its Neoconservatives: The Politics of Tehran's Silent Revolution.* London and New York: I. B. Tauris, 2007.

Eisenstein, Sergei. "A Dialectic Approach to Film Form." *Film Form: Essays in Film Theory.* Trans. Jay Leyda. San Diego and New York: Harvest Books, 1969.

Elena, Alberto. *The Cinema of Abbas Kiarostami.* Trans. Belinda Coombes. London: Saqi, 2005.

Fanon, Frantz. *The Wretched of the Earth.* Trans. Richard Philcox. New York: Grove City Press, 2005.

Farahmand, Azadeh. "Perspectives on Recent (International Acclaim for) Iranian Cinema." In *The New Iranian Cinema: Politics, Representation and Identity*, ed. Richard Tapper, 86–108. London: I. B. Tauris, 2002.

Fischer, Michael M. J. *Mute Dreams, Blind Owls, and Dispersed Knowledges: Persian Poesis in the Transnational Circuitry.* Durham, NC: Duke University Press, 2004.

Floor, Willem M. "The Political Role of Lutis in Iran." In *Modern Iran: The Dialectics of Continuity and Change*, ed. Michael E. Bonine and Nikki R. Keddie, 83–95. Albany: State University of New York Press, 1981.

———. *A Social History of Sexual Relations in Iran.* Washington, DC: Mage, 2008.

BIBLIOGRAPHY

Fozooni, Babak. "Kiarostami Debunked!" *New Cinemas: Journal of Contemporary Film* 2, no. 2 (2004): 73–89.

Gabriel, Teshome H. "Third Cinema as Guardian of Popular Memory: Towards a Third Aesthetics." In *Questions of Third Cinema*, ed. Jim Pines and Paul Willemen. London: British Film Institute, 1989.

———. *Third Cinema in the Third World: The Aesthetics of Liberation*. Ann Arbor, MI: UMI Research Press, 1982.

Ganti, Tejaswini. *Bollywood: A Guidebook to Popular Hindi Cinema*. London: Routledge, 2002.

Ganz, Adam, and Lina Khatib. "Digital Cinema: The Transformation of Film Practices and Aesthetics." *New Cinemas: Journal of Contemporary Film* 4, no. 1 (May 2006): 21–36.

Ghazian, Hossein. "The Crisis in the Iranian Film Industry and the Role of the Government." In *The New Iranian Cinema: Politics, Representation and Identity*, ed. Richard Tapper, 77–84. London: I. B. Tauris, 2002.

Gholamreza Kashi, Abdollah. *Matbu'āt dar 'asr-e Khatami* [Publications during the Khatami Period]. Tehran: Salak, 2000.

Gilloch, Graeme. *Myth and Metropolis: Walter Benjamin and the City*. Cambridge: Polity Press, 1996.

Golestan, Ebrahim. "Qeysar: sar mashq-e kāmeli az Masud Kimiai barā-ye Masud Kimiai" [*Qeysar*: Completed homework by Masud Kimiai for Masud Kimiai]. In *Majmu'eh-ye maqālāt dar naqd va barrasi-ye āsār-e Masud Kimiai* [A collection of critical articles and reviews of the works of Masud Kimiai], ed. Zavan Qukasian, 121–25. Tehran: Entesharāt-e āgāh, 1364/1985.

Graffy, Julian. "Taste of Cherry/Ta'am-e gilas." *Sight and Sound* 8, no. 6 (June 1998): 57.

Grigor, Talinn. "Recultivating 'Good Taste': The Early Pahlavi Modernists and Their Society for National Heritage." *Iranian Studies* 37 (Spring 2004): 17–45.

Guneratne, Anthony R., ed. *Rethinking Third Cinema*. London: Routledge, 2003.

Haeri, Shahla. "Sacred Canopy: Love and Sex Under the Veil." *Iranian Studies* 42, no. 1 (2009): 113–26.

Haglund, John. "Last Night's Best Speech." *Slate*, February 27, 2012, http://www.slate.com/blogs/browbeat/2012/02/27/asghar_farhadi_s_oscar_speech_the_best_of_the_night.html.

Hamid, Rahul. "Review: Under the Skin of the City." *Cineaste* 51 (2003): 50–51.

Haqqdar, Ali Asghar. *Gofteman-e farhangi-siāsi-ye Khatami* [Khatami's cultural-political discourse]. Tehran: Entesharāt-e Shafi'i, 1378/2000.

Hassaninasab, Nima. "Zhānr-e dovom-e Khordād" [The genre of the second of Khordad]. *Film* 19, no. 270 (2001): 10–15.

Hayes, Edmund. "10 × Ten: Kiarostami's Journey Into Modern Iran." *openDemocracy*, 2002, http://www.opendemocracy.net/content/articles/PDF/815.pdf.

Huntington, Samuel. "Clash of Civilizations?" *Foreign Affairs* 72, no. 3 (Summer 1993): 22–49

———. *The Clash of Civilizations and the Remaking of World Order*. New York: Touchstone, 1997.

Hurst, Heike. "Makhmalbaf questionne le pouvoir." *Jeune Cinéma* 247 (May–June 1996): 15–19.

Jahromi, Mohammad Rasul, and Amirreza Porholm. *Khatami-hā*. Tehran: Dādār, 2001.

Jalili, Ahmadreza. "Sinemāgarān dar entekhābāt: ruzegār-e mā . . ." [Filmmakers in the elections: Our Times . . .]. *Film* 20, no. 283 (2002): 18.

BIBLIOGRAPHY

Jehl, Douglas. "Killing of 3 Rebel Writers Turns Hope Into Fear." *New York Times*, December 14, 1998, http://www.nytimes.com/1998/12/14/world/killing-of-3-rebel-writers-turns-hope-to-fear-in-iran.html?src=pm.

Kamrava, Mehran. "The Civil Society Discourse in Iran." *British Journal of Middle Eastern Studies* 28, no. 2 (2001): 165–85.

———. *Iran's Intellectual Revolution*. Cambridge: Cambridge University Press, 2008.

Karimi-Hakkak, Ahmad. "Of Hial and Hounds: The Image of the Iranian Revolution in Recent Persian Literature." *State, Culture, and Society* 1, no. 3 (1985): 148–80.

Kashani-Sabet, Firoozeh. *Frontier Fictions: Shaping the Iranian Nation: 1804–1946*. Princeton, NJ: Princeton University Press, 1999.

Keddie, Nikki R. *Modern Iran: Roots and Results of Revolution*. New Haven, CT: Yale University Press, 2003.

Kepley, Vance, Jr. "Soviet Cinema and State Control: Lenin's Nationalization Decree Reconsidered." *Journal of Film and Video* 42, no. 2 (Summer 1990): 3–14.

Khatami, Mohammad. Address to the UNESCO Roundtable on Dialogue Among Civilizations. September 5, 2000, http://www.unesco.org/dialogue/en/khatami.htm.

———. *Eslām, ruhāniyyat va enqelāb-e Eslāmi* [Islam, the clergy, and the Islamic revolution]. Tehran: Tahr-e no, 1379/2000.

———. *Hazāreh-ye goft-o-gu va tafāhom*. Tehran: Nashr-e Resānash, 1378/2001.

———. *Mardomsālāri* [Democracy]. Tehran: Tahr-e no, 1380/2001.

———. "Women and Men Are Different, but Women Are Not the Second Sex and Men Are Not Superior." *Zan-e ruz* 143 (1997): 8–10.

———. *Zanān va javānān* [Women and youth]. Tehran: Tahr-e no, 2000.

"Khatami Threatens Resignation Over Power Struggle with Hard-Liners." *Daily Star*, July 17, 2003, accessed December 19, 2014, http://www.drsoroush.com/English/News_Archive/E-NWS-20030714-Khatami_Threatens_Resignation-The_Daily_Star.html.

Khomeini, Ruhollah. *Islam and Revolution: Writings and Declarations of Imam Khomeini*. Trans. Hamid Algar. London: Routledge and Paul Kegan, 1981.

Lang, Robert. *New Tunisian Cinema: Allegories of Resistance*. New York: Columbia University Press, 2014.

Lewicki, T. "Al-Ḳazwīnī, zakariyyāʿ b. muḥammad b. maḥmūd Abū Yaḥyā." In *Encyclopaedia of Islam*, ed. P. Bearman, Th. Bianquis, C. E. Bosworth, E. van Donzel, and W. P. Heinrichs. 2nd ed. Brill, 2011, http://www.brillonline.nl.ezproxy.lib.utexas.edu/subscriber/entry?entry=islam_SIM-4093.

Lewis, Bernard. "The Roots of Muslim Rage." *Atlantic Monthly* 266, no. 3 (September 1990): 47–60.

Lewis, Franklin D. *Rumi: Past and Present, East and West: Life, Teaching, and Poetry Jalāl al-Din Rumi*. Oxford: Oneworld, 2000.

Lopate, Philip. "Interview with Abbas Kiarostami." In *Totally, Tenderly, Tragically*, 352–67. New York: Anchor/Doubleday, 1998.

Maafi, Majid. "Siyāsat dar keluz āp" [Politics in close-up]. *Sorush* 27 (28 Khordad 1384 / June 18, 2005): 54.

BIBLIOGRAPHY

Madanipour, Ali. *Tehran: The Making of a Metropolis*. New York: John Wiley & Sons, 1998.

Mahmudi, Ali Reza. *Bist-o-panj sāl-e sinemā-ye Irān: nashriyāt va ketāb-hā-ye sinemāii* [Twenty-five years of Iranian cinema: Cinematic publications and books]. Muzeh-ye Sinemā: Tehran, 1382/2004.

Makhmalbaf, Mohsen. *Gong-e Khābideh: montakhab-e maqāleh-hā, goftogu-hā, va barrasi-hā* [Muted dreams: A selection of articles, interviews, and reviews]. Tehran: Nashr-e ney, 1372/1993.

———. *Nowbat-e 'āsheqi* [Time for love]. Tehran: Neshar-e ney, 1368/1990.

Manovich, Lev. *The Language of New Media*. Cambridge, MA: MIT Press, 2001.

Matin-asgari, Afshin. "Abdolkarim Sorush and the Secularization of Islamic Thought in Iran." *Iranian Studies* 30, nos. 1–2 (Winter/Spring 1997): 95–115.

May, Lary. *Out the Past: The Birth of Mass Culture and the Motion Picture Industry*. Chicago: University of Chicago Press, 1983.

Mcleod, Scott. "The Vote in Iran." *Time*, February 13, 2000, http://content.time.com/time/magazine/article/0,9171,39214,00.html.

Mehrabi, Massoud. "Commitment, Cinema, Construction: An Interview with Rakhshan Bani-Etemad." *Film International* 13, nos. 52–53 (2007): 82–93.

———. *Farhang-e film-hā-ye mostanad-e sinemā-ye Irān: az āghāz tā sāl-e 1375* [A guide to Iranian documentary films: From the beginning to 1997]. Tehran: Daftar-e Pezhuhesh-hā-ye farhangi, 1375/1997.

Milani, Farzaneh. *Veils and Words: The Emerging Voices of Iranian Women Writers*. Syracuse, NY: Syracuse University Press, 1992.

———. *Words, Not Swords: Iranian Women Writers and the Freedom of Movement*. Syracuse, NY: Syracuse University Press, 2011.

Mirbakhtyar, Shahla. *Iranian Cinema and the Islamic Revolution*. London: McFarland, 2006.

Mir-Hosseini, Ziba. "Iranian Cinema: Art, Society and the State." *Middle East Report* 219 (2001): 26–29.

———. "Negotiating the Forbidden: On Women and Sexual Love in Iranian Cinema." *Comparative Studies of South Asia, Africa, and the Middle East* 27 (Fall 2007): 673–79.

Mohassesi, Mohammad Said. "Futbāl bā qavānin-e handbāl" [Soccer according to the rules of handball]. *Film* 361 (2007): 109–11.

Moslem, Mehdi. *Factional Politics in Post-Khomeini Iran*. Syracuse, NY: Syracuse University Press, 2002.

Motlagh, Amy. *Burying the Beloved: Marriage, Realism, and Reform in Modern Iran*. Stanford, CA: Stanford University Press, 2011.

Mottahedeh, Negar. *Displaced Allegories: Post-Revolutionary Iranian Cinema*. Durham, NC: Duke University Press, 2008.

———. "Iranian Cinema in the Twentieth Century: A Sensory History." *Iranian Studies* 42, no. 4 (September 2009): 529–48.

———. *Representing the Unpresentable: Historical Images of National Reform from the Qajars to the Islamic Republic of Iran*. Syracuse, NY: Syracuse University Press, 2008.

BIBLIOGRAPHY

———. "Where Are Kiarostami's Women?" *Subtitles: On the Foreignness of Film*, ed. Atom Egoyan and Ian Balfour. Cambridge, MA: MIT Press, 2004.

Moulthrop, Stuart. "You Say You Want a Revolution? Hypertext and the Laws of Media." *Postmodern Culture* 1, no. 3 (May 1991): 14.

Mulvey, Laura. "Kiarostami's Uncertainty Principle." *Sight and Sound* 8, no. 6 (June 1998): 24–27.

———. "Repetition and Return." *Third Text* 21, no. 1 (January 2007): 19–29.

Naficy, Hamid. *An Accented Cinema: Exilic and Diasporic Filmmaking*. Princeton, NJ: Princeton University Press, 2001.

———. "Cinematic Exchange Relations: Iran and the West." In *Iran and the Surrounding World: Interactions in Culture and Cultural Politics*, ed. Nikki R. Keddie and Rudi Matthee, 254–79. Seattle and London: University of Washington Press, 2002.

———. "Iranian Cinema Under the Islamic Republic." *American Anthropologist* 97, no. 3 (1995): 548–58.

———. "Iranian Cinema Under the Islamic Republic." In *Images of Enchantment: Visual and Performing Arts of the Middle East*, ed. Sherifa Zuhur, 229–45. Cairo and New York: The American University in Cairo Press, 1998.

———. "Iranian Writers, Iranian Cinema, and the Case of 'Dash Akol.'" *Iranian Studies* 18, nos. 2–4 (Spring–Autumn 1985): 231–51.

———. "Islamizing Film Culture in Iran: A Post-Khatami Update." In *The New Iranian Cinema: Politics, Representation and Identity*, ed. Richard Tapper, 26–58. London: I. B. Tauris, 2002.

———. "Kiarostami's *Close-Up*: Questioning Reality, Realism, and Neorealism." In *Film Analysis: A Norton Reader*, ed. Jeffrey Geiger and R. L. Rutsky, 794–812. New York: W. W. Norton, 2005.

———. *A Social History of Iranian Cinema*. Vol. 1, *The Artisanal Era, 1897–1941*. Durham, NC: Duke University Press, 2011.

———. *A Social History of Iranian Cinema*. Vol. 2, *The Industrializing Years, 1941–1978*. Durham, NC: Duke University Press, 2011.

———. *A Social History of Iranian Cinema*. Vol. 3, *The Islamicate Period, 1978–1984*. Durham, NC: Duke University Press, 2012.

———. *A Social History of Iranian Cinema*. Vol. 4, *The Globalizing Era, 1984–2010*. Durham, NC: Duke University Press, 2012.

———. "Veiled Vision/Powerful Presences: Women in Post-Revolutionary Iranian Cinema." In *In the Eye of the Storm: Women in Post-Revolutionary Iran*, ed. Mahnaz Afkhami and Erika Friedl, 131–150. Syracuse, NY: Syracuse University Press, 1994.

———. "Veiled Voice and Vision in Iranian Cinema: The Evolution of Rakhshan Banietemad's Films." In *Ladies and Gentlemen, Boys and Girls: Gender in the Film at the End of the Twentieth Century*, ed. Murray Pomerance, 37–54. Albany, NY: SUNY Press, 2001.

Najmabadi, Afsaneh. *Women with Mustaches and Men Without Beards: Gender and Sexual Anxieties of Iranian Modernity*. Berkeley: University of California Press, 2008.

Newman, Michael Z. *Video Revolutions: On the History of a Medium*. New York: Columbia University Press, 2014.

BIBLIOGRAPHY

"Nezārat bar nemāyesh-e film va eslāyd va vidiyu va sodur-e parvaneh namāyesh-e ānhā" [Supervision over the exhibition of films, slides, and video and issuing their exhibition permits]. *Markez-e pazhuhesh-hā-ye majles-e shurā-ye eslāmi* [Islamic Parliament Research Center], July 3, 1982, http://rc.majlis.ir/fa/law/show/106928.

Nichols, Bill. *Blurred Boundaries: Questions of Meaning in Contemporary Culture*. Bloomington and Indianapolis: Indiana University Press, 1994.

——. "Discovering Form, Inferring Meaning: New Cinema and the Film Festival Circuit." *Film Quarterly* 47, no. 3 (Spring 1994): 16–30.

——. *Introduction to Documentary*. Bloomington and Indianapolis: Indiana University Press, 2001.

——. *Representing Reality: Issues and Concepts in Documentary*. Bloomington and Indianapolis: Indiana University Press, 1991.

Noh, Jean. "Mohsen Makhmalbaf, *The President*." *Screen Daily*, October 5, 2014, http://www.screendaily.com/features/interviews/mohsen-makhmalbaf-the-president/5078286.article.

Nooshin, Laudan. "The Language of Rock: Iranian Youth, Popular Music, and National Identity." In *Media, Culture, and Society in Iran: Living with Globalization and the Islamic State*, ed. Mehdi Samati, 69–93. London and New York: Routledge, 2008.

——. "Underground, Overground: Rock and Youth Discourses in Iran." *Iranian Studies* 38, no. 3 (2005): 462–94.

Okome, Onookome. "Nollywood: Spectatorship, Audience and the Sites of Consumption." *Postcolonial Text* 3, no. 2 (2007): 1–21.

Orgeron, David. *Road Movies: From Muybridge and Méliès to Lynch and Kiarostami*. New York: Palgrave MacMillan, 2008.

Pak-Shiraz, Nacim. "Filmic Discourses on the Role of the Clergy in Iran." *British Journal of Middle Eastern Studies* 34, no. 3 (2007): 331–49.

Parsipur, Shahrnush. *Khāterāt-e zendān* [Prison memoirs]. Stockholm: Baran, 1996.

——. *Zanān bedun-e mardān* [Women without men]. Tehran: Nashr-e noqreh, 1367/1991.

Penz, François. "From Topological Coherence to Creative Geography: Rohmer's *The Aviator's Wife* and Rivette's *Pont du Nord* in Cities in Transition." In *The Moving Image and the Modern Metropolis*, ed. Andrew Webber and Emma Wilson, 123–140. London: Wallflower Press, 2008.

Pines, Jim, and Paul Willemen, eds. *Questions of Third Cinema*. London: British Film Institute, 1989.

Poudeh, Reza J., and M. Reza Shirvani. "Issues and Paradoxes in the Development of Iranian National Cinema: An Overview." *Iranian Studies* 41 (Summer 2008): 323–42.

Price, Michael. "Imagining Life: The Ending of Taste of Cherry." *Sense of Cinema* 17 (November 2001), accessed December 19, 2014, http://sensesofcinema.com/2001/abbas-kiarostami-17/cherry/.

Qukasian, Zavan, ed. *Majmu'eh-ye maqālāt dar naqd va barrasi-ye āsār-e Masud Kimiai* [A collection of critical articles and reviews of the works of Masud Kimiai]. Tehran: Entesharāt-e āgāh, 1364/1985.

Qukasian, Zavan. *Majmu'eh-ye maqālāt dar naqd va mo'arrefi-ye āsār-e Abbas Kiarostami* [A collection of criticism and reviews of Abbas Kiarostami's works]. Tehran: Nashr-e didār, 1375/1997.

BIBLIOGRAPHY

Rahimieh, Nasrin. "Capturing Cultural Transformation on Film: Makhmalbaf's *A Moment of Innocence.*" *Edebiyat: Journal of Middle Eastern Literatures* 12, no. 2 (2001): 195–214.

———. "Overcoming the Orientalist Legacy of Iranian Modernity: Women's Post-Revolutionary Film and Literary Production." *Thamyris/Intersecting* 10 (2003): 147–63.

Rahmani, Bahram. *Afsāneh-ye jāme'eh-ye madani* [The myth of civil society]. Köln: Forugh Books, 2001.

Railton, Diane, and Paul Watson. *Music and the Politics of Representation.* Edinburgh: Edinburgh University Press, 2011.

Rakel, Eva Patricia. "The Political Elite in the Islamic Republic: From Khomeini to Ahmadinejad." *Comparative Studies of South Asia, Africa, and the Middle East* 29, no.1 (2009): 105–25.

Rastegar, Kamran. "Book Review: *Displaced Allegories.*" *Feminist Review* 97, no. 1 (2011): 14–16.

Rosen, Miriam. "The Camera of Art: An Interview with Abbas Kiarostami." *Cineaste* 19, nos. 2–3 (Fall 1992): 40.

Rosenbaum, Jonathan. "Fill in the Blanks." *Chicago Reader,* May 29, 1998.

Rosenbloom, Nancy J. "Between Reform and Regulation: The Struggle Over Film Censorship in Progressive America, 1909–1922." *Film History* 1, no. 4 (1987): 307–25.

Rosenthal, F. "Intiḥār." In *Encyclopaedia of Islam,* ed. P. Bearman, Th. Bianquis, C. E. Bosworth, E. van Donzel, and W. P. Heinrichs. 2nd ed. Brill, 2011, http://www.brillonline.nl.ezproxy.lib.utexas.edu/subscriber/entry?entry=islam_SIM-3581.

Roy, Oliver. "The Crisis of Religious Legitimacy in Iran." *Middle East Journal* 87, no. 2 (Spring 1999): 201–16.

Sadr, Hamid Reza. *Iranian Cinema: A Political History.* London: I. B. Tauris, 2006.

Saeed-Vafa, Mehrnaz, and Jonathan Rosenbaum. *Abbas Kiarostami.* Urbana and Chicago: University of Illinois Press, 2003.

Safaee, Hamed, and Vahid Parsa. "Tehrān: shahr-e bi-hāfezeh" [Tehran: The city that forgets]. *Tehran Avenue* (May 2007), http://www.tehranavenue.com/article.php?id=693.

Samini, Naghmeh. "Rakhshan Bani-Etemad dar yek negāh" [Rakhshan Bani-Etemad at a glance]. *Film* 19, no. 263 (2001): 132.

Schimmel, Annemarie. *As Though a Veil: Mystical Poetry in Islam.* New York: Columbia University Press, 1982.

Sedgwick, Eve Kosofsky. *Epistemology of the Closet.* Berkeley: University of California Press, 1990.

Siavoshi, Sussan. "Cultural Policies and the Islamic Republic: Cinema and Book Production." *International Journal of Middle Eastern Studies* 29, no. 4 (1997): 509–30.

Silverman, Kaja. *The Subject of Semiotics.* New York: Oxford University Press, 1983.

Shahidi, Hossein. *Journalism in Iran: From Mission to Profession.* New York: Routledge, 2007.

Sheibani, Khatereh. "Kiarostami and the Aesthetics of Modern Persian Poetry." *Iranian Studies* 39, no. 4 (2006): 509–37.

———. *The Poetics of Iranian Cinema: Aesthetics, Modernity and Film After the Revolution.* London and New York: I. B. Tauris, 2011.

Shoard, Catherine. "Jafar Panahi Not in Cannes for *This Is Not a Film* Premier." *Guardian,* May 21, 2011, http://www.theguardian.com/film/2011/may/21/jafar-panahi-cannes-not-film-premiere.

BIBLIOGRAPHY

Shohat, Ella, and Robert Stam. *Unthinking Eurocentrism: Multiculturalism and the Media.* London and New York: Routledge, 1994.

Simmon, Scott. "Movies, Reform, and New Women." In *American Cinema in the 1910s: Themes and Variations,* ed. Charlie Keil and Ben Singer, 26–47. New Brunswick, NJ: Rutgers University Press, 2009.

Slackman, Michael. "Winner in Iran Calls for Unity; Reformists Reel." *New York Times,* June 26, 2005.

Soja, Edward. *Postmodern Geographies: The Reassertion of Space in Critical Social Theory.* London: Verso Press, 1989.

Sontag, Susan. *Regarding the Pain of Others.* New York: Picador, 2004.

Soroush, Abdolkarim. "Interview with Dariush Sajjadi." *Homa TV.* March 9, 2006, http://www.drsoroush.com/English/Interviews/E-INT-HomaTV.html.

———. *Qabz va bast-e te'urik-e shari'at: nazarieh-ye takāmol-e ma'refat-e dini* [The theoretical contraction and expansion of religious law: The concept of the evolution of religious knowledge]. Tehran: Mo'aseseh-ye farhang-e sarāt, 1378/1999.

———. *Reason, Freedom, and Democracy in Islam: Essential Writings of 'Abdolkarim Soroush.* Trans. and ed. Mahmoud Sadri and Ahmad Sadri. New York: Oxford University Press, 2000.

Stam, Robert. "Beyond Third Cinema: The Aesthetics of Hybridity." In *Rethinking Third Cinema,* ed. Anthony R. Guneratne, 32–47. London: Routledge, 2003.

Tabari, Keyvan. "The Rule of Law and the Politics of Reform in Post-Revolutionary Iran." *International Sociology* 18, no. 1 (March 2003): 96–113.

Tabemohammadi, Shahram. "Hargez film-e siāsi nakhvāham sākht: goft-o-gu bā Abbas Kiarostami" [I will never make a political film: A conversation with Abbas Kiarostami]. *Film* 19, no. 254 (2001): 42–44.

Talattof, Kamran. *The Politics of Writing in Iran: A History of Modern Persian Literature.* Syracuse, NY: Syracuse University Press, 2000.

Tapper, Richard. *The New Iranian Cinema: Politics, Representation and Identity.* London: I. B. Tauris, 2002.

Tarock, Adam. "The Muzzling of the Liberal Press in Iran." *Third World Quarterly* 22, no. 4 (2001): 585–602.

Tavakoli-Targhi, Mohammad. *Refashioning Iran: Orientalism, Occidentalism, and Historiography.* New York: Palgrave, 2001.

Tavazoi, Jaber. "Jafar va Golnar dar Tehran-e bi-anār: goftogu bā Massoud Bakhshi" [Jafar and Golnar in Tehran without pomegranates: A conversation with Massoud Bakhshi]. *Jām-e jam,* 9 Tir 1388 / June 25, 2009.

Tazmini, Ghancheh. *Khatami's Iran: The Islamic Republic and the Turbulent Path to Reform.* London: I. B. Tauris, 2009.

Vahdat, Farzin. "Religious Modernity in Iran: Dilemmas of Islamic Democracy in the Discourses of Mohammad Khatami." *Comparative Studies of South Asia, Africa, and the Middle East* 25 no. 3 (2005): 650–64.

Varzi, Roxanne. "A Ghost in the Machine: The Cinema of the Iranian Sacred Defense." In *The*

New Iranian Cinema: Politics, Representation and Identity, ed. Richard Tapper, 156–66. London: I. B. Tauris, 2002.

———. *Warring Souls: Youth, Media, and Martyrdom in Post-Revolution Iran*. Durham, NC: Duke University Press, 2006.

Vaziri, Persheng. "Iranian Documentary Cinema Between Reality and Fiction." *Middle East Report* 225 (Winter 2002): 53–54.

Vernallis, Carol. *Experiencing Music Video: Aesthetic and Cultural Context*. New York: Columbia University Press, 2004.

Wees, William C. *Recycled Images: The Art and Politics of Found Footage Films*. New York: Anthology Film Archives, 1993.

Winberger, Stephen. "Neorealism, Iranian Style." *Iranian Studies* 40, no. 1 (2007): 5–16.

Yari, Abbas. "Noqteh-ye 'atf: goftegu bā Seyfollah Dād" [Turning point: A conversation with Seyfollah Dad]. *Film* 15, no. 205 (Khordād 1376 / June 1997): 40–41.

Yau, Ching-Mei Esther. *At Full Speed: Hong Kong Cinema in a Borderless World*. Minneapolis: University of Minnesota Press, 2001.

Yazdi, Ebrahim. *Seh Jomhuri* [Three republics]. Tehran: Jāme'eh-ye Irāniān, 1379/2000.

Youngblood, Denise J. *Soviet Cinema in the Silent Era, 1918–1935*. Austin: University of Texas Press, 1991. Kindle edition.

Zeydabadi-Nejad, Saeed. *The Politics of Iranian Cinema: Film and Society in the Islamic Republic*. London: Routledge, 2010.

Žižek, Slavoj. *The Fright of Real Tears: Kryztof Kieslowski Between Theory and Post-Theory*. London: British Film Institute, 2001.

PERSIAN NEWSPAPERS AND JOURNALS

Abrār (6 Farvardin 1370 / March 26, 1991).
Adineh 72 (Mordād 1371 / August 1992).
Āyeneh-ye andisheh 4 (Bahman 1369 / February 1991).
——— 5 (Esfand 1369 / March 1991).
Ettelā'āt (16 Esfand 1369 / March 6, 1991).
——— (21 Esfand 1369 / March 12, 1991).
——— (27 Esfand 1369 / March 18, 1991).
——— (19 Khordād 1370 / June 9, 1991).
——— (20 Khordād 1370 / June 10, 1991).
——— (21 Khordād 1370 / June 11, 1991).
——— (22 Khordād 1370 / June 12, 1991).
——— (4 Khordād 1371 / May 25, 1992).
——— (12 Ordibehesht 1372 / May 2, 1993).
——— (15 Shahrivar 1372 / September 7, 1993).

BIBLIOGRAPHY

—— (6 Mehr 1372 / September 26, 1993).
—— (12 Mehr 1372 / October 4, 1993).
—— (12 Abān 1372 / November 3, 1993).
—— (4 Dey 1372 / December 25, 1993).
—— (5 Khordād 1377 / May 26, 1998).
Film, no. 34 (Esfand 1364 / March 1986).
——, no. 104 (Farvardin 1370 / March 1991).
——, no. 108 (Tir 1370 / July 1991).
——, no. 125 (Tir 1371 / July 1992).
——, no. 135 (Dey 1381 / January 1993).
——, no. 204 (Khordād 1376 / June 1997).
——, no. 205 (Khordād 1376 / June 1997).
——, no. 207 (Shahrivar 1376 / September 1997).
——, no. 221 (Tir 1377 / July 1998).
——, no. 262 (Āzar 1379 / November 2001).
——, no. 264 (Bahman 1379 / February 2001).
——, no. 270 (Khordād 1380 / June 2001).
——, no. 271 (Tir 1380 / July 2001).
——, no. 272 (Mordād 1380 / August 2001).
——, no. 275 (Mehr 1380 / September 2001).
——, no. 280 (Bahman 1380 / January 2002).
——, no. 287 (Tir 1381 / July 2002).
——, no. 288 (Mordād 1381 / August 2002).
Jām-e jam (9 Tir 1388 / June 25, 2009).
Jomhuri-ye Eslāmi (12 Esfand 1369 / March 3, 1991).
—— (15 Esfand 1369 / March 6, 1991).
—— (23 Esfand 1369 / March 14, 1991).
Kehyān-e farhangi (Bahman 1371 / February 1993).
Keyhān (7 Esfand 1369 / February 26, 1991).
—— (8 Esfand 1369 / February 27, 1991).
—— (12 Esfand 1369 / March 3, 1991).
—— (23 Esfand 1369 / March 14, 1991).
—— (25 Esfand 1369 / March 16, 1991).
—— (26 Esfand 1369 / March 17, 1991).
—— (21 Farvardin 1370 / April 10, 1991).
—— (1 Ordibehesht 1370 / April 21, 1991).
—— (2 Ordibehesht 1370 / April 22, 1991).
—— (5 Ordibehesht 1370) / April 25, 1991).
—— (21 Ordibehesht 1370 / May 11, 1991).
—— (29 Ordibehesht 1370 / May 18, 1991).
—— (30 Ordibehesht 1370 / May 19, 1991).
—— (31 Ordibehesht 1370 / May 20, 1991).

BIBLIOGRAPHY

—— (1 Khordād 1370 / May 22, 1991).
—— (8 Khordād 1370 / May 29, 1991).
Omid (12 Esfand 1369 / March 3, 1991).
—— (19 Esfand 1369 / March 10, 1991).
Resālat (2 Esfand 1369 / February 21, 1991).
—— (5 Esfand 1369 / February 24, 1991).
—— (14 Esfand 1369 / March 7, 1991).
—— (25 Esfand 1369 / March 16, 1991).
—— (7 Farvardin 1370 / March 27, 1991).
—— (10 Farvardin 1369 / March 30, 1991).
—— (14 Farvardin 1370 / April 3, 1991).
—— (4 Ordibehesht 1370 / April 24, 1991).
Rooz Online (2 Aban 1380 / October 24, 2010).
Salām (26 Mordād 1376 / August 17, 1997).
Sorush (28 Khordād 1384 / June 18, 2005).
Zanān (Ordibehesht 1376 / May 1997).

FILMOGRAPHY

Apple / Sib. Samira Makhmalbaf, 1998, Iran/France.
Blue Scarf, The / Rusari-ye ābi. Rakhshan Bani-Etemad, 1993, Iran.
Boycott / Bāykot. Mohsen Makhmalbaf, 1985, Iran.
Bread and Alley / Nān va kucheh. Abbas Kiarostami, 1970, Iran.
Bread, Love, and a 1000cc Motorcycle / Nān o 'eshq o mutur-e hezar. Abulhosssein Davudi, 2001, Iran.
Brick and Mirror / Khesht va āyeneh. Ebrahim Golestan, 1965, Iran.
Circle, The / Dāyereh. Jafar Panahi, 2000, Iran/Switzerland/Italy.
Close-Up / Namā-ye nazdik. Abbas Kiarostami, 1990, Iran.
Cow, The / Gāv. Dariush Mehrjui, 1969, Iran.
Crow, The / Kalāgh. Bahram Beyzaie, 1976, Iran.
Cyclist, The / Bāysikelrān. Mohsen Makhmalbaf, 1989, Iran.
Dash Akol / Dāsh Ākol. Masud Kimiai, 1972, Iran.
Divorce Iranian Style. Kim Longinotto and Ziba Mir-Hosseini, 1998, Iran/UK.
Gilaneh / Gilāneh. Rakhshan Bani-Etemad, 2004, Iran.
Hamun / Hamun. Dariush Mehrjui, 1990, Iran.
House Is Black, The / Khāneh siāh ast. Forugh Farrokhzad, 1962, Iran.
Legend of a Sigh / Afsāneh-ye āh. Tahmineh Milani, 1991, Iran.
Life and Nothing More / Zendegi va digar hich. Abbas Kiarostami, 1992, Iran.
Lor Girl, The / Dokhtar-e Lor. Ardeshir Irani and Abdolhossein Sepanta, 1933, Iran/India.
"Love of Speed" / "'Eshq-e sor'at." Ahmad Kiarostami and Kiosk, 2007, Iran/United States.
Marriage of the Blessed / 'Arusi-ye khubān. Mohsen Makhmalbaf, 1989, Iran.
May Lady / Bānu-ye ordibehesht. Rakhshan Bani-Etemad, 1998, Iran.
Moment of Innocence / Nan va goldān. Mohsen Makhmalbaf, 1996, Iran/France.

FILMOGRAPHY

Mudbrick and Mirror / Khesht va āyeneh. Ebrahim Golestan, 1965, Iran.
Nasuh's Repentance / Towbeh-ye Nasuh. Mohsen Makhmalbaf, 1983, Iran.
Narges. Rakhshan Bani-Etemad, 1992, Iran.
Night It Rained, The / Un shab keh bārun umad. Kamran Shirdel, 1967, Iran.
Nights of the Zayenderud / Shab-hā-ye zāyendeh rud. Mohsen Makhmalbaf, 1991, Iran.
No One Knows About Persian Cats / Kasi az gorbeh-hā-ye Irāni khabar nadārad. Bahman Ghobadi, 2009, Iran.
Nose Iranian Style / Damāgh, beh sabk-e Irāni. Mehrdad Oskouei, 2006, Iran/United States.
Off Limits / Khārej az mahdudeh. Rakhshan Bani-Etemad, 1988, Iran.
Offside / Āfsāyd. Jafar Panahi, 2006, Iran.
Our Times . . . / Ruzegār-e mā . . . . Rakhshan Bani-Etemad, 2002, Iran.
Peddler, The / Dastforush. Mohsen Makhmalbaf, 1986, Iran.
Prince Ehtejab / Shāzdeh ehtejāb. Bahman Farmanara, 1974, Iran.
Protest / E'terāz. Masud Kimiai, 1999, Iran.
Qeysar / Qeysar. Masud Kimiai, 1969, Iran.
Qeysar 40 Years Later / Qeysar 40 sāl-e ba'd. Masud Najafi, 2010, Iran.
Red / Qermez. Ferydun Jeyrani, 1999, Iran.
Smell of Camphor, the Scent of Jasmine / Bu-ye kāfur, 'atr-e yās. Bahman Farmanara, 2000, Iran.
South of the City / Jonub-e shahr. Farrokh Ghaffari, 1958, Iran.
Tall Shadows of the Wind / Sāyeh-hā-ye boland-e bād. Bahman Farmanara, 1978, Iran.
Taste of Cherry / Ta'm-e gilās. Abbas Kiarostami, 1997, Iran/France.
Tehran Is the Capital of Iran / Tehrān pāytakht-e Irān ast. Kamran Shirdel, 1966, Iran.
Tehran Has No More Pomegranates / Tehrān anār nadārad. Massoud Bakhshi, 2007, Iran.
10. Abbas Kiarostami, 2002, Iran/France/United States.
10 on Ten. Abbas Kiarostami, 2004, Iran/France.
This Is Not a Film / In film nist. Mojtaba Mirtahmasb and Jafar Panahi, 2011, Iran.
Through the Olive Trees / Zir-e darakhtān-e zeytun. Abbas Kiarostami, 1994, Iran/France.
Time for Love / Nowbat-e 'āsheqi. Mohsen Makhmalbaf, 1991, Iran/Turkey.
Two Sightless Eyes / Do cheshm-e bisu. Mohsen Makhmalbaf, 1983, Iran.
Under the Skin of the City / Zir-e pust-e shahr. Rakhshan Bani-Etemad, 2000, Iran.
Under the Skin of the Night / Zir-e pust-e shab. Feyridun Goleh, 1974, Iran.
Where Is the Friend's House / Khāneh-ye dust kojāst. Abbas Kiarostami, 1987, Iran.
Who Do You Show These Films to, Anyway? / Beh ki in film-hā ro neshun midin. Rakhshan Bani-Etemad, 1993, Iran.
Wind Will Carry Us, The / Bād mā rā khāhad bord. Abbas Kiarostami, 1999, Iran/France.

INDEX

Abrahamian, Ervand, 18
absolutism, 58, 59; antiabsolutism, 32, 41
accountability, 29–41
Ādam barfi (The snowman) (film), 20
Adineh, Golab, 70, *71*
Adorno, Theodore, 141
aesthetics, 105; Islamic set of, 32; M. Makhmalbaf and, 32, 38; mystic, 54
Afkhami, Behruz, 18, 62
African American cinema, 10
Afsāneh-ye āh (Legend of a sigh) (film), 117
Āfsāyd (Offside) (film), 204
Afsharnaderi, Nader, 67
Ahmad, Jalal Al-e, 155
Ahmadinejad, Mahmoud: Green movement and, 201–2; Majles and, 167; political platform of, 25, 166
Akbari, Mania, 115, 119–20
Alefbā-ye afghan (Afghan alphabet) (film), 21
Alexanian, Janet, 196
Angel of History, 94
Angelus Novus (Klee), 94
antiabsolutism, 32, 41
antidocumentary (*zed-e mostanad*), 168

Anvar, Fakhreddin, 16, 37
Apple (*Sib*) (film), 95–96
archival images, 183
ARK. *See* Association of Revolutionary Cinematography
Armbrust, Walter, 141–42
art-house cinema, 73, 136, 163, 165; censorship and, 141; commercial cinema and, 141–42; digital video and, 121; in Egypt, 141; reality and, 65
Arts University, 126
'Arusi-ye khubān (Marriage of the blessed) (film), 223n60
'āshurā (mourning ceremony), 53
Assad, Bashar al-, 1
assault on culture (*tahājom-e farhangi*), 100, 101
Association of Revolutionary Cinematography (ARK), 8
Ātashbas (*Ceasefire*) (film), 142
Āthār al-bilād wa-akhbār al-'ibād (Monuments of the countries and the history of their inhabitants) (Qazvini), 169
authority, 29–41

INDEX

authorship, 29–41
avant-garde filmmaking, 7
Az Abbas-e Kiarostami motenafferam! (I hate Abbas Kiarostami!) (film), 123

Bād mā rā khāhad bord (*The Wind Will Carry Us*) (film), 115, 118
Bāgh-e ferdaws (Ferdows Garden), 22, 197, 198
Bahār tā bahār (Spring to spring) (documentary), 85
Bakhshi, Massoud, 25, 167, 168, 169, 170, 174, 179
Balut (Oak) (documentary), 67
Bam earthquake, 180
Bani-Etemad, Rakhshan, 21, 70, 84, 90, 121, 141, 185; documentary and, 65–66, 69, 72; housing crisis and, 85; Khatami and, 62; montage and, 79; shot of, 71; social commentary and, 64; time and, 88; urbanism and, 24, 73; women and, 63. *See also specific films*
Bānu-ye ordibehesht (*May Lady*) (film), 62, 218n42
Baqeri, Ebrahim, 74
Bāshu, gharibeh-ye kuchak (Bashu, the little stranger) (film), 13, 17, 29
Battle of Algiers (film), 12
Battle of Chile, The (film), 10
Battle of Karbala, 227n24
Bāykot (*Boycott*) (film), 32, 33
Bazargan, Mehdi, 15
Behesht-e Zahra Cemetery, 2, 3
Beheshti, Mohammad, 16, 198
Benjamin, Walter, 82, 84, 94, 116
Berlin International Film Festival, 147
Beyzaie, Bahram, 13, 29, 182
Board of Censorship of Programs of Motion Pictures Shows, 5
Board of Review, 5
Boffa, Gilda, 213n37
Bonyād-e sinemā-ye Fārābi (Farabi Cinema Foundation), 12, 16, 29, 198
Boycott (*Bāykot*) (film), 32, 33

Bread, Love, and a 1000cc Motorcycle (*Nān o 'eshq o mutur-e hezar*), 163–64
Brown, Wendy, 92
Brown, William, 142
Bu-ye kāfur, 'atr-e yās (*The Smell of Camphor, The Scent of Jasmine*) (film), 24, 96, 123–35, 125, 129, 135

Cameron, James, 163
campaign movies (*film-hā-ye tablighāt-e entekhābāti*), 61–62, 99, 100
Cannes Film Festival, 103, 115, 200, 202, 203
capitalism, 186
Ceasefire (*Ātashbas*) (film), 142
CEDAW. *See* Elimination of All Forms of Discrimination Against Women
censorship, 12, 14, 31, 74, 120, 162; art-house cinema and, 141; in Chinese cinema, 9; digital video and, 102; Ministry of Culture and Islamic Guidance and, 28; modesty laws and, 13; women and, 69, 117
Center for Women's Participation, 119
Certeau, Michel de, 77
China, 9
Cinecittà Film Studio, 1
Cinema House Festival, 63
Cinema Museum (Muzeh-ye sinemā), 21–22, 25, 197–200, 204
cinema-related publishing, 198
Cinema Rex fire, 2
circularity, 109
circular journeys, 104
circumstance, 46–47
city planning, 90
civil society (*jāme'eh-ye madani*), 18–19, 21, 76, 77, 162, 167, 178
clash of civilizations, 59, 216n86
commercial cinemas, 141
commitment, 63–73
Communist Party, 7
Constitutional Revolution (1905–1911), 59
context, 59

246

INDEX

Culture Principles, 36
Culture Revolution Institute, 215n82

Dabashi, Hamid, 128, 129; Derrida and, 215n66; M. Makhmalbaf and, 32, 39, 96; mysticism and, 54; *Protest* and, 139
Dad, Seyfollah, 18, 37, 38, 62, 99, 100, 198
Dah (film), 24
Dahlén, Ashkan, 57
"Dar in bon bast" (In this dead end) (Shamlu), 214n62
Dariush, Hajir, 128, 147
Darvish, Ahmad Reza, 18, 62
Dāsh Ākol (film), 146
dāsh mashti films, 144, 146
Dastforush (The peddler) (film), 32
Dāyereh (The circle) (film), 204
Dāyi jān Nāpol'on (My Uncle Napoleon) (TV series), 182
democratization, of intellectualism, 130
Derrida, Jacques, 215n66
dialogue among civilizations (*goftegu-ye tamaddon-hā*), 18, 19, 21, 59, 93, 127, 200
digital video, 24, 96–97, 102, 121–23
Din Shah, Mozaffar al-, 183
Din Shah, Naser al-, 172, 173, 183
discourses of sobriety, 92
documentary: antidocumentary, 168; Bani-Etemad and, 65–66, 69, 72; commitment, reality and representation and, 63–73; metadocumentary, 181; untimeliness of, 87–94; urban myth and, 73–87. See also specific documentaries
Dokhtar-e Lor (The Lor Girl) (film), 148–49, 182, 183–84
domestic violence, 86
Dos Santos, Nelson Perreira, 2

earthly love (*'eshq-e zamini*), 43–44
earthquakes, 178, 180, 226n10
Ebert, Roger, 103
Egan, Eric, 212n36

Egypt, 141
Eisenstein, Sergei, 8, 9, 79, 168
Elena, Alberto, 116
Elimination of All Forms of Discrimination Against Women (CEDAW), 119
emergency cinema, 1
Ershadi, Homayun, 113
'eshq-e āsemān (heavenly love), 43–44
"Eshq-e sor'at" (Love of speed) (Kiosk), 25, 167, 177, 186–96, *190*, *195*, 227n25
'eshq-e zamini (earthly love), 43–44
eslāhtalabi (political reform), 15
E'terāz (*Protest*) (film), 24–25, 136–40, 145, 156–62
Ettelā'āt (newspaper), 35
Europeanization, 172
exorcism, 55

factionalism, 28, 37, 41, 76
"Fairies (Pariā)" (Shamlu), 214n62
Fajr Film Festival, 29–30, 34, 43, 50, 170
Fanon, Frantz, 10
Farabi Cinema Foundation (Bonyād-e sinemā-ye Fārābi), 12, 16, 29, 198
Farahmand, Azadeh, 103
Farhadi, Asghar, 13–14, 141
Farmanara, Bahman, 21, 24, 96, 103, 123, 124, 126
Farrokhzad, Forugh, 67, 181, 218n42
female characters, 98, 150–51, 218n42
feminism, 166
Ferdows Garden (Bāgh-e ferdaws), 22, 197, 198
Film (journal), 38, 88, 97, 101
film archives, 166–68
film-e ābgushti (stew films), 140
filmfārsi, 137, 140–43, 148, 163
film-hā-ye tablighāt-e entekhābāti (campaign movies), 61–62, 99, 100
financial backing, 31
financial incentive policies, 12
found footage, 169
freedom of press, 131
funerals, 123–35

INDEX

Gabriel, Teshome, 10
Gan, Aleksei, 7
Ganj-e Qarun (Qarun's treasure) (film), 164
Ganz, Adam, 117, 122
Gāv (The cow) (film), 3, 50, 73
Gavazn-hā (The deer) (film), 2
gender: homeownership and, 86; inequalities in, 84, 86; legal relations and, 117; norms of, 146; roles of, 145, 148–50; sexuality and, 151. *See also* masculinity; women
"Genre of the Second of Khordād (Zhānr-e dovom-e khordād)" (Hassaninasab), 97
Getino, Octavio, 10
Ghaffari, Farrokh, 74, 75
gharbzadegi (Westoxicated), 210n10
Ghazali, Al-, 55
Gilāneh (film), 73
globalization, 9; Third Cinema and, 10
goftegu-ye tamaddon-hā (dialogue among civilizations), 18, 19, 21, 59, 93, 127, 200
Golestan, Ebrahim, 67, 127, 147, 152
Golshiri, Hushang, 124
Gong-e khābideh (Muted dreams) (M. Makhmalbaf), 43
Goskino, 7
government, 60, 76
Gozāresh-e 71 (Report of 71) (documentary), 85
Grassa, Marco Della, 108
Green movement (Jonbesh-e sabz), 201–2
Guardian Council, 88, 119
guardianship of the Islamic jurist (*velāyat-e faqih*), 19, 58, 76, 108
guidance (*hedāyat*), 16
Guiterrez Alea, Thomas, 2
Guzman, Patricio, 10, 12

habs-e ta'ziri (suspended sentence), 202
Haeri, Shahla, 45
Hafez, 49
Hajjar, Mitra, 136
halāl (lawful actions), 107
Hallaj (mystical figure), 52

Hamid, Rahul, 72, 79
Hamlet (film), 35
Hamun (film), 29, 50–55, 53, 129
haqiqat (reality), 42, 48, 63–73
harām (prohibited actions), 107
Hassaninasab, Nima, 97–98
heart, logic of, 43–44
heavenly love (*'eshq-e āsemān*), 43–44
hedāyat (guidance), 16
Hedayat, Sadeq, 106
hemāyat (support), 16
Hitchcock, Alfred, 153
hokumat-e qānun (rule of law), 21, 139, 176–77
Hollywood, 9, 11–12
homoeroticism, 151
homosexuality, 152
Hong Kong, 141
Horkheimer, Max, 141
House of Cinema, 19
housing, 84–86
humanism, 59
human knowledge, 57
Huntington, Samuel, 59

identity, Iranian, 56
India, 141
individualization, of filmmaking, 41
individual paths (*tāriqs*), 48
In film-hā ro be ki neshun midin? (*Who Do You Show These Films to, Anyway?*) (documentary), 85
In film nist (*This Is Not a Film*) (film), 25–26, 200, 201, 203–5
innovation, 184; cultural, 27; technological, 96
intellectualism, 43, 53, 58, 123–35
interface, 72
international cinemas, 141
Internet, 196
iPhones, 204
Irani, Ardeshir, 182, 183
Iranian identity, 56

INDEX

Iran-Iraq War (1980–1988), 6, 11–14, 23, 28, 52, 54, 98, 100
Islam, 107; Shi'i, 15, 32, 34, 53; Sufism, 42, 48, 52, 58, 105, 109
Islamic Revolution (1978–1979), 2, 3, 6, 14, 59

jāheli films, 144, 146
jāme'eh-ye madani (civil society), 18–19, 21, 76, 77, 162, 167, 178
Jannati, Ahmad, 35–36, 37
Japan, 141
javāmardi, 144
Jens-e dovom (Second sex) (journal), 119
Jodāi-ye Nader az Simin (*A Separation*) (film), 13
Jomhuriye Eslāmi, 30
Jonbesh-e dovome Khordād (Second of Khordād movement), 18, 96, 97–98, 105, 121, 135
Jonbesh-e sabz (Green movement), 201–2
Jonub-e shahr (*South of the City*) (documentary), 74
journeys, 104, 108–9
Joussee, Thierry, 147

Kabir, Amir, 173, 174
Kadivar, Mohsen, 19, 76
Kafka, Franz, 130
Kalāgh (The crow) (film), 182
Kant, Immanuel, 56
Karimi, Nosrat, 169, 182
Karoubi, Mehdi, 202
Kavusi, Amirhushang, 140
Kennedy, John F., 61
Kepley, Vance J., 7
Keyhān (newspaper), 33, 39, 131
Keyhān Publishing House, 40
Khāk-e āshenāi (Familiar soil) (film), 126
Khāneh'i ru-ye āb (A house on water) (film), 126
Khāneh siāh ast (The house is black) (documentary), 67

Khāneh-ye dust kojāst? (Where is the friend's house?) (film), 50, 105, 226n10
Kharābābād (Ruinville) (documentary), 67
Khatami, Seyyed Mohammad, 15–16, 55, 75–77, 88, 94, 104; Bani-Etemad and, 62; campaign movies and, 61–62, 99, 100; Cinema Museum and, 21–22; cultural innovation and, 27; dialogue among civilizations and, 19, 59, 93, 127; Farmanara and, 124; intellectualism and, 129–30, 133–34; Jannati and, 36–37; Khomeini and, 28, 41; M. Makhmalbaf and, 18; Ministry of Culture and Islamic Guidance and, 17, 22, 28; Motamedi and, 35; mysticism and, 59–60; political platform of, 18–19, 76, 107–8, 111, 139, 161; popular cinema and, 24; presidency of, 20–21; relativity and, 41; resignation of, 27; Second of Khordād movement and, 18, 97–98; technology and, 24; *Time for Love* and, 23, 30, 35, 37, 39–41; tough-guy films and, 163–65; *Under the Skin of the City* and, 62, 131–32; video spectatorship and, 102; women and, 118–21
Khatib, Lina, 117, 122
Khayyam, Omar, 106
Khesht va āyeneh (*Mudbrick and Mirror*) (film), 127–28
Khomeini, Ayatollah Ruhollah, 2, 3, 4, 7, 40, 59, 77, 187, 202; death of, 14, 15, 17, 23, 37, 54; Khatami and, 28, 41; *velāyat-e faqih* and, 58
Khosrow, Naser, 143
Kiarostami, Abbas, 20, 24–25, 50, 65, 96, 102, 103, 186; digital video and, 21, 121–23; women and, 117. *See also specific films*
Kimiai, Masud, 2, 21, 24, 137, 139–40, 145–46, 153
Kimiavi, Parviz, 67
King, Rodney, 102
Kiosk (band), 25, 167, 177, 186–87, 189, 191, 227n25
Klee, Paul, 94
knowing God (*ma'refat*), 42, 48
knowledge, 57, 68
Kosari, Baran, 70

249

INDEX

Lang, Robert, 11
Larijani, Ali, 100
Latin America, 1
lawful actions (*halāl*), 107
legal system, 49
Lenin, Vladimir, 7, 8
Lewis, Franklin, 42
liberation movements, 9, 10
lip-synching, 191, 192
logic of the mind–logic of the heart (*manteq-e sar–manteq-e del*), 43–44
Lor Girl, The (*Dokhtar-e Lor*) (film), 148–49, 182, 183–84
Los Angeles riots, 102
love stories, 30
Love's Turn, 213n37
Lumet, Sidney, 147
luti, 143–44, 145, 159
lutigari, 144

Madanipour, Ali, 80, 90
Mahdiar, N., 34
Majles (parliament), 16, 27, 40, 131, 167
Makhmalbaf, Mohsen, 21, 37, 202, 212n36; aesthetics and, 32, 38; Dabashi and, 32, 39, 96; early career of, 13; Khatami and, 18; logic and, 43–44; mysticism and, 54, 59; Nasrabadi and, 32–33, 39–40; perfectionism and, 49; Rahimipur and, 38; relativism and, 57; Rumi and, 42, 46, 48; women and, 33. *See also specific films*
Makhmalbaf, Samira, 95, 102
manteq-e sar–manteq-e del (logic of the mind–logic of the heart), 43–44
ma'refat (knowing God), 42, 48
marginalized characters, 84, 110
masculinity, 137, 138, 145, 148, 160, 224n16; music and, 161; violence and, 151
Masnavi-ye ma'navi (Rumi), 42, 143
Matin-asgari, Afshin, 55, 56
May Lady (*Bānu-ye ordibehesht*) (film), 62, 218n42

Mehrjui, Dariush, 3, 29, 50, 73, 129, 141
metadocumentary, 181
Milani, Farzaneh, 85, 142
Milani, Tahmineh, 117
Ministry of Art and Culture, 67
Ministry of Culture and Islamic Guidance (Vezārat-e farhang-o-ershād-e Islāmi), 12, 23, 30, 32, 123, 171, 181; censorship and, 28; Cinema Museum and, 197–98; commandments for looking and, 120; Dad and, 99; Khatami and, 17, 22, 28; liberalization of, 29; music and, 188; press and, 131; *Time for Love* and, 35, 37, 38, 40–41; women and, 34
Ministry of the Interior, 68
Mirbaqeri, Davud, 20
Mirtahmasb, Mojtaba, 26, 200, 203
mobtazal (campy), 140
modernity, 84, 146, 160, 190, 191
modernization, 74, 75
modesty, 117, 121; laws, 13, 120; rule of, 34
Mohammad (prophet), 107
monharef (deviant), 140
montage, 79, 168, 183
Montreal Film Festival, 202
Moqaddam, Jajal, 128
moral antiabsolutism, 32, 41
morality, 33, 45, 49, 55
moral relativism (*nasbiyat-e akhlāq*), 46, 58, 59, 213n50
Motahhari, Ali, 33, 46, 214n50
motorcycle phenomenon (*padideh-ye motorsiklet*), 176
Mottahedeh, Negar, 4
Mousavi, Mir-Hossein, 28, 202
movie theaters, 2
Mudbrick and Mirror (*Khesht va āyeneh*) (film), 127–28
Mulvey, Laura, 106
music, 161, 187–88, 227n18
music videos, 186–87, 189, 191, 192, 227n22
Mussolini, Benito, 1

250

INDEX

Muzeh-ye sinemā (Cinema Museum), 21–22, 25, 197–200, 204
mysticism, 27–29, 213n37; cine-mysticism, 42, 54–55, 60; Dabashi and, 54; Khatami and, 59–60; love and, 23, 41–50; politics of ownership and, 29–41; revival of, 50–60; Soroush and, 55–56, 58; women and, 55
myth, urban, 73–87

Naficy, Hamid, 3, 4, 10, 30, 43, 139, 140, 142; populist cinema and, 141; tough-guy films and, 145, 146, 224n16; women and, 216n6
Nakhl (Palm) (documentary), 67
Namā-ye nazdik (Close-up) (film), 65
Nān o 'eshq o mutur-e hezar (*Bread, Love, and a 1000cc Motorcycle*), 163–64
nasbiyat-e akhlāq (moral relativism), 46, 58, 59, 213n50
Nasuh's Repentance (*Towbeh-ye Nasuh*) (film), 13, 32, 33, 38
Nateq-Nouri, Ali Akbar, 131
National Library, 17
neorealism, 70
New Economic Policy (1917–1922), 7, 9
Newman, Michael Z., 100
New Tunisian Cinema (Lang), 11
New Wave movement, 67, 126, 138
nezārat (supervision), 12, 16
"Nezārat bar nemāyesh-e film va eslāyd va vidiyu va sodur-e parvaneh namāyesh-e ānhā" (Supervision over the exhibition of films, slides, and video and issuing their exhibition permits), 16
Nichols, Bill, 66–67, 92
Nigeria, 141
Night It Rained, The (*Un shab keh bārun umad*) (documentary), 67–68, 168–69
NITV, 102
Nixon, Richard, 61
Nooshin, Laudan, 187, 188
Nowbat-e 'āsheqi (film). See *Time for Love*

online videos, 166–68
ostād (spiritual guide), 52
Our Times . . . (*Ruzegār-e mā . . .*) (documentary), 62–63, 87–94, 91, 174, 218n33

padideh-ye motorsiklet (motorcycle phenomenon), 176
Pahlavi, Mohammad Reza, 2, 3, 11, 74, 145, 152, 155, 175
Panahi, Jafar, 25–26, 200, 202–4
"Pariā" (Fairies) (Shamlu), 214n62
parliament (Majles), 16, 27, 40, 131, 167
Parsipur, Shahrnush, 28, 33, 86
Partow, Maziar, 152
Peh mesl-e pelikān (P as in pelican) (documentary), 67
perfectionism, 49, 58
perplexity (*hayrat*), 56
plastic surgery, 192
"Plato's Pharmacy" (Derrida), 215n66
pluralism, 57, 58, 214n50
political content, 98
political reform (*eslāhtalabi*), 15
Pontecorvo, Gillo, 12
pop music, 161, 187–88, 227n18
popular cinema, 24, 164–65
popular reform movement, 14
populist cinema, 141
post-revolutionary Iranian cinema, 3–4
presidential campaigns, 61–62
press liberalization, 131
Prince Ehtejab (*Shāzdeh ehtejāb*) (film), 126, 127
private space, 92
Progressive Era, 5–6
prohibited actions (*harām*), 107
propaganda, 1, 5, 7
Protest (*E'terāz*) (film), 24–25, 136–40, 145, 156–62
Psycho (film), 153, *154*
publishing, 198
Pudovkin, Vsevolod, 9

INDEX

qabz (contraction), 56
Qabz va bast-e te'urik-e shari'at: nazarieh-ye takāmol-e ma'refat-e dini (The theoretical contraction and expansion of religious law: the concept of the evolution of religious knowledge) (Soroush), 56, 57
Qajar, Ahmad Faruqi, 182
Qajar, Mohammad Shah, 197
Qajar Dynasty, 144, 175, 179, 183
qatlhā-ye zanjireh'i (serial murders), 133–34
Qazvini, Zakariya, 169, 180
Qeysar (film), 24, 137, 138–39, 145, 147, *149*, 149–51, 157; as *jāheli* film, 146; similarity to *Psycho* and, 153, *154*; violence in, 148, 152–53, 155, 156

Rafsanjani, Akbar Hashemi, 166, 174
Rahimipur, Rahim, 38
Rasoulof, Mohammad, 202
Rastegar, Kamran, 141
reality (*haqiqat*), 42, 48, 63–73
reason, 57
reformist philosophy, 41–50
refugee children, 21
relativism, 57; moral, 46, 58, 59, 213n50
relativity, 41
religion, 57
representation, 63–73
Reqābat dar shahr (Rivalry in the city) (documentary), 74
Resālat (Mission) (newspaper), 32
Reypur, Bahram, 128
Ritm (Rhythm) (documentary), 67
Rocha, Glauber, 2
Roy, Olivier, 58, 107
Rudbar earthquake, 180, 226n10
rule of law (*hokumat-e qānun*), 21, 139, 176–77
rule of modesty, 34
Rumi, Jalal al-Din, 37, 143, 213n37; M. Makhmalbaf and, 42, 46, 48; Soroush and, 55
runaway girls, 219n44

Russian Civil War (1917–1922), 6
Russian Revolution (1917), 6, 7
Ruzegār-e mā . . . (Our Times . . .) (documentary), 62–63, 87–94, *91*, 174, 218n33

Sadr, Hamid Reza, 139, 184
Saeed-Vafa, Mehrnaz, 103
Saffar-Harandi, Hossein, 166
Salām (newspaper), 131
Saltaneh, Mirza Ebrahim Akkasbashi Sani al-, 182
Satrapi, Marjane, 202
SAVAK, 133
Sāyeh-hā-ye boland-e bād (*Tall Shadows of the Wind*) (film), 126
Schimmel, Annemarie, 42
science, 56
Search for Common Ground (SFCG), 19
Second of Khordād movement (Jonbesh-e dovome Khordād), 18, 96, 97–98, 105, 121, 135
secularism, 166
Sedgwick, Eve Kosofsky, 151
Sepanta, Abdolhossein, 182, 183
Separation, A (*Jodāi-ye Nader az Simin*) (film), 13
serial murders (*qatlhā-ye zanjireh'i*), 133–34
sexuality, 55, 148, 152–53; gender and, 151; homosexuality, 152; *Time for Love* and, 44–46; of women, 33
SFCG. *See* Search for Common Ground
Shahid-Saless, Sohrab, 128
Shamlu, Ahmad, 214n62
Shariati, Ali, 155
Shāzdeh ehtejāb (*Prince Ehtejab*) (film), 126, 127
Shi'i Islam, 15, 32, 34, 53
Shirdel, Kamran, 67–68, 75, 168, 169, 182
Shohat, Ella, 10
Shojai, Zohreh, 119
Sib (*Apple*) (film), 95–96
Sierra Leone, 133

INDEX

Sight and Sound, 62
silence, 108–9
silent cinema, 8
Silverman, Kaja, 153
Simmon, Scott, 6
Smell of Camphor, The Scent of Jasmine, The (Bu-ye kāfur, 'atr-e yās) (film), 24, 96, 123–35, *125*, *129*, *135*
social experiment, 106
Social Films Festival, 63
Social History of Iranian Cinema, A (Naficy), 142
socialist realism, 7–8
social structures, 78
Solanas, Fernando, 10
Soroush, Abdolkarim, 29, 108, 212n36, 215n82, 221n39; moral relativism and, 46; mysticism and, 55–56, 58; reason and, 57; Rumi and, 55; science and, 56; Shi'i Islam and, 15; *Time for Love* and, 33, 41–43, 46–47, 55, 57–59
"Sorud-e Ebrāhim dar ātash" (The song of Abraham in the fire) (Shamlu), 214n62
sound, 183
South of the City (Jonub-e shahr) (documentary), 74
Soviet Union, 6–7, 8, 9
Sovinko, 7
spiritual guide (*ostād*), 52
stagnation, 109, 110
Stam, Robert, 10
stew films (*film-e ābgushti*), 140
subsidies, 31
Sufism, 42, 48, 52, 58, 105, 109
suicide, 106–7, 111
supervision (*nezārat*), 12, 16
"Supervision over the exhibition of films, slides, and video and issuing their exhibition permits" ("Ezārat bar nemāyesh-e film va eslāyd va vidiyu va sodur-e parvaneh namāyesh-e ānhā"), 16
support (*hemāyat*), 16

suspended sentence (*habs-e ta'ziri*), 202
Syria, 1

Tabari, Keyvan, 108
Tabemohammadi, Shahram, 121
Taft, William, 5
tahājom-e farhangi (assault on culture), 100, 101
Talā-ye sorkh (Crimson gold) (film), 204
Tall Shadows of the Wind (Sāyeh-hā-ye boland-e bād) (film), 126
Ta'm-e gilās (Taste of Cherry) (film), 20, 24, 96, 103–16, *113*, *115*, 176
Taqvai, Naser, 67
tāriqs (individual paths), 48
Taste of Cherry (Ta'm-e gilās) (film), 20, 24, 96, 103–16, *113*, *115*, 176
tax breaks, 31
Tayab, Manuchehr, 67
technology: innovations of, 96; Khatami and, 24; video, 23, 24
Tehran, 23, 63, 73–74, 77–81, *81*, 82, 83, 87, 112; density problem of, 178; housing in, 84–86; mapping of, 87–94; spatiality of, 75
Tehrān anār nadārad (Tehran Has No More Pomegranates) (film), 25, 167, 168–85, *182*, 194, *195*, 205
Tehrān-e emruz (Tehran today) (film), 182
Tehrān pāytakht-e Irān ast (Tehran Is the Capital of Iran) (documentary), 67, 75, 182
temporality, 59
10 (film), 114–21
10 on Ten (film), 122
Theoretical Contraction and Expansion of Religious Law, The: The Concept of the Evolution of Religious Knowledge (Qabz va bast-e te'urik-e shari'at: nazarieh-ye takāmol-e ma'refat-e dini) (Soroush), 56, 57
"Theses on the Philosophy of History" (Benjamin), 94
Third Cinema, 1, 9–10, 11, 139
Third World, 11

INDEX

This Is Not a Film (*In film nist*) (film), 25–26, 200, 201, 203–5
"Three Fish, The" (Rumi), 213n37
time: perceptions of, 23; reconfiguration of, 88; untimeliness, 87–94
Time (magazine), 61, 104
Time for Love (*Nowbat-e 'āsheqi*) (film), 17, 29, 30–34, 36, 54; episodic structure of, 49; Khatami and, 23, 30, 35, 37, 39–41; Ministry of Culture and Islamic Guidance and, 35, 37, 38, 40–41; mystic love and, 41–50; pluralism and, 57–58; sexuality and, 44–46; Soroush and, 41–43, 46–47, 55, 57–59
Titanic (film), 163
tough-guy films, 24, 136–40; death of genre, 140–46; Khatami and, 163–65; Naficy and, 145, 146, 224n16; *Protest* and, 156–62; *Qeysar* and, 147–56
"Toward a Theory of Third Cinema" (Solanas and Getino), 10
Towbeh-ye Nasuh (*Nasuh's Repentance*) (film), 13, 32, 33, 38
tradition, 190, 191
Tuba va ma'nā-ye shab (Tuba and the meaning of night) (Parsipur), 86
Turkey, 32

UN. *See* United Nations
uncertainty, 37
underground music scene, 187–88
Under the Skin of the City (*Zir-e pust-e shahr*) (film), 24, 62, 83, 87, 94, 176; acclaim for, 63; Adineh in, *71*; commitment and, 63–73; first shot of, *71*; housing and, 84–86; interface and, 72; Khatami and, 62, 131–32; montage and, 79; narrative of, 69; reality and, 63–73; representation and, 63–73; social structures in, 78; Tehran and, 63, 73, 75, 77–83, *81*; women in, 117
United Nations (UN), 19, 59–60
United States (U.S.), 5–6, 11, 19–20

University of Isfahan, 132
Un shab keh bārun umad (*The Night It Rained*) (documentary), 67–68, 168–69
untimeliness, 87–94
urbanism, 62, 73
urban myth, 73–87
U.S. *See* United States
US-Iran Cinema Exchange, 19

VCRs, 101
velāyat-e faqih (guardianship of the Islamic jurist), 19, 58, 76, 108
Vernallis, Carol, 188, 189, 192
Vertov, Dziga, 7, 9
Vezārat-e farhang-o-ershād-e Islāmi. *See* Ministry of Culture and Islamic Guidance
video: cameras, 123–35; spectatorship, 102, 113, 116; technology, 23, 24; VCRs, 101
video democracies, 95–98, 117–23; funerals and, 123–35; intellectualism and, 123–35; *Taste of Cherry* and, 103–16; video cameras and, 123–35; videotape histories and, 99–103
videotape histories, 99–103
violence, 52, 139; domestic, 86; masculinity and, 151; in *Protest*, 156–57; in *Qeysar*, 148, 152–53, 155, 156; against women, 86–87
Vosuqi, Behruz, 149, 152

Wees, William C., 183
Westernization, 172, 175
Westoxicated (*gharbzade*), 210n10
White Revolution, 152
Who Do You Show These Films to, Anyway? (*In film-hā ro be ki neshun midin?*) (documentary), 85
Wind Will Carry Us, The (*Bād mā rā khāhad bord*) (film), 115, 118
women, 70, 88, 219n45; Bani-Etemad and, 63; censorship and, 69, 117; civil society and,

19; clothing of, 228n27; female characters, 98, 150–51, 218n42; idealized, 34; Khatami and, 118–21; Kiarostami and, 117; M. Makhmalbaf and, 33; modesty and, 13, 34, 117, 120, 121; mysticism and, 55; Naficy and, 216n6; sexuality of, 33; violence against, 86–87
Women Without Men (*Zanān bedun-e mardān*) (Parsipur), 28, 33
workshops, 12
World War I, 6
Wretched of the Earth, The (Fanon), 10

Yek bus-e kuchulu (A little kiss) (film), 126
Youngblood, Denise J., 7, 8
YouTube, 186, 196, 227n22

Zanān (Women) (journal), 19, 118, 219n45
Zanān bedun-e mardān (*Women Without Men*) (Parsipur), 28, 33
Zanān va javānān (Women and youth) (Khatami), 118
zed-e mostanad (antidocumentary), 168
Zendegi va digar hich (Life and nothing more) (film), 50, 105, 226n10
Zeydabadi-nejad, Saeed, 16
"Zhānr-e dovom-e khordād" (Genre of the Second of Khordād) (Hassaninasab), 97
Zir-e darakhtān-e zeytun (*Through the Olive Trees*) (film), 50
Zir-e pust-e shahr (film). *See Under the Skin of the City*
Žižek, Slavoj, 72

FILM AND CULTURE SERIES

What Made Pistachio Nuts? Early Sound Comedy and the Vaudeville Aesthetic
    Henry Jenkins
Showstoppers: Busby Berkeley and the Tradition of Spectacle
    Martin Rubin
Projections of War: Hollywood, American Culture, and World War II
    Thomas Doherty
Laughing Screaming: Modern Hollywood Horror and Comedy
    William Paul
Laughing Hysterically: American Screen Comedy of the 1950s
    Ed Sikov
Primitive Passions: Visuality, Sexuality, Ethnography, and Contemporary Chinese Cinema
    Rey Chow
The Cinema of Max Ophuls: Magisterial Vision and the Figure of Woman
    Susan M. White
Black Women as Cultural Readers
    Jacqueline Bobo
Picturing Japaneseness: Monumental Style, National Identity, Japanese Film
    Darrell William Davis
Attack of the Leading Ladies: Gender, Sexuality, and Spectatorship in Classic Horror Cinema
    Rhona J. Berenstein
This Mad Masquerade: Stardom and Masculinity in the Jazz Age
    Gaylyn Studlar
Sexual Politics and Narrative Film: Hollywood and Beyond
    Robin Wood
The Sounds of Commerce: Marketing Popular Film Music
    Jeff Smith
Orson Welles, Shakespeare, and Popular Culture
    Michael Anderegg
Pre-Code Hollywood: Sex, Immorality, and Insurrection in American Cinema, 1930–1934
    Thomas Doherty
Sound Technology and the American Cinema: Perception, Representation, Modernity
    James Lastra

Melodrama and Modernity: Early Sensational Cinema and Its Contexts
    Ben Singer
Wondrous Difference: Cinema, Anthropology, and Turn-of-the-Century Visual Culture
    Alison Griffiths
Hearst Over Hollywood: Power, Passion, and Propaganda in the Movies
    Louis Pizzitola
Masculine Interests: Homoerotics in Hollywood Film
    Robert Lang
Special Effects: Still in Search of Wonder
    Michele Pierson
Designing Women: Cinema, Art Deco, and the Female Form
    Lucy Fischer
Cold War, Cool Medium: Television, McCarthyism, and American Culture
    Thomas Doherty
Katharine Hepburn: Star as Feminist
    Andrew Britton
Silent Film Sound
    Rick Altman
Home in Hollywood: The Imaginary Geography of Hollywood
    Elisabeth Bronfen
Hollywood and the Culture Elite: How the Movies Became American
    Peter Decherney
Taiwan Film Directors: A Treasure Island
    Emilie Yueh-yu Yeh and Darrell William Davis
Shocking Representation: Historical Trauma, National Cinema, and the Modern Horror Film
    Adam Lowenstein
China on Screen: Cinema and Nation
    Chris Berry and Mary Farquhar
The New European Cinema: Redrawing the Map
    Rosalind Galt
George Gallup in Hollywood
    Susan Ohmer
Electric Sounds: Technological Change and the Rise of Corporate Mass Media
    Steve J. Wurtzler

The Impossible David Lynch
  Todd McGowan

Sentimental Fabulations, Contemporary Chinese Films: Attachment in the Age of Global Visibility   Rey Chow

Hitchcock's Romantic Irony
  Richard Allen

Intelligence Work: The Politics of American Documentary
  Jonathan Kahana

Eye of the Century: Film, Experience, Modernity
  Francesco Casetti

Shivers down Your Spine: Cinema, Museums, and the Immersive View
  Alison Griffiths

Weimar Cinema: An Essential Guide to Classic Films of the Era
  Edited by Noah Isenberg

African Film and Literature: Adapting Violence to the Screen
  Lindiwe Dovey

Film, a Sound Art
  Michel Chion

Film Studies: An Introduction
  Ed Sikov

Hollywood Lighting from the Silent Era to Film Noir
  Patrick Keating

Levinas and the Cinema of Redemption: Time, Ethics, and the Feminine
  Sam B. Girgus

Counter-Archive: Film, the Everyday, and Albert Kahn's Archives de la Planète
  Paula Amad

Indie: An American Film Culture
  Michael Z. Newman

Pretty: Film and the Decorative Image
  Rosalind Galt

Film and Stereotype: A Challenge for Cinema and Theory
  Jörg Schweinitz

Chinese Women's Cinema: Transnational Contexts
  Edited by Lingzhen Wang

Hideous Progeny: Disability, Eugenics, and Classic Horror Cinema
    Angela M. Smith

Hollywood's Copyright Wars: From Edison to the Internet
    Peter Decherney

Electric Dreamland: Amusement Parks, Movies, and American Modernity
    Lauren Rabinovitz

Where Film Meets Philosophy: Godard, Resnais, and Experiments in Cinematic Thinking
    Hunter Vaughan

The Utopia of Film: Cinema and Its Futures in Godard, Kluge, and Tahimik
    Christopher Pavsek

Hollywood and Hitler, 1933–1939
    Thomas Doherty

Cinematic Appeals: The Experience of New Movie Technologies
    Ariel Rogers

Continental Strangers: German Exile Cinema, 1933–1951
    Gerd Gemünden

Deathwatch: American Film, Technology, and the End of Life
    C. Scott Combs

After the Silents: Hollywood Film Music in the Early Sound Era, 1926–1934
    Michael Slowik

"It's the Pictures That Got Small": Charles Brackett on Billy Wilder and Hollywood's Golden Age
    Edited by Anthony Slide

Plastic Reality: Special Effects, Technology, and the Emergence of 1970s Blockbuster Aesthetics
    Julie A. Turnock

Maya Deren: Incomplete Control
    Sarah Keller

Dreaming of Cinema: Spectatorship, Surrealism, and the Age of Digital Media
    Adam Lowenstein

Motion(less) Pictures: The Cinema of Stasis
    Justin Remes

The Lumière Galaxy: Seven Key Words for the Cinema to Come
    Francesco Casetti

The End of Cinema? A Medium in Crisis in the Digital Age
 André Gaudreault and Philippe Marion
Studios Before the System: Architecture, Technology, and the Emergence of Cinematic Space
 Brian R. Jacobson
Impersonal Enunciation, or the Place of Film
 Christian Metz
When Movies Were Theater: Architecture, Exhibition, and the Evolution of American Film
 William Paul
Carceral Fantasies: Cinema and Prison in Early Twentieth-Century America
 Alison Griffiths
Living History: Experiencing the Past Through Film
 William Guynn

GPSR Authorized Representative: Easy Access System Europe, Mustamäe tee
50, 10621 Tallinn, Estonia, gpsr.requests@easproject.com

www.ingramcontent.com/pod-product-compliance
Lightning Source LLC
Chambersburg PA
CBHW021357290426
44108CB00010B/284